Femmes

Recent Writings on French Women

G. K. Hall
WOMEN'S STUDIES
Publications

Barbara Haber
Editor

Femmes

Recent Writings on French Women

MARGARET COLLINS WEITZ

G.K.HALL&CO.
70 LINCOLN STREET, BOSTON, MASS.

All Rights Reserved
Copyright © 1985 by Margaret Collins Weitz

Library of Congress Cataloging in Publication Data

Weitz, Margaret Collins.
  Femmes : recent writings on French women.

  (G.K. Hall women's studies publication)
  Bibliography: p.
  Includes index.
  1. Women—France—Bibliography 2. Feminism—France—
Bibliography I. Title. II. Series.
Z7964.F8W44 1985   [HQ1617]   016.3054'0944   84-25246
ISBN 0-8161-8475-5

This publication is printed on permanent/durable acid-free paper
MANUFACTURED IN THE UNITED STATES OF AMERICA

Contents

The Author vii

Foreword ix

Preface
    Purpose xi
    Period Covered xii
    Problematics xiii
    Selection xiv
    Categories xv
    Format xvii
        Reference and Archival Materials. xviii
        Bibliographies. xviii
        Dictionaries and Encyclopedias. xix

Acknowledgments. xxiii

Introduction
    The Past 1
    Enfranchisement: Into the Political Process 4
    Divorce. 11
    <u>L'ecole des femmes</u>: School for Women/Wives. 13
        Higher Education. 20
    Family Planning 22
    Recent Developments. 25

Women in French History 31
    General Studies 34
    Biographies and Autobiographies. 45

French Views on American Women 67

French Feminisms
    General and Theoretical Studies. 69
    Creativity 71
    Journalism, The Feminist Press, and Advertising. 72

Contents

Sexual Politics
    Sexuality 111
    Reproductive Rights, Family Planning, and Abortion. 112
    Prostitution 113
    Rape 114

Women in French Society
    The Family and Children 131
    Education and Sex Roles 134
    Religion 136

Politics, Law, and Crime 159
    Politics and Law 162
    Crime 169

Women and Work 171

Bibliography of Earlier Works, 1830-1969 193

Subject Index 231

Author Index 235

Title Index 239

The Author

Margaret Collins Weitz is associate professor and chair of humanities and modern languages at Suffolk University, and research associate at the Center for European Studies at Harvard University. She has written on literature, language, French Civilization, and Women's Studies. Recent publications include Femmes et Métiers (Cambridge: Harvard Modern Language Center, 1979; Jeffrey Norton, 1982, co-author Judith G. Frommer). Forthcoming is Some Notable French Women, a collection of interviews. Professor Weitz has held grants from the Bunting Institute of Radcliffe College, the American Philosophical Society, the American Council of Learned Societies, and the Polaroid Foundation as well as residency fellowships at the Rockefeller Foundation, Bellagio, and the Camargo Foundation, Cassis.

Foreword

In folklore and romance French women have often been cast as "men's women" par excellence, embodiments of sophisticated femininity, projections of the Frenchman's ideal, the admiring, desirable, malleable woman. So it may have been a shock to the "heroes" of the 1968 student rebellion when a small group of their female companions walked out on them denouncing their assumptions of male supremacy and female domesticity. The contemporary French feminist movement took off from that incident and, in the seventies, rapidly took precedence over all other causes. At least such is the scenario sometimes described. Why the movement burgeoned so energetically in the next ten years seems to require further explanation. Margaret Weitz's book deals with the phenomenon indirectly by bringing into focus and examining the outpouring of publications of all kinds that accompanied the vigorous and successful movement of the seventies.

Post-World War II French feminism has been in essence many-faceted, and yet it has been a central force in shaping the changing cultural patterns of contemporary France. Convinced that no single approach to this phenomenon can be satisfactory unless it takes into account a much broader context, Margaret Weitz has put together a reference work that gives access to the abundant literature on the topic. I use the word "literature" here in its broader sense of "writing." Literature proper, Weitz notes quite rightly, has been widely translated, studied, and discussed in academic circles. As has been noted, the contemporary French women's movement is made up of a number of "movements," sometimes crisscrossing, sometimes in conflict, sometimes combining in a temporary community of thought and action. It has its roots in a past that had dropped out of view in France's cultural horizon, but that has gradually been recovered as the movement gained momentum.

Femmes: Recent Writings on French Women deals with that complexity, hence its organization does not follow the usual patterns of bibliographical reference works. It develops rather like a mosaic, each of its parts contributing to an overall design. As Weitz explains in her preface, it does not claim to be exhaustive but is designed to orient further investigations into the historical, socio-

Foreword

political, and institutional conditions that French women have challenged over many years. What she has done is to draw on specific archives and collections devoted to feminine history and feminine texts. Briefly, her purpose was to "fill in" the gaps in our knowledge of the French feminine presence and role and to promote in the same volume indications of research done in various specialized areas concerning French women. At the outset she provides valuable information on the archives and collections available to the researcher. An unannotated bibliography at the end of the book lists some of the many volumes published between 1830 and 1969.

In her introductory chapter, Weitz presents an overall view of the historical phases of a struggle for women's rights that spans the centuries. It sets the stage for assessing the quality and vitality of a tradition that survived many disappointments and stubbornly persisted. The bulk of her book deals with the abundant feminist publications of the nineteen seventies. It is divided into seven sections, each centering on a specific topic announced in a chapter heading that allows for several subsections: for instance, "Women in French History," "Sexual Politics," or "Women and Work." A brief essay introduces each section and is followed by bibliographical entries. These are particularly interesting and useful since the materials are not readily available. In her annotations Weitz provides background, summarizes and briefly evaluates the content of the works cited; in addition, she furnishes information on the writers in succinct but sympathetic character sketches. Because she has worked in this area for some years and has interviewed some of the women mentioned, her book has an unusual richness and variety.

An invaluable aid to research for those engaged in Women's Studies, whether as historians, social scientists, or theoreticians, it offers a surprisingly wide range of factual information. A book of this kind requires of its author scrupulous scholarship. It is designed to be consulted, not read as a discursive text. Margaret Weitz's sympathetic interest in the themes, personalities, and texts she presents gives this reference book a personal note that adds greatly to its readability without impinging on its scrupulous objectivity.

Germaine Brée
Kenan Professor of the Humanities
Wake Forest University

Preface

Many see the changing condition of women—the many legal rights recently granted them, their admission to institutions of higher learning, their continuing entry into the work force and their advancement into higher level positions, their gradual involvement in the political forum, and, perhaps most revolutionary of all, their ability to control their reproductive capacities—as the most important social phenomenon of our time. Such a view is particularly appropriate to France. It would be no exaggeration to say that French women have attained as much in the past few years as they have in the past few centuries. This dramatic change is reflected in the many works by and about women that have been published recently to present women's views, voice their demands and concerns, and give them the place in history they so demonstrably deserve.

PURPOSE

My conviction of the need for an interdisciplinary listing of studies dealing with various aspects of women's status published in France in the 1970s grew out of research for several articles: "Cherchez la femme: recherches sur les femmes," French Review, February 1978; "The Status of Women in France Today," and "An Annotated Bibliography of Recent Studies on French Women," Contemporary French Civilization, Fall 1978 and Spring 1979. In preparing these pieces I became aware of the many French studies devoted to women: histories, biographies and autobiographies, essays and reports. At the same time, it became apparent that the majority of these French works on women were unknown to the general English-speaking public, in part because of the difficulties entailed in finding them. Yet apart from their inherent interest, these studies share concerns common to women elsewhere. There were no comprehensive listings in English of these studies, works that in some cases resulted from what might be termed the Franco-American dialogue on feminism.

Preface

This book is an effort to fill that need. Its aim is to provide English-speaking scholars and researchers in various disciplines with references to recent French studies on women. These works deal with different aspects of French women: their role in history, politics, society, and work. For the most part literary works have been omitted, although the writings of some women authors and studies about literature have been included when they relate to the role of women in French society.

Together these studies provide a fairly comprehensive view of French women's concerns. There are many entries for sexual issues and employment. This emphasis is historically accurate. Efforts to obtain rights in these domains have served as catalysts in the women's movement in France today. Obviously some areas such as family and sexuality are vast and many titles are found for these topics. To have attempted to include them all would have meant an entire volume devoted to the subject undertaken by an expert in the field. This volume provides only an introductory listing of works that are the product of recent feminist research.

PERIOD COVERED

The entries concentrate on volumes, books, or works relating to French women published in France during the decade 1970-79. In a few instances earlier works have been included. Deemed significant, still authoritative, or useful for comparative purposes, they present views of earlier periods.

The decade covered in this volume is not based upon arbitrary or artificial choice. The latest stage in the French feminist movement (neo-feminism as some term it, or feminisms: I use the term <u>feminism</u> in a broad sense to apply to those working for women's concerns) is the direct outgrowth of what are referred to as the "events" of May 1968, the uprising of students, later joined by factory workers, to protest conditions in the country. Rimbaud's cry, "<u>Changer la vie</u>" (change life), was proclaimed throughout the land. This challenge was heard by eager audiences. In the collective responses and endeavors that followed this revolt, women found that they were not treated as equals. They were assigned the traditional roles of taking notes, typing tracts, etc. More importantly, women found that their most pressing concerns were not always shared by men.

A second major factor in French women's growing awareness of their problems was the work of American feminists Betty Friedan and Kate Millett (who for their part had been inspired by Simone de Beauvoir's now classic <u>The Second Sex</u> [1949]). Their works were translated into French almost immediately. They themselves visited France.

Preface

Groups of French women began to meet to discuss how best to attain their aims. Out of these gatherings came small demonstrations and protests. As one of the early 1970s journals, Le Torchon brûle, puts it:

> It is a question of recounting one's life, of discussing the meaning our personal experience may have with that of all women; of verbalizing what must be done. Freeing this discourse is the basis of our actions so that each woman may change her life; so that together women may transform themselves in order to radically transform society; so that capitalist and feudal patriarchy may be abolished; so that new relations may be created among people.[1]

Following the American example, the French press designated the activities of these women's groups as the MLF (Mouvement de Libération des Femmes). This label was first used in August 1970 to describe a handful of women who attempted to place a wreath on the Tomb of the Unknown Soldier, the shrine of French patriotism. The wreath was inscribed "To one more unknown than the soldier, his wife." There were a number of demonstrations in the next few years. In addition, the popular women's magazine Elle sponsored the Estates General of Women in the fall of 1970 and again in the spring of 1971. In April of that year the "Manifesto of 343" appeared. Women publicly proclaimed that they had undergone abortions, then a crime in France. There were also campaigns against pornography, tribunals denouncing "crimes against women," and trials over abortion and rape. Activities expanded, as did the number of participants. In a short compass much took place.

To place the renascent feminist movement in France in context for those not conversant with French history, the Introduction provides a brief survey that focuses on French women's long struggle to enter the political process and on their efforts to obtain the same education as men. The long, acrimonious struggle for reproductive rights is outlined. These events are not well known. For those just interested in a particular topic, a brief summary is provided at the beginning of each major division.

PROBLEMATICS

The many steps on the long, laborious route to these gains must be understood. French women have had much to overcome in order to be recognized at last as adults, "of age." Any attempt to explain what makes French women different from other women leads only to further questions. Their relations with men, their struggle for legal and intellectual emancipation, and their views of themselves are not

Preface

identical with their counterparts in other countries. A great deal of research remains to be done before in-depth comparative histories of women may be undertaken. The many recent French studies just appearing and under way attest to that fact. The complexity of the problem is stressed by historian Theodore Zeldin in his review of Françoise Mayeur's L'enseignement secondaire des jeunes filles sous la Troisième République (Times Literary Supplement [London], 7 October 1977).

Until quite recently there were few comprehensive studies, few studies in general devoted to the "second sex." Women were hidden from history. Fortunately there is much documentation in France, even for the pre-Revolutionary period, the ancien régime. The records are extensive and vast. They encompass national and departmental archives, parish and notary registries, and court records, including judicial depositions and police reports. The problem is how the extant documents are to be interpreted.

Personal documents such as memoirs, journals, and diaries provide insights into the lives of the nobles and well-to-do. The historical demography of the poor, however, is limited largely to the crucial events of life as they were recorded in the parish registries: birth, marriage, death. Tracts, pamphlets and essays provide some measure of women's concerns, problems, and aspirations. So too does the feminist press. Until quite recently, the traditional view of women's role in French society was drawn from literary sources. Today the subject of French women is one of major importance. Many studies treating the topic have been published in the last decade. And they continue to be published. Fiction is now giving way to fact.

SELECTION

The problem of selecting--or more accurately of finding--these titles proved particularly difficult. Several trips were made to France to consult official lists of books in print, visit publishing firms, and check libraries. The main difficulty encountered was that while the category "woman" now exists for published books, it is far from being inclusive. Many works are listed under other headings such as ethnography, folklore, and manners and customs. Further, there is often little information about the content of works published. To cite but one example, the promising Questions des femmes (women's questions) proved to be just that: questions women ask their doctors. Every entry had to be checked.

Inevitably there are titles missing. In some cases this omission is deliberate. It was not possible to include the many official French government reports and publications, nor all the dissertations and theses. Although a rich source for materials, official

Preface

publications and academic works are often difficult to obtain. Some are highly specialized. Nevertheless it should be possible to locate these documents through consulting the initial section devoted to research. For consistency, translated works were also omitted. This group includes important studies by well-known figures such as Françoise Giroud and Évelyne Sullerot. Works have no doubt been included that will subsequently appear in English. Since there is no listing of translations in progress, this is inevitable. It seemed preferable to err on the side of inclusion even at the risk of repetition.

In a few cases it was not possible to examine the work. In these instances basic information about the content was obtained and collated from at least two sources, primarily publisher's information. At the end of some sections there are titles listed with a brief or no annotation. These were books whose existence had been verified but for which no detailed information was available. Bibliographical data was checked through French publication listings and the National Union Catalogue. All unexamined listings are marked with an asterisk.

To make this as complete a reference work as possible, a listing of works published between 1830 and 1969 has been included at the end of the volume.

CATEGORIES

It proved somewhat difficult to classify the works published from 1970 to 1979. Many combine personal testimony reinforced by research, surveys, facts, and figures. This form of presentation has become the most widely used for setting forth women's issues. Its format, the essay, has a long and distinguished history in France. Montaigne first developed the genre in order to "essay," to try his views and observations on a wide-ranging number of topics, including that of women. The essay provides for discussion of a number of different areas within a given topic and permits considerable latitude. Women are now using it to good advantage.

As the number of entries increased, some obvious categories did emerge. They are centered upon issues central to French women's concerns, not traditional academic disciplines. Further, some studies might justifiably have found their place in several of the categories. When there was no clear demarcation line, they were placed in the category where they appeared to make the most important contribution. Other guiding categories and cross-references are indicated in the index.

The rationale behind the various divisions is the following: <u>Women in French History</u> contains both general studies and biographies and autobiographies. This section was placed first because it seemed

Preface

the most obvious and appropriate way to introduce the subject of women in France.

<u>French Views on American Women</u>. While there are only a few titles in this group, a separate section seemed warranted. Earlier French writings on American women will be found in the bibliography of works published from 1830 to 1969.

<u>French Feminisms</u>. The entries under this heading best exemplify works described as essays. Some might conceivably have been included under more specific rubrics. However, rather than foreclose upon their rich, open quality by defining them narrowly, I chose to include these volumes in a more general category. References and citations in these works do not always follow American scholarly practice. In some cases there is little critical apparatus and references are not given. Works with a strong feminist orientation and works that set forth feminist ideologies were placed here.

<u>Sexual Politics</u> includes works on family planning and abortion. These topics are generally found together in French works, even in official government reports. The explanation for this linking is that until the late 1960s contraception was illegal in France. Consequently abortion was often the unfortunate result of this strict pronatalist policy. Also found here are some of the many works on sexuality that have been published. To include them all would have meant a volume devoted to that subject alone. Here there are titles with a more feminist orientation.

<u>Women in French Society</u> includes a number of topics such as the family, religion, and politics, as well as education. Here too, many titles have come out recently. Those listed are works relevant to the subject of this volume. The subheading "Education and Sex Roles" contains few entries. This puzzling fact can be attributed to France's highly centralized and organized national education system. There is little opportunity for outside observers to affect educational policies. Nevertheless, feminists have undertaken a number of investigations of school texts, those books used during the important early formative years. Not surprisingly sexual stereotypes were found to prevail. In general, the presentation of women in these texts was neither favorable nor accurate.

<u>Politics, Law, and Crime</u>. This subsection contains a number of entries--at times somewhat loosely linked--that deal with French women vis-à-vis the legal system, and efforts to effect changes in the political system. By publicly proclaiming that they had broken the law, as did the 343 who signed the manifesto saying they had undergone an abortion, and by bringing concerns such as rape to public trial, French women transformed what had been formerly felt to be private and personal into the political.

Preface

Women and Work. Obviously work is one aspect of women in society. However, for such an important group of entries it seemed advisable to provide a separate section. Under work will be found studies of French peasants. Peasant is both a social classification and an occupation. I chose to place studies on peasants under the latter heading to facilitate comparisons.

FORMAT

The entry lists the title followed by an approximate English translation in brackets. Where there was a question of choosing between literal accuracy or literary elegance in translating, I opted for accuracy, admittedly not always an easy matter. At times several meanings are provided. These are cases of deliberate ambiguity or double entendre. The fact that the term femme means both woman and wife in French graphically illustrates the problem of translation. And perhaps in a more general way it indicates some of the problems of French women. A 1974 article of the review Tel Quel was entitled "La femme, ce n'est jamais ça" (Woman can never be defined). Although there were many cognates in the titles, they were translated for consistency in presentation. Elsewhere in the texts, however, such obvious cognates as libération and civilisation were not translated.

The date of publication may vary in listings found elsewhere by a year or two because of copyright or other factors. The National Union Catalogue precedes all French publication dates with c.

ANNOTATIONS

An effort was made in the annotations to state the general contents of the book--for most will never be translated--and to indicate aspects of the work that would be of most interest. My aim was to present materials relating to the situation of women in France, past and present, and to offer views of or on French women and on the issues that preoccupy French feminists. Unless otherwise indicated, the passages quoted are my rendering of the original French.

The difficulties enumerated in first obtaining the titles and then copies of the works themselves necessarily preclude any claim to completeness. It is my hope that the entries included in this volume will provide enough references to permit meaningful scholarly research into the topic of women in France. At the same time, it should encourage others to continue and expand bibliographical work on this timely and important topic.

Preface

RESOURCES

Reference and Archival Materials

Knowledge about French archival practice can greatly aid full utilization of the country's vast and extensive documents. It is invaluable to the scholar seeking the most likely location of materials on a particular topic. <u>Research Resources: France (Libraries and Archives in France)</u> is a helpful handbook published in 1973 and revised in 1979 by the Council for European Studies. Pertinent information on various major libraries and archives is provided. There is also practical information: address, public transportation, telephone, hours, possibility of access, etc.

The major resource for work on feminism and women in France is the Bibliothèque Marguerite Durand in the town hall of the fifth arrondissement (Mairie du 5e, Place du Panthéon, Paris 5). The prominent feminist Marguerite Durand gave her papers to the city of Paris. These materials cover the years 1896 to 1932 and form the nucleus of the collection. Since that time holdings have been augmented through purchase and gifts. There is a substantial collection of French feminist documents, including press files and periodicals dating from the mid-1880s to the present. There are also manuscripts, letters, feminist posters, publications, and microfilms.

Bibliographies

Les femmes [Women]. 2 vols. Paris: Documentation Française, 1975, no pagination.
    This bibliographical guide was prepared as a contribution to the International Year of Woman. It contains over two thousand listings of books, studies, journals, and government reports. While it is not devoted to French women exclusively, many of the works included do treat aspects of the women's situation in that country. Many specialized studies are listed that are not generally found elsewhere. Some of the works are annotated. Summaries of the articles in important periodicals enhance the value of this research tool. In some instances, articles of particular interest in daily papers have been included. The index lists both authors and titles.
    (Note: the code <u>US</u> used in the bibliography means "usuel," the classification the works bear in the reading room of the Documentation Française, 29-31 Quai Voltaire, Paris 75340.)

GUILBERT, MADELEINE, NICOLE LOWIT, and MARIE-HÉLÈNE ZYLBERBERG-HOCQUARD. Travail et condition féminine: bibliographie commentée [Work and woman's status: an annotated bibliography]. Paris: Éditions de la Courtille, 1977, 247 pp.

Preface

Published with the assistance of the CNRS (Centre National de Recherche Scientifique), this comprehensive bibliography contains over a thousand entries. The entries have been divided chronologically into three groups: I, Before 1914; II, 1914-45; III, 1945-76. Brief summaries are provided for the periods as well as for the entries. Many are not well known. To further facilitate research, the call numbers for French libraries such as the Bibliothèque Nationale have been included for early studies. In some cases, they refer to the only extant copy. These references not only call attention to rare materials but save time locating the works.

If the emphasis is on the problem of women and work, the listings far exceed that framework. Attempts to obtain employment have been a prime motivating factor in the women's movement.

HOULE, GHISLAINE. La femme et la société québécoise [Woman and Québec society]. Québec: Bibliothèque Nationale de Québec, 1975, 288 pp.

This is another contribution to UNESCO's International Year of Woman. There are over 1,400 entries listed. A few are annotated. Most entries concentrate on Québec women although some are French publications involving comparisons with women in France. The imposing number of works enumerated not only show the importance of cultural, social, and economic research on women in society but also the richness of reflection on the topic.

SAMSON, MARCELLE GERMAIN. Des livres et des femmes [On books and women]. Québec: Conseil du Statut de la Femme, Gouvernement de Québec, 1978, 254 pp.

There are some 1,300 entries in this partially annotated bibliography. Some are translations, a few, works in English. The entries dealing with French feminism are arranged chronologically. Many studies refuse to be confined to one category. Nevertheless there are some subcategories, including politics, law, work, and education. Most titles were published between 1940 and 1978, although earlier works have been included. The majority of this last group deals with women in Québec.

Dictionaries, Encyclopedias, and Histories

BARDÈCHE, MAURICE. Histoire des femmes [History of women]. 2 vols. Paris: Stock, 1968.

BERTRAND, MICHELINE, ed. Nouvelle encyclopédie de la femme [New encyclopedia on women]. Paris: Ferdinand Nathan, 1966, 355 pp.

BORGAL, CLÉMENT. Quinze femmes célèbres [Fifteen famous women]. Paris: Gauthier-Langerau, 1975, 220 pp.

Preface

CASTELOT, ANDRÉ. Femmes tragiques de l'histoire [Tragic women of history]. Paris: Presses Pocket, 1969, 317 pp.

CHIAPPE, JEAN-FRANÇOIS. Le monde au féminin: encyclopédie des femmes célèbres [The feminine world: encyclopedia of famous women]. Paris: Somogy, 1976, 296 pp.
   Well-known historian and radio-TV producer Jean-François Chiappe and eleven collaborators have put together a compendium of notable women. France contributes half the 499 entries. A picture or portrait accompanies the brief biographies. Most have attained prominence in social spheres. There are few creative women or feminists. This is consistent with the editor's view that women have seldom appeared in the public and political spheres. Women are credited with being able to seize the "unseizable," having a particular aptitude for intuition and psychology.

DÉCAUX, ALAIN. Histoire des Françaises [History of French women]. 10 vols. Paris: Librairie Académique Perrin, 1972.
   Alain Décaux is a popular historian well known to the French television public. His extensive work portrays women of all classes. There are many interesting details and references. The tone of the work is light and amusing, not pedantic or overly scholarly. It is intended for the general public.

DUFOUR, ANTOINE. Les vies des femmes célèbres [The lives of famous women]. Geneva: Droz, 1970, 214 pp.

Histoire illustrée de la femme [Illustrated history of women]. 3 vols. Paris: Lidis, 1963.

GRIMAL, PIERRE. Histoire mondiale de la femme [World history of woman]. 4 vols. Paris: Nouvelle Librairie de France, 1965-67.
   Classical scholar Pierre Grimal and his collaborators survey women from prehistoric times on. The factual information presented is still valid. The volumes are devoted to: 1) Prehistory and Antiquity; 2) The Western World from the Celts to the Renaissance; 3) The East, Black Africa, Asia, and Contemporary Societies.

JOURCIN, ALBERT, and PHILIPPE VAN TIEGHEM, eds. Dictionnaire des femmes célèbres [Dictionary of famous women]. Paris: Larousse, 1969, 255 pp.

REY, PIERRE LOUIS, ed. La femme: de la belle Hélène au mouvement de libération des femmes [Woman: from beautiful Helen to the women's liberation movement]. Paris: Bordas, 1972, 207 pp.
   This is another work for a more general public. It contains a history of women; an outline of women and the major currents of

Preface

contemporary thought; an outline of the status of women in contemporary French society; and a selection of texts from Homer on.

Several bibliographies were published while the one at the end of this volume was being compiled. A special issue of Third Republic/ Troisième République 3-4 (Spring/Fall 1977) was devoted to scholarship on the woman question in France between 1870 and 1940. This little-known journal is available in microfiche from its editor, William Logue, c/o Department of History, Northern Illinois University, De Kalb, IL 60015. This issue includes Charles Sowerwine's extensive and extremely useful bibliography "Women, Socialism and Feminism, 1872-1922" and Karen Offen's helpful assessment of current scholarship in a bibliographical essay entitled "The Woman Question as a Social Issue in Republican France before 1914."

Each year sees the publication of one or two important historical studies that usually provide lengthy bibliographies. Works of particular interest published in the last few years include: Patrick K. Bidelman's Pariahs Stand Up! The Founding of the Liberal Feminist Movement in France: 1858-1889 (Guilford: Greenwood Press, 1982); James McMillan's Housewife or Harlot: The Place of Women in French Society, 1870-1940 (New York: St. Martin's Press, 1981); Priscilla Robertson's An Experience of Women: Pattern and Change in Nineteenth Century Europe (Philadelphia: Temple University Press, 1982) and Charles Sowerwine's Sisters or Citizens: Women and Socialism in France since 1876 (Cambridge and New York: Cambridge University Press, 1982).

Two recent anthologies offer English translations of French texts dealing with the woman question and feminist issues. Susan Groag Bell and Karen Offen's Women, the Family, and Freedom: The Debate in Documents (1750-1950), 2 vols. (Stanford University Press, 1983) is an extensive, incisive collection of 264 primary documents chronicling the public debate that raged in Europe and America over the role of women in Western society. Elaine Marks and Isabelle de Courtivron's New French Feminisms (University of Massachusetts Press, 1980) contains over fifty selections of recent French feminist writings. Both works provide substantive essays to introduce the materials.

NOTES

1. "Cause toujours!" Le Torchon brûle, no. 4. Cited in Danièle Leger, Le féminisme en France (Paris: Sycamore, 1982), 16.

Acknowledgments

Any work of this nature is but the continuation of the scholarship and support of many. My work draws both upon the many volumes included in this study and upon the works listed in the Introduction. Beyond that, my sincere appreciation is extended to Professors Bernard Quinn and Douglas J. Daniels of the journal <u>Contemporary French Civilization</u>, which first published the three articles that form the basis of this work. Acknowledgment must also be made to Xavier North, cultural attaché and André-Jean Libourel, cultural counselor of the French Embassy in New York for having arranged a "mission" to Paris that provided support for my research. I am also indebted to the Rockefeller Foundation for granting me a scholar-in-residence post at the Bellagio Study and Conference Center. The setting and the solicitude of the director, Roberto Celli, and the staff gave me a "room of my own" and the time to write the essays in this volume.

The press services of a number of French publishing firms provided me with materials. They include Denoël/Gonthier, the first firm to bring out a special collection on women (under the direction of Colette Audry), Seuil, Stock, Gallimard, Payot, Maspero, P.U.F., Syros, and Éditions Sociales.

Professor Germaine Brée was generous enough to write a foreword for her former student. Virginia Hules of Wellesley College and Linda Clark of Millersville State College provided welcome professional expertise. In particular, Karen Offen of the Center for Research on Women at Stanford University took time to read the entire manuscript and offered a number of very useful scholarly suggestions. However, I alone bear full responsibility for any errors or shortcomings.

The patience and support of G.K. Hall and its editors--in particular my friend and advisory editor Barbara Haber--went well beyond professional concern. They have my sincere thanks.

Without the understanding of my children, Richard, David, and Catherine, this project could not have been completed. Finally, there was the support and encouragement of my late husband.

Introduction

The last few years have seen dramatic gains in the position of women in French society. In fact, it would be no exaggeration to say that French women have obtained almost as much in recent years as they have in the past few centuries. Many opportunities have at last opened up for women. Many long overdue legal changes have been implemented. Nevertheless, the details of the situation of French women are not always known to non-French specialists. The history of the efforts that led to their achievements and the final granting of equal rights to women is not that familiar. French women have had many obstacles to overcome in order to be considered "of age," to become full citizens with equal opportunities to education and work and to become involved to some extent in the decision making that affects every facet of their lives.[1]

THE PAST

Throughout antiquity and the Middle Ages women in France were considered inferior to men. However, from the eleventh century on, under the influence of German law, upper-class women were accorded certain rights, such as titulaires de fief. The châtelaine or lady of the manor could sit in justice in the absence of her husband. Women of this rank could also name delegates to meetings of the Estates General, the assembly the king summoned at his discretion (but rarely did). The assembly brought together representatives of the three Estates in pre-Revolutionary France: the clergy, the nobility, and the third estate, which consisted of the bourgeoisie, the city dwellers, and le peuple, the future proletariat.

Nevertheless, from the Renaissance on--in spite of figures such as Marguerite de Navarre (1492-1549), Catherine de Médicis (1519-89), and Anne d'Autriche (1602-66), all of whom governed France (although as regents only) at one time or other--women's rights were increasingly "contested." Vestiges of Roman law were reintroduced to strengthen recent legislation. The overall effect of these measures

Introduction

was to strengthen patriarchal authority, a "domestic" monarchy. A few voices of protest were raised over this development. Marie de Gournay (1566-1645), Montaigne's "adopted" daughter, claimed that to women "all good things were forbidden, freedom was refused and virtues denied."[2]

Throughout the sixteenth and seventeenth centuries, a rhetorical tradition continued those works of the Middle Ages that had celebrated or condemned women. These were tours de force on a paradoxical subject, not efforts at critical thought or attempts to refute prejudice. Some take the form of alphabets, with A standing for "very avid animal" or "angelic," depending upon the side chosen. Others were historical compendiums drawn up to demonstrate the depravity or superiority, the virtues or defects of women.

Towards the end of the seventeenth century one of the first intelligent male voices to champion women's rights was heard. François Poullain de la Barre (1647-1723) set forth enlightened views in De l'inégalité des sexes (1673). During this century, France's golden age of letters, women presided over salons. The précieuses (whom Molière ridiculed for their excesses in Les Précieuses ridicules [1659]) attempted to purify both social conduct and language. Language and literature were favored topics of conversation at these gatherings. This was the period when the French language was evolving into its modern form. Women's contribution to this evolution may be seen in the suggestions of one of the principal arbiters of grammar of the time, Vaugelas. When in doubt over questions of language he held it best to consult women. As Caroline Lougee has shown, the salons played a central role in the process of social mobility in the upper classes.[3]

There were also outstanding women writers in France at the time, including Mme de La Fayette (1634-93), who wrote the first classical French novel, La princesse de Clèves (published anonymously in 1678). The letters of Mme de Sévigné (1626-96) are important social documents as well as models of the epistolary genre. But the vast majority of women in France's "splendid century" had little education and limited opportunities to participate in political activities. This state of affairs did not noticeably improve in the age of the Enlightenment, the eighteenth century. However, ideas were discussed at this time that would help bring about the French Revolution and women's growing awareness of their common concerns.

In the stratified society of eighteenth-century France, a woman's place was initially defined by birth, that is, through her family's situation. Then, for most women, it was defined through marriage when the husband's rank was assumed. Since their place was determined by family or spouse, women had less opportunity to participate in the social mobility that was slowly, almost imperceptibly, taking place throughout the century. The older hierarchies were being eroded by social and economic change.

Introduction

The <u>Philosophes</u> and other enlightened figures of the period affirmed the equality of the sexes, albeit in some cases with nuances. But these affirmations were generally declarations of principles rather than practical proposals for obtaining equality in society as it then existed. France's laws were not yet codified in the eighteenth century. There were considerable regional differences. Concern over the institution of slavery started in the 1760s. The inevitable comparison between women and slaves was made. As a woman observed in 1766, girls are born slaves of prejudice; their only accepted place in society is married or cloistered. According to <u>Philosophe</u> Denis Diderot (1713-84) women were "eternal minors," treated like "imbecile children."[4] At that time, the testimony of three women did not equal that of two men. Wherever they lived, the legal status of French women left much to be desired, as did their situation in general. In virtually all matters the husband and father exercised both legal and actual power over the person and property of his wife and children.

On the threshold of the French Revolution the legal and political status of French women was determined by both Roman law and local customs, the latter reinforced by the Pauline strictures of the Catholic church, which were particularly hard on women. Their fundamental inferiority is exemplified in the notorious edict issued by Henri II in 1556, which made the single or widowed mother of a child who died before receiving the sacrament of baptism subject to the death penalty. Women who attempted to conceal their pregnancy were publicly whipped. The edict was passed in an effort to control illegitimate births and infanticide. Periodic efforts were made to see that it was enforced when it was felt that application was being relaxed. Louis XIV, for example, insisted in 1708 that it be read every few months in all churches. It was not until 1731 that the death penalty was commuted to banishment. As the seduced Marceline in Beaumarchais's <u>Marriage of Figaro</u> (1784) points out, men should be punished rather than their victims. Women are treated as minors when it comes to their merits, but as adults in regard to their faults.

Women and their rights became a matter of public concern during the Revolution and the period following. No longer was it a question of a few outstanding figures. The upheaval and profound transformations in French society of that time permitted women limited participation in the newly evolving order.

<u>Cahiers de doléances</u> (Notebooks of grievances)[5] were drawn up as working papers for the various committees of the Estates General. (The opening session of the Estates called for May 5, 1789, the first session since 1614, marked the outbreak of the Revolution.) Women drew up some notebooks--admittedly a small number of the total. They provide information on women's demands of the time: divorce, education, more midwives in the rural areas, etc. While political equality and the right to divorce were sought, the focus was on more

Introduction

general and more pressing problems such as poverty, prostitution and lack of education.

Olympe de Gouges (1755-93) set forth women's demands in Déclaration des droits de la femme et de la citoyenne (1791), a declaration based upon the Déclaration des droits de l'homme et du citoyen adopted by the National Assembly in 1789 to proclaim the rights newly acquired through the Revolution. Her preamble maintains that "the Revolution will not be complete until all women are fully aware of their deplorable fate and of the rights that they have lost in society."[6] The first Article states that "woman is born free and remains equal to man in all rights. Social distinctions may be based only upon common good." Women had the right to be heard she maintained, for they had the right to the scaffold, a "right" she herself was to experience. Other women revolutionary figures included Claire Lacombe, Pauline Léon, and Théroigne de Méricourt.

During this period--as throughout French history--the women of the people courageously engaged in the struggle. The Romantic historian Jules Michelet (1798-1874) saw women as the vanguard of the Revolution itself.[7] They suffered many privations and bore the burden of the extravagances of the rich. What little material goods they possessed they gladly gave to the Constituent Assembly to further the cause of the Revolution. While awaiting their eventual political rights as citoyennes, they demonstrated in public street gatherings at Versailles and Paris, including at the Bastille. Feminist pamphlets circulated and a number of feminist clubs were formed. They included the Club of Women Friends of Truth, the Club of Revolutionary Citizen-Women, and the Patriotic Society of the Friends of Liberty. The goals of these clubs were to uproot the last despotism, free women from the "chains" of marriage, give them the same education as men and admit them to the same employments. It was felt that laws should be as common to the two sexes as are the air and the sun.

ENFRANCHISEMENT: INTO THE POLITICAL PROCESS

The Revolution's concerns with women were short-lived. The wait for suffrage proved long indeed. Antoine-Nicolas de Condorcet (1743-93) was one of the few leaders of this time to openly espouse the cause of women. In Sur l'admission des femmes au droit de cité (1790), he protested against the violation of the principles set forth in the Déclaration des droits de l'homme. These violations, he argued, deprived half the human race of the right to vote and the right to participate in the political process.

The reaction that followed the Revolution under the Convention (1792-95) was particularly hard on women. The changes envisioned for

Introduction

French society by figures such as Marat and Robespierre did not extend to women. In 1793 women were forbidden to attend political assemblies, even as spectators. They were restricted to their homes and meetings of more than five women were banned. The situation did not perceptibly improve during the Directory (1795-99).

Under Napoleon the status of women reached its nadir. Like a number of military figures, he was strongly antifeminist. His viewpoint is expressed in his frequently quoted saying "Woman is not made to realize herself, but to serve." Woman's place in his sociomilitary hierarchy was under her husband, to whom she owed "complete obedience." Article 213 of the Civil Code stated that the husband owes protection to the wife, the wife, obedience to her husband (who could exercise his authority with a military hand).[8] This article is but the legal expression of Napoleon's general view that "woman is given to man in order to have children. Thus she is his property as the fruit tree is that of the gardener."[9] This reinforcement of authority aimed at protecting the legitimate family.

The French Civil Code, or Napoleonic Code, was drawn up in 1804; it is part of the Napoleonic Code, which also includes penal, commercial, civil and criminal procedure. From that time on it has been the basis of French civil law. The code's impact has not been limited to France. It played a considerable part in the drafting of laws in Belgium, Luxembourg, Greece, Italy, certain Latin countries, and the province of Québec (where women have been subject to double discrimination under the French code and British law; Canadian women were accorded the vote in 1920, but women in Québec did not receive that right until 1940).[10]

The Napoleonic Code, referred to as the "paper Bastille" by early feminists, has been a formidable barrier in the long, laborious efforts of French women to obtain their rights, including the right to vote. It also impeded efforts to obtain more extensive legal rights. The code represents an implicit consensus of views regarding the status of women inherited from the ancien régime that have been reinforced by the conservative views of the ascending bourgeoisie. Concerns for protecting legitimate birth and inheritance date back to feudal times.

Under the Civil Code women are divided into two groups, the married and the single. They are treated quite separately. Married women were most affected by its provisions. Until quite recently they had fewer rights than did their predecessors in medieval times. Article 1124 forbade married women from entering into legal contracts. They were placed in the same "unfit" category as minors, the insane, and ex-convicts.[11] The code's restrictions were only gradually changed, with the most improvement made in the past few decades. Previously married women were regarded by the law as their husband's dependents. They were unable to undertake activities such as opening a bank account or traveling abroad without their husband's

Introduction

consent. Fortunately the doctrine of tacit consent mitigated women's legal incapacity. Women were generally "presumed" to be acting with their husband's approval. Overall though, the Civil Code restricted women's rights in France for almost a century and a half. It codified their subordination.

As the nineteenth century progressed, various tendencies in the struggle for women's rights emerged. Perhaps the most paradoxical phenomenon is that of the various utopian socialits such as Charles Fourier, "Père" Enfantin, Étienne Cabet, and their followers, the Saint-Simoniens.

Social reformer Charles Fourier (1772-1837) is thought to have been the first to use the term feminism in French in 1837. Fourier envisioned an ideal society called Harmony. During the reign of Harmony, women would be autonomous (Théories des quatre mouvements et des destinées générales [1808; 2d ed., 1841]. Some of Fourier's more practical ideas were incorporated into social communities, the phalanstères. These were basically agrarian cooperatives, ideally, of 100 families. There were a number of short-lived attempts to set up such communities in France.

Like a few enlightened thinkers before him, Fourier felt that the freedom permitted women was the touchstone of progress or decline in the social order. The granting of rights to women was the basic principle of all social progress.[12] This idea was treated as yet another utopian concept.

Le Père (Father) Prosper Enfantin (1796-1864) elaborated a new religion based upon the socialist utopian views promulgated by the social philosopher Henri de Saint-Simon (1760-1825) and Fourier. Enfantin was the self-appointed pontiff of the "new Christianity" that worshipped a divinely androgynous god. In the early 1830s, women from the bourgeoisie and working classes were attracted to the services of the charismatic leader. Their enthusiasm was short-lived. When the women saw that they were once again being exploited, disillusionment set in. This was predictable given the contradictions inherent in the movement. Women's freedom was linked to sexual freedom. The mystical tenets of the faith were further undercut by the abusive authority of the "Father." The public and press attacked the immorality of the "Family." And among themselves, the women could not accept any woman as leader. The pilgrimage to the Orient in quest of the female Messiah was not successful. Yet the saint-simonien experience contributed to many women's feminist development. It was the first opportunity many had had to meet and discuss their ideas and concerns. Journals were published. Campaigns were undertaken to aid the underprivileged, the poor, and the prostitutes. The Saint-Simonien proletariats, as they called themselves, were to find a more fruitful field for their activities in syndicalism and socialism. Among this group were Flora Tristan, Jeanne Deroin, and Pauline Roland, who linked the problems of women to those of the working class.

Introduction

Influenced by Robert Owens, Étienne Cabet (1785-1856) made three efforts to establish an ideal community in America called Icarie, after his socialist romance, Voyage en Icarie (1842). The departure song of the Icarians urged "Up, women of God, let us part full of zeal to regenerate the universe. . . . Let us found the temple of Equality."[13] But dreams proved difficult to transpose into reality and the noble experiment failed.

One of the underlying problems of these visionaries was the disparity between their visions and the limited scope they permitted women in their brave new worlds. Women were then viewed in French society as idealized vestals, at least in theory. As the often reprinted homage, Le mérite des femmes (1801) of Gabriel Legouvé, professor at the College de France puts it: "Fall at the feet of that sex to which you owe your mother."[14] But the women of these groups--including Claire Bazard, Eugénie Niboyet and Suzanne Voilquin (1801-76)--wanted equality, not adoration. As Voilquin remarked, deep down the male Saint-Simoniens proved to be more males than good Saint-Simoniens.

During the reign of Louis Philippe (1830-48), the ascendant bourgeoisie continued to idolize woman, provided, of course, that she remain in her assigned place--at home in the family. The conservative woman's aspirations were expressed thus in a prayer of the time. "Lord, You have given me a spouse to whom You have united me, a guide for my inexperience, a protector for my weakness. Deign that after the happiness of pleasing You, the attachment to my husband, the concern to render him happy, occupy me completely. Deign that through denial of the will, through deference to his least desires, I may make his life pleasant and agreeable."[15]

Between vestal and victim, there were more balanced views of women in this period of clashing, contradictory currents. In general women were seen as "domestic beings." The distinguished rector of the University (France's higher education system), Victor Cousin (1792-1867), described them thus. Man he termed the "public personage." The ideology of domesticity and the doctrine of separate spheres of activity were continually evoked.

Early French feminists had to brave hostile public opinion, particularly in regard to their liberal stance on morals. A few advocated free love marriages in addition to the right to divorce. They also faced strong antifeminist opposition. Pierre-Joseph Proudhon (1809-65), one of the most outspoken of the misogynist group, placed women in the degrading dilemma of having a choice between being either harlots or housewives (courtisans ou ménagères). He went so far as to "scientifically" calculate women's presumed inferiority in the formula 8/27, the 27 representing the male to be sure. When women obstinately continued in their efforts to obtain the vote and other rights, he indignantly set forth his views in print: De la justice dans la Révolution et dans l'Église (1858) and La pornocratie, ou les femmes dans les temps modernes (1875; published posthumously).

Introduction

During the Revolution of 1848, as in 1789, women combined forces to seek political rights. Their secondary aim was for better conditions for the working woman. To this end the provisional government of 1848 admitted a few working class women as delegates to the Commission on Work. That same year France granted universal suffrage--to men. The following year Jeanne Deroin ([1805-94], a former worker and saint-simonien who had taught herself to read and write), dared to present herself as a candidate in legislative elections. Her platform was based upon the right to vote and hold office. For these and other efforts on behalf of human rights--including founding a women's club and a feminist newspaper--she obtained fifteen votes and, eventually, a prison sentence.

Throughout French history each major upheaval has brought women's demands to the fore. Such was the case in the uprising of 1871, the Commune. It offered women the chance to fight for their rights after the unfavorable interval of the Second Empire (1852-70). Women's specific demands included pensions for women with three or more children, the reestablishment of divorce, and the elimination of prostitution. The need for education was stressed by Louise Michel (1830-1905), the heroine of the Commune, among others. A teacher herself, Michel spoke from experience. During the last decades of the century women began to assume some minor official positions for the first time. Generally, however, their needs were viewed and treated as subservient to those of French society as a whole.

Papers and journals played an important part in disseminating the demands and views of women. The first, La Muse Historique, appeared in 1650. These journals continued to appear although they were generally short-lived and changed names and staffs frequently. The spectacular outpouring of women's pamphlets and reviews published between 1830 and 1848 was not to be equaled until the 1970s. At the end of the century La Fronde (the slingshot) appeared. This was the first feminist daily directed, administered, edited, and produced uniquely by women. Founded in 1897 by Marguerite Durand, it had an initial press run of over 200,000, perhaps in an effort to obtain subscribers. La Fronde was not afraid to take a stand on political issues. It supported Dreyfus during the Affair.

Marguerite Durand (1864-1936) was an important French feminist figure. She gave her papers to the city of Paris. They form the core of the women's library there, which bears her name. Another notable feminist journalist with La Fronde and other papers was Caroline Rémy (1857-1929), known as Séverine.

Towards the end of the century suffragettes made their appearance. The most prominent was Hubertine Auclert (1838-1914). Involved initially with Le Droit des femmes, a periodical founded in 1869 by Léon Richer (1824-1911) and Maria Deraismes (1824-94), Auclert founded a weekly, La Citoyenne, which she published from 1881 to 1891, making it the longest in duration of these nineteenth-

Introduction

century feminist journals.[16] La Citoyenne concentrated on obtaining suffrage. Militant, anticlerical, Hubertine spoke at the 1879 socialist congress in Marseilles as the "slave delegate representing nine million slaves." In addition to her publishing endeavors and her political activism, Auclert's stance on taxes brought considerable public attention and legal harassment. She refused to pay her taxes on the grounds that, as she wrote to the Prefect, "I have no rights, therefore I have no responsibilities. I do not vote, [therefore] I do not pay [taxes]."[17]

Maria Deraismes and Léon Richer established the Association pour le Droit des Femmes in 1870. Official objections to the name made them change the title to the Association pour l'Avenir de la Femme. The name was changed again, to Société pour l'Amélioration du Sort de la femme in 1875 when the Association joined the New York-based International Women's League. Le Droit des femmes was obliged to appear in the 1870s as L'Avenir des femmes. The Society organized the first French congress for women's rights (Congrès international du droit des femmes) in conjunction with the international exposition held in Paris in 1878.

During the 1880s, however, Deraismes and Richer split over strategy: the former became more aggressive and wanted to include suffrage among her goals, while the latter endeavored to work for reforms within the Civil Code. Consequently Richer founded the Ligue Française pour le Droit des Femmes in 1882.[18] His journal had resumed its earlier title of Le Droit des femmes. Soon the League became the largest of the French feminist groups. Undoubtedly its more moderate stance appealed to a wider public: the majority of members were bourgeois. Richer spelled out the League's most pressing demands for reform in a handbook, Le Code des femmes (1883). This was the last of four works devoted to the woman question by a man who devoted his life to feminism. The League's exclusion of suffrage from its demands was consonant with bourgeois feminism of the time. It was caught in the dilemma of reconciling women's demands with concerns that the new Third Republic flourish and prosper. More militant feminists such as Hubertine Auclert believed that women's right to vote took precedence, but they were in the minority. Deraismes and Richer were able to reconcile their differences and organize the second French International Congress for Women's Rights in 1889, in conjunction with the centennial celebration of the French Revolution. The 1889 congress was followed by a second generation of feminists. One of this group was Jane Misme (1865-1935) who organized the group La Française (The French Woman) in 1906. Misme advocated a more moderate stance, as did Jeanne Schmahl (1846-1916) initially. She worked for legal reforms, including the first married woman's property act and legislation permitting women to testify in official public acts. Finding it a long and difficult undertaking to implement legislation, she founded the Union Française pour le Suffrage des Femmes in 1909, to focus on the suffrage. The Union did

Introduction

not last long once its major goal was achieved in 1945. The Union encompassed a number of groups: members ranged from Catholics to socialists.

The League--which exists to this day--flourished under Maria Vérone (1874-1948). A distinguished lawyer, Vérone was the first French woman to plead before the Assises, this in 1908. Other feminists groups continued to appear and some demonstrations were organized, although they were timid by Anglo-Saxon standards. An unofficial referendum undertaken by Le Journal (unfortunately on the eve of the outbreak of the war) in 1914 received over 500,000 votes in favor of suffrage for women. Attempts were made to elect partisans of women's suffrage to Parliament. The most important group in the prewar period was the Conseil National des Femmes Françaises, the CNFF. This council of French women was composed of liberal feminists and Protestant moral reformers. By 1912 the CNFF claimed over 100,000 members in over 100 groups.

In the years preceding the First World War there were few male public figures who spoke out for women. The majority of French males still did not consider woman's suffrage a serious question. This attitude, along with the fact that many poor and peasant women were unaware of the issues, accounted for the defeat of measures in 1901, 1906, and 1914 that would have permitted women to vote in municipal elections.

Like their English counterparts, French women found the opportunity to show their capabilities when they replaced men in many activities during the war. With their fine patriotic record it seemed that their efforts, like those of women in other countries, would bring about enfranchisement. In 1919 a motion to obtain the vote for women passed the National Assembly only to be defeated three long years later in the Senate. The pattern was to be repeated three more times until the end of the Second World War in 1925, 1932, and 1935. Each time, the motion passed the Assembly only to be defeated in the more conservative Senate. It is conceivable that the Assembly was aware of this when it boldly passed these bills in favor of women's right to vote.

In 1936 the Assembly voted 488 to 1 in favor of the measure. Employing the tactics of the English suffragettes, Louise Weiss (1893-1983) organized a gathering of several thousand women. Two years earlier this political activist and journalist (one of the first women agrégée, an advanced degree holder) had founded a league, Femme Nouvelle. Political machinations prevented reports of the league demonstrations being mentioned in the popular press. Then, as throughout the long campaign for the vote and education, loyalties were confused. The Right was fearful that enfranchised women would become militant leftists and libre-penseuses, freethinkers. At the very least they would be manipulated by the Left. For its part, the

Introduction

Left was apprehensive lest the clergy ultimately control the women's vote. The impasse continued.

If they could not vote they could at least serve. The paradoxical situation existed in 1936 during the Popular Front when there were three women under secretaries of state at a time when women could neither vote nor stand for office. Starting in 1935, a number of municipalities took the expedient move of utilizing special powers to appoint women municipal counselors. This permitted women some political and civic activity. It took their demonstrated courage and capability in yet another war before French women were at last accorded the vote.

The provisional government at Algiers voted French women suffrage and eligibility, equality in political law, in April 1944. The following year, in the same month, women voted for the first time in municipal elections. Women's right to vote was formally inscribed in the Constitution of 1946, and again, in the Constitution of 1958. The articles spell out women's equality. The preamble proclaims that "The law guarantees a woman rights equal to those of a man in all domains."

French women's enfranchisement following the Second World War was justified by General de Gaulle in military terms. Women had "earned" the vote by their bravery during the war, as indeed they had. The histories and memoirs of the Resistance amply document this claim. When their country was defeated and occupied women of all economic, social, religious, and political persuasions joined together to continue the struggle in a clandestine war, the Resistance. But this was certainly not the first time that the women of France had participated in their country's struggles.

For most civilized nations the right to vote is viewed as the hallmark of the citizen. French women had many obstacles to overcome before they were finally accorded that fundamental right. And this in a country that took the lead in granting universal male suffrage. The long, laborious efforts of French women to obtain the right to vote exemplify concurrent efforts to obtain divorce, and their subsequent efforts to obtain more extensive legal rights. These followed a similar, somewhat slower pattern.

DIVORCE

Like the battle for suffrage, the history of efforts to obtain the right to divorce, and once possible, to divorce under less difficult conditions, offers further insights into the secondary status accorded women in France over the centuries.

Introduction

Until the sixteenth century the Catholic church was reticent to join the state in making regulations governing marriage. It viewed any secular requirements as restrictions upon the total freedom necessary to enter into the holy sacrament of matrimony. Only with the Council of Trent (1545-63) were the priest and a specific location, the parish church of one of the partners, required. The church has always insisted upon the impossibility of dissolving the bonds of marriage. Annulments were sanctioned but they were few indeed and their grounds were limited. The marriage of priests, monks, and nuns during the Reformation undermined the Church's views on marriage. A royal decree of 1579 equated the marriage of a minor (under twenty-five at that time) without parental permission to the crime of kidnapping, a crime subject to the death penalty. In most cases a young woman could not reject the partner chosen by her parents.

The husband's legal authority was gradually strenthened. At the same time, women were increasingly subjected to severe punishment for adultery. The bourgeoisie, like the aristocracy, a class concerned with inheritance and legitimate birth was on the rise. This social group encompassed a wide spectrum, from the jurists and financiers to modest shopkeepers trying to establish themselves. In these milieus there was generally a high moral tone along with an insistence upon parental authority. A freer, more tolerant attitude toward sexual dalliance was found in the aristocracy. The eighteenth-century Philosophes condemned the indissolubility of religious marriages. In his Spirit of the Laws (1748) Montesquieu stated that divorce held great political value.

The notebooks of grievances and various petitions drawn up for the Estates General contained repeated demands for divorce. The Constitution of 1791 first made marriage an obligatory civil contract, thus making divorce possible. An initial, albeit limited, law permitting divorce had passed in 1752, but divorce was not generally possible in France until 1792. The wide grounds permitted by the law passed that year included mutual consent, mutual incompatability, desertion for at least two years, etc. The year after the law passed, one of three Parisian marriages ended in divorce. This high rate gave support to those who argued for the inviolability of marriage.

Divorce was incorporated into the Civil Code, but the grounds were made more limited. The double standard was codified in the stipulation of grounds for adultery. A man was guilty of adultery if he housed his mistress in the conjugal domicile. The wife could simply be denounced by her husband. She was subject to a prison sentence of from three months to two years (commuted if her husband agreed to take her back). Her "guilty" partner risked the same prison sentence along with a fine. The husband, on the other other hand, incurred only a modest fine if found guilty of adultery (Article 339). The intent of these laws that penalized women more severely than men was to protect legitimate progeny.

Introduction

The restoration of the Bourbon monarchy in 1815 saw Catholicism proclaimed the state religion again. The next year the law sanctioning divorce was repealed by the Catholic-dominated Parliament. Both the Church and the bourgeoisie had sought the repeal. One of the principal opponents of divorce, Louis de Bonald (1754-1840), maintained that divorce was in harmony with democracy. As a royalist and a Catholic, he believed that democracy had been in power far too long in France, with disastrous results.

From 1816 to 1884 divorce was illegal in France. Grounds for separation were restricted. They were based upon the principle of fault. Adultery was automatic grounds for separation. Violence and serious injury were admissible as grounds--at the discretion of the judge. The demand for divorce was a constant during this period, a period that saw women's expanded economic participation and increased feminist activity.

In 1884, after four years of unsuccessful efforts, Alfred Naquet (1834-1916), a deputy who was trained as a physician but left his practice to devote himself to radical political activities, succeeded in passing a law permitting divorce (known after its sponsor as the Naquet law). This law, with some amendments, remained in vigor until 1975 when, at women's insistence, it was amended to make divorce possible under less rigid and time-consuming conditions. Continued feminist pressure has brought further modifications to the divorce law in the past few years. Now the law is written in accessible, contemporary language. The word "adultery" has been excluded. The principal unresolved problem is that of making the former husband pay alimony when a judgment has been made. In 1982, mothers who did not receive their alimony payments after two months were made eligible for "orphan" benefits. Two years later, special study bureaus were set up in Paris, Lille, and Crétail to study this problem.

Divorce legislation is but one of three significant legislative victories of the past few years that have done much to ameliorate women's situation in France. The other two are the right to birth control information and devices (1974) and the right to abortion (under certain circumstances). Passed provisionally in 1975, this law was made permanent in 1979.

L'ÉCOLE DES FEMMES: SCHOOL FOR WOMEN/WIVES

Education is inextricably linked to women's participation in every area of French society. Many are familiar with Molière's dramatization of the problem of education for women in L'école des femmes (1662). The concerns he presents are not limited to his period. The question of just how much to educate women has been a longstanding one in French history. It dates back to medieval times.

Introduction

The Catholic church played a major role in this debate: education was long linked to moral concerns. And women's morals were viewed as a very serious matter. Further, during the Middle Ages, education in France was organized and controlled exclusively by the church. While a few young women received some education during this time, they were those of privileged families. And their accomplishments were not applauded by all. Phillip de Navarre wrote a moral treatise in 1250 in which he argued that women should not be permitted to learn to read or write. Only then, he believed, could they be prevented from writing love letters.

Christine de Pizan (c. 1365-1430) was the outstanding figure of this period. She knew several languages and was well educated. Widowed at an early age, she became the first woman to live by her pen as she endeavored to support herself and her children. Christine's output was remarkable. Early love poems express her love for her late husband in graphic physical terms that strike a modern note. Christine undertook serious writing in order to defend her interests in financial litigations. This experience made her a firm advocate of education for women, an education that would also include the rudiments of common law. She also maintained that science should be taught to girls. Women lacked education, not aptitude. All girls needed were the same educational opportunities as boys.

Public recognition came to Christine when she took up the cause of women in a dispute sometimes referred to as the "Querelle des dames," women's quarrel. Following the rhetorical tradition, long lists of the presumed virtues or faults of women were drawn up. Historical references to famed ladies reinforced the claims, particularly those of the putative champions of women, for their claims went against the general consensus. Subsequently Christine became the first women chronicler of the court when Philip of Burgundy commissioned her to record the rule of the Valois king Charles V. And, by defending herself against attacks, she became the first woman to participate in a literary debate, to justify the capacities of women to express their own opinions.

<u>La cité des dames</u> (1405) is the best presentation of her feminist claims. The major part of this lengthy work is allegorical, in the tradition of the times. Nevertheless her own experience and good sense enter into play. The <u>Cité</u> is the first clear, logical expression of feminist concerns. In their recent history of French feminism, Albistur and Armogathe call her the first "emancipated" woman in the history of feminism. Christine's public interventions to rehabilitate women both as moral and social beings were seconded by her personal struggle to attain social and economic independence. She argued for education for women from personal conviction and experience.

With the rise of the universities in the thirteenth century, education started to break away from ecclesiastical domination, a

Introduction

trend the Renaissance was to reinforce. Generally, the few girls who were educated did not learn Latin, as did boys. This situation was institutionalized with the creation of grammar or "French" schools where no Latin was taught. These schools received some girls from the twelfth century on. Unfortunately these modest gains in the education of women were set back by the plague of 1348 and the devastating Hundred Years War, critical events in French history that had profound effects on all of society.

The Renaissance concern with education was fundamental. Humanists envisioned the seemingly limitless capacities of man. But one finds little mention in the works of sixteenth-century figures such as Rabelais and Montaigne about the education of women. Again, during this period, it was the young girls of the nobility, sometimes those from the upper bourgeoisie, who were taking part in the new learning. Catherine de Médicis surrounded herself with cultivated women. Salons were formed. Yet humanistic culture was essentially aristocratic and masculine.[19]

The "quarrel" about women reappeared. There were many tracts and polemics. Education was one of the central issues. A "protectionist" pedagogy appeared. Reason and prudence were among the virtues stressed for the female sex, virtues that differed from those encouraged in males. In general, education was only approved for women with means, those whose lives would not be filled with domestic tasks. This was consonant with the French fear of déclassement, and their view of women in general. See, for example, Fénelon's L'éducation des filles (1687). To educate young women who did not have leisure might set up false expectations, it was argued. The Protestant Reformers limited girls' education to what was considered essential to bringing up children in a Christian fashion and managing a household.

The seventeenth century, the "grand siècle," saw a gradual extension of instruction to women, although it was still largely restricted to the more favored classes. At the same time, however, women began to play a greater part in the education--in the larger sense of the word--of France. They led and animated the salons, which flourished. Literature and language were the principal topics of conversation at these gatherings. As noted, it was during this period that the French language was evolving into its modern form and French classical literature reached its apogee. French women played an important part in these achievements.

Toward the end of the century royal decrees were passed directed at extending education to girls. But these decrees were basically ineffectual since means were not provided for their implementation. During this time Catholic spokesmen advocated education for women. Their concerns reflected the need to respond to the pressures of the changing society of the time. Further, religious orders--some such as the Ursulines founded specifically

Introduction

for the education of women—endeavored to address the problems of educating their charges. At least twenty-five religious orders devoted themselves to this end. Their programs, however, were basically practical in orientation; conceived as earlier efforts to improve morals and to ensure that women became good wives and mothers. Still there was a slow but perceptible increase in interest in letting women of the upper classes share in the new knowledge being acquired. Popular works, such as <u>Les avantages que les femmes peuvent recevoir de la philosophie</u>, appeared. (Philosophy is construed here in the sense of how to conduct oneself in society.) To accompany and complement these written texts, lectures were given that women might attend. While such efforts were positive, results were limited. Serious scholarship remained the domain of a few privileged women. Along with others of his time, Molière poked fun at the pretentions of "scholarly women" in <u>Les femmes savantes</u> (1672). The target was not necessarily intelligent women, but rather women who viewed literary creation and scholarship as but worldly diversions.[20] The most cursory survey of the literary output of France's golden age of letters shows the important contribution of women to seventeenth-century literature.

The Cartesian François Poullain de la Barre rigorously argued his claims for women. Higher education and university courses were necessary for women if they were to undertake the professions he felt them qualified for. These included political, military, even ecclesiastical careers. In the following century Poullain's work was influential. He was frequently "honored" by being plagiarized.[21] It has been argued that some of the ideas he proposed in works such as <u>De l'égalité des deux sexes</u> (1673) and <u>De l'éducation des dames</u> (1674) are to be found in Simone de Beauvoir's epochal work, <u>The Second Sex</u>.

Eighteenth-century France is often referred to as the century of progress. Early in the century Louis XV set forth an ordinance calling for compulsory education (1724). But, as there were no accompanying provisions for implementing such a program, there was little progress. One of three articles entitled "Woman" in the <u>Encyclopedia</u> (1750-80), the major intellectual project of the century, notes that since women's education had been so neglected, the fact that so many had been able to distinguish themselves by erudition and writing was a significant accomplishment.[22] Diderot's views on women vary with his writings. He did hold that lack of education was perhaps the principal reason for women being perceived as intellectually inferior to men. The eminent mathematician and philosopher Condorcet had no reservations. He saw education, not nature, as the main reason for differences between the sexes. For the Legislative Assembly's Committee on Education he wrote five monographs on public instruction (1790). Condorcet insists that public education is an absolute right of mankind. His advocacy of co-education was deemed yet another revolutionary idea.

Introduction

Choderlos de Laclos (1741-1803) wrote three essays on De l'éducation des femmes in 1783 (they were not published, however, until the early 1900s). He examines physiological questions in order to understand human nature and to shed prejudice. Women needed education so that they could read and be conversant in social gatherings, he felt.

Rousseau's (1712-78) Émile (1762) is frequently read in education courses and is considered one of the classic treatises on the subject. The fifth book of Émile is devoted to Sophie' Émile's idealized companion. Her education spells out Rousseau's ideas on women's education, which emphasize making her subservient to man. Her role is to please and be subjugated. Science, Rousseau claims, is beyond women's capacities. And, since women's lives are bound to contain many interruptions, they should not be introduced to endeavors that require continuity and sustained effort.[23]

The Cahiers de doléances that women drew up and circulated at the outset of the Revolution (admittedly, only a small number of the total prepared) stressed the need for education for women. This demand was second only to one for more midwives for rural areas. The education women sought was primary education. Little was said about secondary courses. On balance, as the Goncourt brothers noted in their study of women in the eighteenth century, La femme au XVIIIe siècle (1862), women in that century continued to receive an education that oscillated between wordliness and renunciation, between development of their talents and retreat, between etiquette lessons and meditation.

In the period following the Revolution, vast reforms were drawn up to radically change French society. Various measures and projects pertaining to education were examined. The first law providing for public instruction in France was passed in 1795. Named after Lakanal, the legislator who elaborated it, this law set up segregated classes. Since parents were required to pay teachers' salaries, potential gains for women were considerably weakened. Then--as even today--priority was given to boys in the family if finances were a problem. Few but the wealthy could, or would, make financial sacrifices for their daughters.

Napoleon's views on women's education were consistent with his views on women in general. They should be taught "perpetual resignation." They could be no better educated than by their mothers. "Public education is not suited for them at all because they are not destined to lead public lives. . . . Marriage is their only destination."[24] Napoleon's stormy relations with internationally known Mme de Staël (Anne-Louise Germaine Necker [1766-1817]), whom he exiled, are but one example of his abhorrence of "women who reason," intellectual women. Women's calling was procreation, not creation.

Introduction

During the emperor's reign, the Imperial University was completely reorganized. This name refers to the public education system of the country. The university held authority over the secondary and higher education establishments: <u>lycées</u>; <u>collèges</u>; and <u>Grandes Écoles</u> (state-run institutions offering specialized training for careers in various professions such as archivist, diplomat, etc.). The aim of the Imperial University was to produce the efficient cadres needed by French society. This initial state monopoly on boys' secondary education was relaxed with the restoration of the Bourbon monarchy in 1815. It was officially terminated with the Falloux law of 1850 which permitted lay and religious secondary schools in addition to those of the state. During this earlier period, there had been some private secular and religious secondary schools. They included <u>lycées</u>, municipal colleges, and <u>petits séminaires</u>, not all of whose students were destined for the priesthood.

To a large extent, the Catholic church continued to furnish the personnel entrusted with the education of girls. Feminist Claire Démar noted in 1833 that the young girls of the people if they went to school at all, went probably to the good sisters who taught them prayers and hymns which they did not understand. By the end of the eighteenth century mothers had become more involved in the upbringing of their own children. Concern arose that the mother-educators (mères-éducatrices) have some rudiments of education. Many tracts of the period attest to the concern with the mother's "privileged" role as teacher. It was the mother's "duty" to instruct her offspring in both elementary subjects and catechism.

Throughout the nineteenth century there was a protracted struggle between the church and the traditional establishment on the one hand, and the liberals and anticlerics on the other. At issue was the control of women's education. The former group sought to "preserve" young girls, a concern that did not always extend to the poorer classes. The liberals wanted to "free" young girls (and women) from the influence of the church. In essence this was yet another phase of the conflict between those in power in the <u>ancien régime</u> and the people, between the church and the republicans.

In 1833 boys' public primary schools were instituted through the Guizot law, part of conservative Protestant François Guizot's efforts to institute nationwide primary education for boys. But these primary schools were neither free nor compulsory, and no mention was made of girls' education. The Pellet law of 1836 stipulated that girls should also be included in the elementary schools that the 1833 law decreed be set up. But there were no provisions for their implementation. The following decade the philosopher Victor Cousin was Minister for Public Instruction. He did much to organize education, but if he advocated coeducation it was because it was more economical to build single rather than separate schools. In the early part of the century, then, French girls could attend public primary schools. However, there were few such schools. The Falloux law of 1850 made

Introduction

public primary education compulsory for both sexes in communities of over 800 inhabitants. This figure was reduced to 500 in 1867. These schools were separate. And they were not free. Further, the church gained control of the majority of the schools that were set up, in part because the religious were not required to have the certificates required of lay teachers. In theory the schools of the church and of special interest groups were subject to state inspection. But this provision was not fully enforced until 1881 when a certificate was required of all teachers. This measure effectively abolished the church's long monopoly over women's education.

The campaign for secondary schooling for girls was even more arduous. When first efforts were made to establish state secondary schools in the 1860s Monseigneur Dupanloup, Bishop of Orleans, became the church's principal spokesman. The theologian protested vigorously these measures to infringe on the what the church perceived as its monopoly. "Young girls are destined for private life. I insist that they should not be permitted access to the courses, exams and diplomas that prepare men for the public life. I demand that we do not prepare free-thinking women for the future," he declared.[25] These first special secondary schools for girls were set up by Victor Duruy in the late 1860s. His daring move, part of a program to reform and extend state education, provoked strong reaction from the church and the conservative establishment. But their boycotts were only part of the explanation for the very modest success of these first girls' secondary schools. Organization was another. Municipalities had no previous experience in the matter. And many of the well-to-do young ladies were not truly interested in learning.

Women's education was largely implemented in the first years of the Third Republic, the "Republic of Professors." Under ministers such as Jules Ferry, Paul Bert, and Camille Sée, the French educational system was consolidated under general principles that still hold today. Political considerations were a major factor in this development. Ferry voiced the sentiments of many liberals in their efforts to laicize education in France when he stated that whoever controls women controls all. The bishops were aware of this, which is why the church wished to hold them back.[26]

Elementary education became free for both sexes from ages six to thirteen in 1881 and compulsory in 1882. For the first time elementary schooling in France was truly democratic. (Secondary schools did not become free until 1933.) In 1882 and 1883 the first <u>lycées</u> (state secondary schools) were set up for young women under the provisions of the Sée law of 1880. However, the degrees they offered were certificates of completion of studies, not the <u>baccalauréats</u> needed for entrance to higher education establishments that boys received in their <u>lycées</u>. To provide the teachers needed for the girls' schools, Écoles Normales Supérieures were created: Fontenay-aux-Roses in 1880 to train women for the departmental primary schools and Sèvres in 1881 to teach secondary school teachers. Growth in

Introduction

these state secondary schools for girls was slow at first. Masculine and feminine programs, that is, different subjects and different emphases, were not eliminated until 1924.[27] There are now slightly more girls than boys in state secondary schools. Complete equality of hours, courses, and preparation for university entrance in secondary schools was not established until 1937.

Pressures brought to bear by women helped in this long struggle to obtain public education for girls. The main factor, however, was the concern to ensure the values of the republic. Political ambitions were also involved. Conservatives wanted women's education to enable them to fulfill their "divine mission" as wives and mothers. Instruction should help make them modest, pious, reserved, charitable, and frugal. The liberal ministers who championed the cause of women's education were concerned about the control the church exercised over women, hence over their children, and indirectly, over their husbands. Neither group seriously contemplated women's higher education as preparation for entering the professions. Economic factors and the First World War brought this change about. Astute women of modest means took advantage of this opportunity. Education helped them to earn a living. Slowly but surely women entered various liberal professions. Access--even with the appropriate degree--proved difficult nevertheless. Not to be deterred, women continued to pursue higher education and eliminate barriers so that in this past decade, they finally have all the same educational opportunities as men.

Higher Education

Julie Daubié (1824-74), the first woman candidate for the baccalauréat, faced the tenacious opposition of the rector of Paris who refused to be "ridiculed" by permitting a woman to present her candidacy for that degree. After various legal battles she was finally permitted to enroll in the University of Lyons where she received her degree in 1861--at the age of thirty-seven. Daubié went on to win the Academy of Lyons' prize for her serious, scholarly investigation into the condition of women workers. The subject proposed by the academy was "The means of increasing the salary of women to equal that of men, for equal work, and how to open new careers to women." These concerns have a contemporary echo. La femme pauvre au XIXe siècle (1866), Daubié's carefully documented study, offered specific solutions to concrete problems, not just observations. The low pay of the urban woman worker, she maintained, at times drove her to prostitution. Like many French women past and present, Julie Daubié put her education to practical use in order to try to better women's lot. In 1874 she founded an association for woman's emancipation.

While the first women (mainly foreigners) were admitted to the Medical Faculty in 1867, the Sorbonne (the Faculty of Letters of the University of Paris) did not fully admit women until 1880. A few outstanding women had been able to sit in on courses at the university

Introduction

level from the 1860s on. The Collège de France (founded in 1530) permitted women to attend its famed lectures, but the College has no examinations and does not offer degrees. And even after they had obtained the necessary degrees from institutions that did grant them, access to the professions was difficult.

There were a series of "firsts" eagerly hailed by the press. In this list of early successes it is worth noting that many of these early women scholars were scientists. Madeleine Brès (1839-1925) became the first French woman doctor. Her 1875 thesis was on nursing. Like many women doctors, she concentrated on the problems of women and children. Although women could study law from 1884 on, it was not until 1900 that the all-male bar admitted women. Marie Curie held the Sorbonne chair in physics in 1906. The following year Mlle Robert became the first woman agrégée (one who holds a graduate degree) in the field of natural sciences. Of the women awarded doctorates between 1870 and 1930, 522 were in medicine, 55 in science, 53 in law, 19 in humanities, and 14 in pharmacy. Today the majority of young women in France's universities are pursuing majors in the "traditional" fields of the humanities.

Women now constitute about half of the university population. And, while they have had a slow and difficult time making their way into the more prestigious Grandes Écoles, they are somewhat ahead of their American counterparts. The proportion of women occupying liberal professions reflects this achievement. When women were first admitted to the École Polytechnique (a scientific and technical school that emphasizes engineering, long considered a male enclave) in 1972, a young woman had the highest score in the competitive entry exam. Recent figures show some rise in the number of women studying science and technology. However, all such figures must be viewed within the context of the French education system. Enrollment cannot be equated with matriculation, nor even less, with a position in one's field. Still France's education system—that includes écoles maternelles, free noncompulsory nursery schools—has played a major part in women's attainments.

The student uprising in May 1968 sought educational reform. One of the results was the Higher Educational Act passed in November of that same year. The act reiterates traditional goals. At the same time, it sets forth a concept relatively new to French universities, education to give one greater control over one's destiny. How this will be implemented is ever the problem. Attempts at educational reform in both the previous and present regimes have encountered stiff—at times violent—opposition. Financial constraints are but one part of the complex problem.

French universities are now becoming involved for the first time in guidance, professional training, and continuing education. This last area has wide ramifications for women. Courses are being offered by radio and television for those unable to attend classes. A

Introduction

recent law recognizes the time women have spent "educating" their children and dispenses them from some of the formal entry requirements to university studies--provided that they pass the entrance exams. Professional work is also being given academic credit. The national educational system is at last taking notice of the difficulties women encounter in pursuing higher education, education indispensable for so many careers. The problem now appearing is that of the disparity between the aspirations professional training brings and actual employment. Women in France are finally able to participate fully in the vast national educational system just at a time when professional opportunities are being adversely affected.

Note: see Françoise Mayeur's books for further details about the development of women's education in France in the nineteenth century.

FAMILY PLANNING

At the beginning of the nineteenth century France was the most densely populated country in Europe. A hundred and fifty years later it had barely doubled the number of inhabitants while neighboring Great Britain had increased fivefold during the same period. Although not openly acknowledged, limitation of family size was obviously taking place. This low birth rate in French society has been ascribed both to the growing awareness of the child as an autonomous individual, the concept of childhood as a stage in life, and to the view that women were more than just vehicles for procreation. In spite of the strong position of the Catholic church against birth control, marriage was increasingly being separated from procreation.

Comparatively reliable family planning occurred initially in the more favored segments of society but, by the end of the nineteenth century, it had spread to the lower classes as well. Confessional manuals indicate that it was already a concern during the Middle Ages. This change in family size appears to have helped feminist activities. Nineteenth-century feminists were mainly bourgeois women with few children. Later, working-class women participated in women's activities when contraception became more widespread and they were somewhat able to limit their family size. At the same time, however, France became more concerned with the declining birthrate. Émile Zola's (1804-1902) Fécondité (1899) is the best-known of the literary expressions of this preoccupation.

The increasingly private practice of family limitation had its counterpart in the implementation of increasingly pronatatalist state policies. The long-standing concern of French conservatives for large, legitimate families was buttressed by France's tragic loss of a million and a half men in the First World War. Since the birthrate remained low throughout the Third Republic, firm measures seemed

Introduction

indicated. With little public awareness, the right wing Bloc National voted a law on 31 July 1920 designed to repress abortion and anticonceptual propaganda. Another, less well-known law was passed in 1923 to make certain that the 1920 law be vigorously applied. Abortion was changed from a felony to a misdemeanor, to take it from jury trial, where there were many acquittals, to stricter judges. The result of these laws was that many women underwent clandestine abortions in the following decades with grave, sometimes fatal consequences.

What is striking in retrospect is that these laws (as Karen Offen has shown was also the case for earlier debate on the topic) were seen only in terms of France's need to increase the population. That women are the ones who bear children appears not to have been considered. Nelly Roussel (1878-1922), an ardent advocate of women's rights and birth control, took up the suggestion of earlier neo-Malthusian Marie Huot, who had worked with militant communard Paule Mink (1839-1901) for women's concerns, and in 1919 proposed a reproductive strike, "une grève des ventres," against the aggressive pronatalist policies of the government.28 That same year she noted that all the promotion of large families was done without reference to women. As it turned out, the restrictive laws did not have the desired effect. The birthrate continued to decline during the interwar period.

Prior to the First World War birth control had been promoted by small radical groups, neo-Malthusians (who advocated contraception, not continence), and free-love advocates. Among the neo-Malthusians was Paul Robin, author of La question sexuelle (1878) and founder of the Ligue pour la Régénération Humaine. Eugène Humbert joined him to publish the review Génération consciente. Their efforts were attacked by the church, the medical corps, and the law. The war effectively ended their campaign.

It was middle-class women who took up the campaign for family planning and sex information in the period between the wars. Most young girls remained in ignorance of the most elemental knowledge of physiology. Educator Henriette Alquier was brought to trial in 1929 for teaching sex education. She had also incurred official wrath for pointing out that abortion was a class crime. For the poor—who were generally unaware of modern birth control methods—it was but a means of contraception. The support of the entire feminist press helped secure her acquittal. Humbert joined Manuel Devaldès in the movement Génération Consciente, founded in 1921. They endeavored to publicize foreign experiences in this domain during the next few years. Both Humbert and his wife Jeanne served prison terms for their advocacy of birth control. Other tentative efforts were made to circumvent the law.

At the initiative of Bertie Albrecht the Assemby of the World League for Sexual Reform met in Paris in 1932. Bertie Albrecht

Introduction

(1895-1943) was from a well-to-do background. Yet she was committed to helping others less fortunate. She worked in a factory at one point. Later she travelled abroad to find out more about recent research in family planning. Ultimately she gave her life in the Resistance after playing a vital role in that war within a war.

After meeting Sylvia Pankhurst in London Albrecht founded the review Problème sexuel in 1932. The aim of this short-lived journal was to publicize foreign clinical experiences and to work to change the laws on contraception. But these efforts, like the earlier ones, were interrupted once again by a global conflict.

Changes in postwar France, along with scientific advances in birth control methods, made the problem current and pressing. Further, the legislation prohibiting abortion and female contraception was reinforced in the mid-1950s, even though this move was contrary to prevailing preferences. In 1956 Dr. Marie Andrée Lagroua Weill-Hallé, a young woman physician from a militant Catholic background, founded Maternité Heureuse (which later became Planning Familial) with feminists Evelyne Sullerot and Catherine Valabrègue. They were joined by doctors from the Left who continued the efforts of Dr. Jean Dalsace, who had set up the first French birth control consultation center in 1937. At this same time, journalist Jacques Derogy brought out his book Des enfants malgré nous? (1956).

These early efforts were condemned by the church, the medical establishment, demographers, the popular press, and others. The Planning Familial endeavored to keep the movement out of the control of the conservative male medical corps. A first clinic was opened at Grenoble in 1960. Two years later presidential candidate François Mitterrand proposed a law to rescind that of 1920. After much deliberation, a national law was passed in 1967 which modified somewhat the notorious law of 1920. Known for Neuwirth, the legislator who sponsored it, this law provided for the distribution of contraceptives on doctors' orders. A special registry similar to that required for narcotics had to be maintained. The medical establishment further restricted implementation of the legislation. Dissemination of family planning information and commercial publicity on the topic continued to be prohibited. It was not surprising, then, that a survey taken in 1974 found only ten percent of French women were using modern contraceptive methods.

The newly emerging French feminist movement of the 1970s concentrated upon sexual issues, those concerning women's control of their bodies: sexuality, birth control, and abortion. Sexual politics brought many women together. The old taboos of silence over subjects relating to women, to reproduction, were broken. Radical and reformist feminists alike worked to call attention to women's demands. In April 1971 the "Manifesto of the 343" was published in Le Nouvel observateur. The manifesto contained the names of women who publicly admitted to having undergone abortions, declarations

Introduction

heretofore kept secret. Since abortion was then a crime in France, these women openly challenged the authorities to prosecute them. In point of fact, some of these women had not actually undergone abortions. They signed in solidarity, for abortion was a possiblity all French women faced because information on contraception was so restricted.

To protect these women and all those accused of abortion and to mobilize the immense response and abundant mail the provocation had aroused, the organization Choisir la Cause des Femmes was formed by Simone de Beauvoir and Gisèle Halimi, both signers of the manifesto, and the eminent biologist Jean Rostand. The group used the highly publicized trial at Bobigny in 1972 to try the law of abortion itself. Militant lawyer Gisèle Halimi undertook the defense of a young girl who had undergone an abortion after seduction and of those charged with her, her mother and several friends. In an election year politicians were forced to address the issue. Many noted specialists, including Nobel laureate Jacques Monod, were brought in by the defense.

Popular and respected Minister of Health and the Family in Giscard d'Estaing's Center-Right government, Simone Veil was charged by the president to introduce a more liberal law on contraception in 1974. The measure passed quickly; it was long overdue. The parliamentarians assumed that this would stem the movement in favor of abortion. With consummate political skill, Simone Veil put forth a bill supporting abortion just a few months later. The government had decided to accept a fait accompli. In spite of the opposition of the church and the Council of the Order of Physicians, the bill passed for a five-year trial period. Women demonstrated and rallied to ensure its permanent adoption in 1979.

This law on abortion (referred to as the Veil law), included provisions for the establishment of maternity information centers. Abortion is no substitute for contraception. Under the newly renamed Ministry of Women's Rights, vigorous efforts are under way to provide free family planning information. There are spots on the public radio and TV stations, signs in the métro and brochures in post offices and social security bureaus. Concern now focuses on making these three major bills--concerning divorce, contraception, and abortion--and other recent legislation more fully responsive to women's needs. For as it is often pointed out, it is easier to change the laws than to change what the French call les mentalités, preconceived ideas.

RECENT DEVELOPMENTS

A government of the Left recently came to power in France for the first time in twenty-five years. With control of both the presidency

Introduction

and the parliament, the Socialist party has a mandate to profoundly change French society. What is noteworthy is the fact that it was the women's vote that put the Socialists in power. Now French women have expectations from that government. Historically the socialists have been favorable to women's concerns. The problem today is the serious economic situation. Women want financial autonomy and participation, on an equal basis with men, in the economic life of their country. There will have to be accommodation.

French women have become more pragmatic in their approach, a change from the many earlier theoretical and separatist ideologies. Psychanalyse et Politique organized a political rally and urged its followers to vote for Mitterrand on the first round. This was the first time in more than a decade that those who had vowed to have nothing to do with the patriarchal state entered into the political process, at least on the national level. At the same time, Psych et Po legally assumed the name Mouvement de Libération des Femmes. This move brought dissension in the feminist ranks. Other French women's groups contend that the name belongs to all women. Women's liberation in France today must represent the "thousand and one tendencies of the Movement of the Liberation of Women . . . that are not trademarked."[29] The tendency to coteries, chapelles, among French feminist movements has reasserted itself. It seems probable, then, that new impetus for change in women's status will come from official governmental directives. In particular, the newly renamed Ministry of Women's Rights seems destined to play a major role.

The Minister Delegate to the Prime Minister for Women's Rights is Yvette Roudy, a feminist and socialist of long-standing. In 1964 she translated Betty Friedan's The Feminine Mystique into French. This work served as a catalyst for the emerging new French feminist movement. She has written other works, including La femme en marge (q.v.). François Mitterrand wrote the preface to this book. He noted that whether it is the minimum salary, the right to work, the length and conditions of work, the problems of the old and young, or the rise in prices, it is always women who are the first, and most affected, victims of crises. There can only be a true socialist society, he maintains, when women will not just be recognized as equal with men, but also as different. Men should not impose the patriarchal model. They must allow women to invent the model best suited to their needs so that women too may contribute fully to the new society he envisions.

Yvette Roudy insisted that her ministry be changed from that of women's condition to that of women's rights. It is better to speak of rights, she insists, than a condition for the issue is one of individual liberties and human dignity. She would like France to become the country of women's rights. Her plans call for "positive discrimination" for women. Women have internalized their submissive state. The struggle is against a whole series of specific inequalities. Her program has been viewed as one of "vast ambitions." This

26

Introduction

is consistent with her mandate that states: "Mme Roudy is charged with setting forth measures destined to make women's rights respected in society, with causing all discrimination against them to be eliminated, and with increasing the guarantees of equality in the political, economic, social, and cultural realms."[30]

Information has become one of the key areas of her ministry. Historically, women have not been apprised of their rights. Ignorance can also lead to fear. Women must become familiar with their rights and the world they live in. They can reach civic maturity only when they know the laws. This achieved, women will be able to participate in the political process as full and equal citizens.

History, particularly women's history, which is just now being written or rewritten, will provide the perspective necessary to assess fully the many changes that have taken place in the situation of women in France in the past decade. Simone de Beauvoir foresees the impact of contraception as comparable to that of the introduction of the printing press.[31] Françoise Giroud voices the opinion of many in seeing the evolution of women as the most important social phenomenon of our time. The traditional persists. But fundamental changes are taking place. These changes and the reflections provoked by these changes are now being committed to paper. This discourse is no longer subaltern, continually erased and effaced. It must be heard and heeded if half of humanity is to achieve economic and cultural emancipation.

NOTES

1. The information presented in this essay has been drawn from the books included in this volume and from documents and materials supplied by the French Embassy Cultural Services and the Ministry for Women's Rights. The histories by Armogathe and Albistur, Huguette Bouchardeau, and Jean Rabaut are useful French works. Of particular interest are the books and articles of historians Patrick Kay Bidelman, James McMillan, Karen Offen, and Charles Sowerwine. Further resources will be found in the section on research.

2. Elise Boulding, The Underside of History (Boulder: Westview Press, 1977), 545. Cited in Andrée Michel, Le féminisme (Paris: P.U.F., 1979), 42.

3. Caroline C. Lougee, Le Paradis des Femmes: Women, Salons, and Social Stratification in Seventeenth-Century France (Princeton: Princeton University Press, 1976).

4. Arthur M. Wilson, "Treated Like Imbecile Children (Diderot): The Enlightenment and the Status of Women," in Woman in the 18th Century and Other Essays, ed. Paul S. Fritz and Richard Morton (Toronto and Sarasota: Samuel Stevens Hakkert, 1976), 89-118.

Introduction

    5. An anthology entitled Cahiers de doléances des femmes en 1789 et autres textes was published by des femmes in 1981.
    6. Olympe de Gouges, "Déclarations des droits de la femme et de la citoyenne," in Women in France, ed. Marie Collins and Sylvie Weil Sayre (New York: Scribners, 1974), 46.
    7. Jules Michelet, Les femmes dans la Révolution (Paris: A. Delhays, 1854).
    8. The inferior status of married women was long institutionalized in the Civil Code. For example, until 1927 women--but not men--lost their nationality when they married a partner not a French citizen. Only in 1938 could they exercise their full capacities as citizens; not until 1965 did they obtain real legal emancipation. Married women's legal incapacity during this long period was attenuated somewhat by the doctrine of "tacit consent," a legal presumption that married women acted with their husband's authorization. See James McMillan, Housewife or Harlot: The Place of Women in French Society, 1870-1940 (New York: St. Martin's Press, 1981), 129.
    9. Monique A. Piettre, La condition féminine à travers les âges (Paris: Marabout, 1974), 185.
    10. The literature on the Code is extensive, and there are many editions of the law itself. To fully comprehend the situation of French women since the Code was drawn up in 1804, one needs to know its provisions. A contemporary summary is Auguste-Charles Guichard, Le code des femmes: de leurs droits, privilèges, devoirs et obligations; ou, récits et entretiens dont la simple lecture leur apprend, en peu d'heures et sans nulle fatigue, ce qu'il importe le plus de savoir pour être en état de diriger elles-mêmes leurs affaires, de stipuler et défendre leur intérêts, dans toutes les circonstances de la vie. . ., 2 vols. (Paris: N. Pichard, 1823). On the development of French matrimonial law prior to 1914 see Charles Lefebvre, Cours de doctorat sur l'histoire du droit matrimonial français, 3 vols. (Paris: L. Larose & L. Terrin, 1906-1923), condensed in La famille en France, dans le droit et dans les moeurs (Paris: M. Giard, 1920). For the theory behind the framing of the Code see P.-A. Fenet, Recueil complet des travaux prépatoires du Code civil, vol. 1 (1836; reprint, Osnabruck: Zeller, 1968). Revisions of the Code within the structure of the patriarchal family are set forth in Ernest Legouvé, Histoire morale des femmes (Paris: Sandré, 1849). Feminist responses to the Code are elaborated in Léon Richer, Le Code des femmes (Paris: E. Dentu, 1883) and Maria Vérone, La femme et la loi (Paris: Larousse, 1920). As Karen M. Offen notes, the treatises written by the first two women to obtain doctorates from the Paris Faculty of Law are of particular interest for the development of women's history. They are: Sarmisa D. Bilcesco, De la condition légale de la mère en droit romain et en droit français (Paris: A. Rousseau, 1890) and Jeanne Chauvin, Des professeurs accessibles aux femmes en droit romain et en droit français (Paris: V. Giard & E. Brière, 1892). For additional references and background, see Offen's excellent article "The 'Woman Question' as a Social Issue in Nineteenth-Century France: A Bibliographical Essay" (Stanford: CROW, 1977) reproduced from Third Republic/Troisième République, nos. 3-4 (Spring/Fall 1977).

Introduction

11. Article 1124: "Les incapables de contracter sont: les mineurs, les interdits, les femmes mariées." Montlosier wrote in Observations sur le projet de Code Civil, "Women, minor children, and servants can have no property for they themselves are property." Cited in André-Jean Arnaud, Essai d'analyse structurale du Code civil français: la règle du jeu dans la paix bourgeoise (Paris: Librairie Générale du Droit et de Jurisprudence, 1973), 82.

12. See Susan Groag Bell and Karen M. Offen, eds., Women, the Family, and Freedom: The Debate in Documents, 1750-1950, vol. 1 (Stanford: Stanford University Press, 1983).

13. Le Romantisme, 1966. Cited in Jean Rabaut, Histoire des féminismes français (Paris: Stock, 1978), 116.

14. Rabaut, 79.

15. Comtesse de Flavigny, Recueil de prières, de méditations et de lectures. Cited in Pierre Grimal, Histoire mondiale de la femme (Paris: Nouvelle Librairie de France, 1965-67), 4:110.

16. A study of Hubertine Auclert and the Citoyenne was brought out by Edith Taüb in Paris, 1982. See also the chapter devoted to her in Patrick Kay Bidelman, Pariahs Stand Up! The Founding of the Liberal Feminist Movement in France, 1858-1889 (Westport, Conn.: Greenwood, 1982).

17. "Je n'ai pas de droits, donc je n'ai pas de charges; je ne vote pas, je ne paye pas." Hubertine Auclert, Le vote des femmes (Paris: V. Giard & E. Brière, 1908), 137.

18. Bidelman's Pariahs Stand Up! details the founding of the League. This thoroughly researched study of the various feminist groups and figures in the later decades of the nineteenth century contains English translations of several major documents. Léon Richer's L'avenir des femmes (1876) lists the actual law and women's proposed revisions on the opposite page.

19. In addition to Lougee's Le Paradis des femmes, see Joan Kelly-Gadol, "Did Women Have a Renaissance?" in Becoming Visible: Women in European History," ed. Renate Bridenthal and Claudia Koonz (Boston: Houghton Mifflin, 1978).

20. According to Frances I. Clark, women's qualifications to serve as arbiters on matters of language seemed to have rested on oral rather than a written basis of knowledge. Women then--including kings' daughters--lacked a firm grounding in the elements of knowledge. The Position of Women in Contemporary France (London, 1937; rpt. Westport, Conn.: Hyperion, 1981), 108-9.

21. Albistur and Armogathe, 1:239-40.

22. See the article by Louis, Chevalier de Jaucourt (1704-79), who is responsible for many of the Encyclopedia's articles translated in Bell and Offen. Their two volumes provide English versions of the major feminist documents. Jaucourt maintained that the legal codes erred in invariably subjecting a wife to her husband.

23. "Ainsi toute l'éducation des femmes doit être relative aux hommes. Leur plaire, leur être utiles, se faire aimer et honorer d'eux, les élever jeunes, les soigner grands, les conseiller, les consoler, leur rendre la vie agréable et douce; voilà les devoirs

Introduction

des femmes dans tous les temps." Jean-Jacques Rousseau, Émile, ou de l'éducation (Paris: Didot l'aîné & Didot, 1817), 21.

24. M. Gontard, L'enseignement primaire en France, 1789-1833 (Paris: Belles Lettres, 1959), 237. Monseigneur Dupanloup repeated this claim.

25. Rabaut, 150. See also Charles Fourrier, L'enseignement français de 1789 à 1945 (Paris: Institut Pédagogique National) and Monseigneur Dupanloup, M. Duruy et l'éducation des filles, lettre de Mgr l'évêque d'Orléans à un de ses collègues.

26. See the translation of Ferry in Groag and Bell for the further views of Ferry (1832-93), minister of education in 1879 and twice premier during the 1880s. There are selections from Ferry in Antoine Prost's excellent survey Histoire de l'enseignement en France, 1800-1967 (Paris: A. Colin, 1968). Further legislation of this campaign is detailed in Evelyn M. Acomb, The French Laic Laws (1879-1889): The First Anti-Clerical Campaign of the Third French Republic (New York: Octagon, 1967).

27. Prior to this time young French women were technically eligible to take the examinations for the bac, but they had to prepare for it independently. Their schools did not offer Greek and Latin, both required subjects. See Karen Offen, "The Second Sex and the Baccalauréat in Republican France, 1880-1924," French Historical Studies 13, no. 2 (Fall 1983).

28. A recent study is Francis Ronsin, La grève des ventres: propagande néo-malthusienne et baisse de natalité française, XIXe-XXe siècles (Paris: Aubier-Montaigne, 1980).

29. Cited in Le Monde, 11 March 1980. For articles on French feminism see the Spring 1981 and Fall 1981 issues of Contemporary French Civilization, and Dorothy Kaufmann-McCall, "Politics of Difference: The Women's Movement in France from May 1968 to Mitterrand," Signs, Winter 1983.

30. Le Monde, 1 July 1981.

31. Her compatriots share this view. In a 1984 survey of F Magazine, over 11,000 women ranked the availability of contraception--now possible because of the liberalization of earlier legislation--as the factor that had most profoundly affected the daily lives of French women during the last fifteen years.

Women in French History

The observations of Juliette Lamber in 1861 are still largely valid today. She wrote in response to Proudhon, who taxed women with inferiority in virtually all domains. History, Lamber insisted, is the history of men in humanity. And what does this history contain? Battles, massacres, torrents of blood, oppression, injustices, betrayals, retreats, sterile revolutions, shameful responses, and, in the center of all that, a few glimmers of love, devotion, charity, fraternity, piety, and virtues, all cultivated and sustained by woman, woman who has virtually no assigned role in history.

Like their counterparts elsewhere, French women are now attempting to retrieve their history and commit it to writing. Theirs is a history that has been largely ignored in the histories written by men. Men were more educated in the past; they dominated and determined the discipline. Too often women have been caricatured, their presence recognized only during the days of revolution and struggle. A few outstanding figures are presented at the expense of the many less flamboyant but no less courageous and committed. For example, many believe that the militant feminist tradition of the nineteenth century remained dormant until the early 1970s. The histories of Albistur and Armogathe, Bouchardeau, Rabaut, and others show that such was not the case.

Archivists are now reviewing France's rich resources: written documents, iconography, and more recently, the audiovisual record. What may be largely lost is the oral tradition. Much of the history of French women--at least in the lower classes--was oral history. Theirs was an original and independent tradition carried on through tales told at <u>veillées</u>, evening gatherings where women met to continue their domestic occupations and chores, such as sewing, weaving, etc. Contemporary feminists are setting up feminist documentation centers in order to guard the memory of women's struggles, to classify and analyze what is being said, written, and invented pertaining to women, particularly what emanates from them. In French women's search for their identity, history is central.

Women in French History

The history of women in France, their efforts to obtain the vote, to receive an education, and their continuing efforts to participate more fully in their society were sketched in the introductory essay. The books included in this section provide a fuller understanding of this rich and complex history. The general studies treat various periods or movements. The biographies and autobiographies introduce the individual women who have played a part in this history--the plot and characters, so to speak.

The portrayal of women in French history has varied with academic styles. In the early nineteenth century, romantic history exemplified by Jules Michelet (1789-1874) offered a mystical-spiritual view of woman. She was the inspiration and counterpoint of man, imbued with creative powers and allied to Nature. She represented all that was not amenable to the rational. At the same time, he stated in La femme (1860) that women needed marriage and a household.

In the later part of the century the emphasis in historical writing shifted to the public and political domains. Since women were generally not included in the public sphere, they received little attention in these works. When various social groups were analyzed, the range of history was extended--as was the role of women at that time. Nevertheless, as the noted historian Michelle Perrot has observed, it was possible to analyze such institutions without considering the other half of humanity. Only when the family became the object of study did women receive some attention. The work of anthropologist Lévi-Strauss has greatly enlarged the scope of these studies.

In the earlier decades of this century, those who studied women tended to be scholars outside formal academic milieus. French academic history today tends to be quite traditional. It has lagged behind that of Anglo-Saxons in recognizing the sexual dimensions of history, an approach that did not get underway there until the 1970s.

Only with the recent emergence of the French neofeminist movement with its ensuing multiple interrogations about women's role, can women be said to be moving to the center stage of French academic history. A few--like Flora Tristan and Louise Michel--had known brief periods of celebrity as romantic heroines during the period of utopian movements and the aspirations of 1848 and the Commune, only to be subsequently forgotten. If Flora Tristan was remembered at all, it was as Gauguin's grandmother. Louise Michel was the Communard.

French academic history is now being rewritten with a fundamental reappraisal at last under way.[1] At the same time, the writings, journals, and memoirs of important but little known figures--Claire Démar, Suzanne Voilquin, and Hubertine Auclert--are now being reissued. New editions of neglected works are also being issued. The records and writings of contemporary feminists and recent academic

Women in French History

studies are advancing the recording of the present and the rescue of the women of France's past from the annals of anonymity.

NOTES

1. See in particular Michelle Perrot, "Sur l'histoire des femmes en France," Revue du Nord, July-September 1981.

Women in French History

GENERAL STUDIES

ALBISTUR, MAÏTÉ, and DANIEL ARMOGATHE. Histoire du féminisme français [History of French feminism]. 2 vols. Collection pour chacune. Paris: Éditions des femmes, 1977, 1:352 pp.; 2:384 pp. Also issued as a single volume, 528 pp.

This authoritative work synthesizes the complaints of women and feminist concerns through the ages. The authors' research reveals that the feminist demands heard today have a long history; these claims are substantiated by their extensive documentation, much of it previously little known.

The exposé of the "querelle des dames" is divided into four major sections. During the period of "Elitist Feminism," from the sixth century to 1789, feminist discourse is first articulated. However, it has little impact upon concrete action. Christine de Pizan (c. 1346-c. 1430), Louise Labé (c. 1525-1565), Marie de Gournay (1566-1645), and François Poullain de la Barre (1647-1723) are among the best-known figures of this group. Then comes "Feminism on the move" (1789-1871), marked by three successive revolutions and a civil war. During these uprisings women from all conditions organized effectively. But their action tended to be subsumed into collective heroic efforts. Some were involved in utopian socialism. The results of these activities were not commensurate with the sacrifices so many women made. "Bourgeois and Reformist Feminism" (1871-1945) covers a period of more visible attainments. Women entered into male preserves: They worked and, finally, they voted. But abstract laws do not ensure equality. The last period, that of "Radical Feminism," was inaugurated with the publication of The Second Sex (1949). Both theoretical and organizational efforts are now being made to overturn the existing order and seek the specific sources of oppression. In this struggle against male domination, the authors contend that one of the main problems has been that women lack the language, the social discourse, to voice their claims.

This book contains an extensive bibliography as well as many footnotes along with lists of pamphlets, significant dates, and titles of works relevant to the long history of feminist activity in France. While it does not specifically analyze the status of women there, such a portrait is indirectly drawn.

_____. Le grief des femmes [Women's grievances]. 2 vols. Paris: Éditions Hier & Demain, 1978.

Albistur and Armogathe have assembled two volumes of documents to complement their history. These anthologies contain 800 years of French women's complaints and concerns. Texts and images, testimony and portraits are included in an effort to fill in the missing iconography as well as the missing history of women in France.

The first volume offers feminist materials from the end of the Middle Ages to the Second Republic. The period from the Second

Empire to the present is covered in the second volume. The materials offered had not been readily available. The feminist texts are enhanced by portraits, photos, cartoons, and leaflets. Scholarly references are placed at the end of each chapter. Relevant critical studies are also listed. The texts themselves serve as a good introduction to the history of women in France for both scholars and students.

BOUCHARDEAU, HUGUETTE. Pas d'histoire, les femmes: 50 ans d'histoire des femmes, 1918-1968 [No history, women: 50 years of women's history, 1918-1968]. Paris: Syros, 1977, 145 pp.

Huguette Bouchardeau sets forth the continuing history of women's efforts to ameliorate the condition of their sex, focusing on the early part of the twentieth century, a period less well known than others. This volume helps fill in the lacunae of the fifty-year period under study. Now at last women such as Cécile Brunschvicg (1897-1946), Nelly Roussel (1878-1922), and others are finding their deserved place in French history.

There are chapters devoted to the struggle for suffrage, the pitfalls of volunteer activities, war against war, prochoice motherhood, and working women. Brief outlines at the end highlight the significant dates in French women's efforts to obtain the vote; in women's pacifist movements from 1915 to 1940; and in the birth control campaign from 1918 to 1971. There is also a list of some noted French feminists with brief biographical information and a summary of French women's organizations.

BRION, HÉLÈNE. La voie féministe [The feminist way]. Collection mémoires des femmes. Paris: Syros, 1978, 117 pp. (Preface, notes and commentary by Huguette Bouchardeau. Voie is a homonym for voix, voice.)

Militant feminist and socialist Hélène Brion (1887-1962) became secretary of the Syndical Federation of Teachers in 1914 and also helped actively in the Confédération Générale du Travail (CGT). Pacifist activities brought about her arrest in 1917 and subsequent trial for "defeatism." The trial was held before a military tribunal; it attracted wide attention. In the end she received a suspended sentence but lost her teaching post. A key factor in obtaining the comparatively favorable outcome was the testimony of numerous feminist personalities.

This manifesto, written about the same time as her trial, treats the relationship between socialism, trade unions, and feminism. With passion Hélène Brion denounced her male socialist and union comrades who are incapable of integrating the goals of women's struggle for emancipation into their political perspectives. "If you do not call women to aid you, the new world you presume to inaugurate will be just as chaotic and unjust as the preceding one was."

There is, she insists, a feminist way that will lead to the radical transformation of social relations. To the most "advanced" of the male militants she issues a call for understanding, comprehension, and cooperation in women's struggle. More than sixty years later, that appeal is still valid.

Hélène Brion's text is accompanied by extensive notes and documentation. There is a chapter outlining the conditions of women teachers in the first decades of the century and another describing the pacifist campaign in France prior to her trial.

CHATEL, NICOLE. Des femmes dans la Résistance [Women in the Resistance]. Collection la Résistance par ceux qui l'ont faite. Paris: Julliard, 1972, 242 pp. (Narratives gathered and presented by Nicole Chatel with the assistance of Annie Boulineau, under the patronage of the National Association of Veterans of the Resistance. Preface by Jean Cassou.)

Nine women from varied backgrounds, social conditions, and convictions recount how they gave themselves wholeheartedly, even at the risk of their lives, to hinder the Nazi occupants of their country. While their vision of the future of France varied, these women were united in their aim to reestablish honor and peace in their beloved country. Some left not only families but also young children, as was the case for militant Communist and trade unionist "Mère" Desrumaux. Claude Gérard held officer rank and assumed military responsibilities. At the end of the war she was named head of female personnel of the Armée de Terre.

For all, this experience totally changed their lives. In those dramatic times they accepted full responsibility for the role that they felt they could and should play next to the men. Theirs was a full and equal role.

CONSTANT, LOUIS, ed. Mémoire de femmes: mémoire du peuple [Women's memoir: the people's memoir]. Paris: Maspero, 1979, 157 pp.

This anthology presents the writings of a group of nineteenth-century women who shared a concern for the proletariat. Some were from the lower classes; others were actively committed to helping this group. The majority of the women were French; all wrote in French. Taken together, the selections provide some idea of women's activities in social and revolutionary activities, including the Commune, in nineteenth-century France.

Suzanne Voilquin, "a woman of the people," endeavored to enlist the aid of the people of Lyon in the Saint-Simonien expedition to the Promised Land in quest of the Femme-Mère, the female Messiah. Flora Tristan is represented by a selection of her Tour de France (1843-44), a crusade she undertook across France on behalf of workers, an undertaking to which she literally gave her life.

Victorine Brocher describes the "living death" she encountered as an ambulance driver during the Commune. She writes of deplorable working conditions, of the striking contrast between luxury and misery. The profound impact of Victor Hugo's Les misérables (1864) is noted, as are efforts to organize study groups and found cooperatives. The name of Alix Payen, a young woman from a bourgeois republican family, is little known. With great difficulty she managed to become a front-line nurse during the worst fighting of the Commune. Selections from her letters describe those events in April-May 1871. Louise Michel, the self-declared anarchist, was often on trial and in jail. Nevertheless she did find much time to write memoirs, novels, and poetry. Here she is represented by a short portrait of Béatrix Excoffans, one of the so-called "pétroleuses," or incendiary women.

CROZET, RENÉ. La sorcellerie en Auvergne [Sorcery in Auvergne]. Roanne: Horvath, 1978, 99 pp.

Auvergne is a comparatively isolated, geographically enclosed region in central France. Thus it is somewhat behind the times. Old customs prevail longer there. The area has a long history of persecution of witchcraft. The trials here presented start with that of the Countess of Deux-Forts in 1150. She was found guilty of witchcraft and executed, along with her servants. The majority of the accused were women. Throughout these trials one hears the echoes of women in revolt.

DUHET, PAULE-MARIE. Les femmes et la Révolution, 1789-1794 [Women and the Revolution, 1789-1794]. Paris: Julliard, 1971, 240 pp.

This study was just being prepared when the new "revolution" of women in France was getting under way. The epigraph from Choderlos de Laclos's De l'éducation des femmes (1783) is still pertinent. "Learn that only through a major revolution can one arise from slavery. Is such a revolution possible? It is for you women to respond, for it depends upon your courage."

Women's contribution to the French Revolution, an event whose impact extended far beyond France, is succinctly outlined. Paule-Marie Duhet has used many original documents for her study. They include a number of projected programs for women's education set forth by Talleyrand, Condorcet, and Lakanal. In the compass of a few years a great deal happened. When the National Assembly adopted the Déclaration des droits de l'homme et du citoyen (1789), women contended that "man" meant mankind. They too had worked hard and sacrificed much to realize common goals.

The careers of demi-mondaines and grandes dames such as Mme de Staël and Mme Roland are included, as are those of a remarkable group who shared both boldness and social ostracism: Théroigne de Méricourt, Etta Palm, Olympe de Gouges, and Claire Lacombe.

Les femmes dans la Résistance [Women in the Resistance]. Acts of the colloquium held at the Sorbonne under the initiative of the Union des Femmes Françaises. Paris: Édition du Rocher, 1977, 312 pp.

In November 1975 a colloquium was organized under the auspices of the Union des Femmes Françaises. This group came into being during the Occupation, when various Resistance elements combined. Shortly after the war the Union had well over 600,000 members.

Since that time the number has declined considerably. (The views of these women are found in its weekly, <u>Heures Claires</u>, which has a large printing.) These women have not forgotten their former commitment. They want to remind all of the role that French women played in their country's worst hours since the Revolution.

The three main themes of the presentations at the colloquium are: the participation of women in all activities of the Resistance; the specific activities of women in the Resistance; and the Resistance as an important step in the evolution of the feminine condition. Under each of these headings are to be found papers that range from personal testimony and firsthand accounts to more general observations from those who were involved in the French underground movement, men as well as women. The many brief interventions offer fascinating insights into the multiple activities, heroic endeavors, and all-pervasive presence of French women in this war within a war. All the various tendencies of the Resistance in both zones are represented. The work does assume a general knowledge of the events and of French politics. The U.F.F. is dominated by the French Communist Party.

FRANCOS, ANIA. <u>Il était des femmes dans la Résistance</u> [There were women in the Resistance]. Paris: Stock, 1978, 484 pp.

Only after French women had demonstrated their patriotism (once again) in the Second World War were they finally accorded the vote. During the war years women of all political persuasions were able to work together for a common goal, to refuse the unacceptable. The men, on the other hand, were often divided by irreconcilable differences.

The women who participated in the Resistance came from all classes of French society: De Gaulle's niece, the daughter of a wealthy industrialist, Communist workers, students, and housewives. They served in many capacities. Ania Francos interviewed some of these women or, in the case of those who gave their lives to the cause, their families or friends. Their respective destinies during the Occupation are recounted. Some led a "double life" and were never suspected; others were caught or betrayed early on and imprisoned, tortured, or executed.

The chapters on the prison camps are difficult to read. Under inhumane conditions, some women came to terms with their captors. The vast majority, however, helped one another to survive. These women have much to tell.

<u>L'histoire sans qualités: essais</u> [History without qualities: essays]. Paris: Galilée, 1979, 223 pp. (Essays by Christine Dufrancatel, Arlette Farge, Christine Faure, Geneviève Fraisse, Michelle Perrot, Elisabeth Salvaresi, and Pascale Werner.)

This is history without "qualities," that is, without the qualities acknowledged by male-dominated history: accomplishments, nobility, etc. This is a different history, one that reveals that women basically have not been passive or submissive in the past.

Arlette Farge writes of women of the lower classes in pre-Revolutionary society. Sexual codes were not fixed then. The "irregular" voices of Flora Tristan and George Sand are analyzed by Pascale Werner. Exact contemporaries, Tristan and Sand were both illegitimate daughters of aristocratic fathers and plebian mothers. Both led "irregular" lives in the new society that evolved after the 1840 revolution. The theme of the woman of the people, victim of bourgeois man, the man of leisure, is traced in Christine Dufranctel's essay on the "imaginary woman" of men. Geneviève Fraisse considers "les bavardes," women chatterers. Their speech is marked by moralism. Fraisse views this as a tactic to reassure the masculine world. Feminism should not frighten.

Historian Michelle Perrot's essay on "the rebellious woman of the people" offers much material for reflection. She sets forth the various forms of activity lower-class women used in their daily struggle to ensure their families' existence. Their concerns focused on bread, shelter, and salary. At times they took to the streets to voice their concerns: price hikes, overcharging, etc. They intervened with their very bodies during the troubled periods of 1816-17, 1828, 1839-40, 1847-48, and 1870-71, and throughout the century in uprisings for subsistence.

Proletarian women invested the city spaces. In contrast, upper-class women were sequestered, hence virtual prisoners. In addition to being workplaces, washing places served a social function. They were places of practical feminism. Mutual help was extended. These networks of women's communications frightened the authorities of the developing industrial society. Efforts were made to restrict women's spaces. Proletarian women's speech and gestures were irrespectful and rich in subversion (grosse, i.e., pregnant). However, their male comrades wanted dignified action; they were suspicious of women's volatile interruptions. Thus it was that these women of the people became "missing persons" in nineteenth-century working-class organizations. But they were neither silent nor submissive. They had, as Perrot shows, other gestures and other words to affirm their presence and their rights. The history of these lower-class women is one of daily practices of concrete forms of resistance. Since it is another history, a different history, it has been largely ignored.

MANDROU, ROBERT. Possession et sorcellerie au XVIIe siècle: textes inédits [Possession and witchcraft in the seventeenth century: unpublished texts]. Paris: Arthème Fayard, 1979, 348 pp.

Ten years after the appearance of his dissertation, Magistrats et sorciers dans la France du XVIIe siècle historian Robert Mandrou published some of the texts used in the earlier study, a historical and psychological work. In general, he subscribes to Michelet's thesis set forth in La sorcière (1862), for it presents a plausible and coherent explanation based upon the role women played in rural communities, a role that brought them into conflict with masculine powers vested in law and jurisprudence. Women organized a counterpower in face of the male order symbolized by the lord and the priest. Men were jealous of women's countersociety; they were in command and wished to stay there. Consequently women were seen as a threat to the male establishment. The notion long prevailed that women undertook nocturnal activities; these might involve revenge against their oppressors.

Michelet--a man ahead of his time, currently being reappraised --focused on the trials of peasant women. Mandrou includes some major trials of the century, those involving figures from higher levels of society. He notes the crucial role of doctors in analyzing the phenomenon of witchcraft. Here they were in an area of presumed competence. He also traces the slow evolution of religion in the face of a phenomenon that was obviously disturbing yet did not fit into traditional theological schemata. The texts published here have provided new material for the debate over the sociological role of the trials of sorceresses in pre-Revolutionary France.

MARKALE, JEAN. La femme celte: mythe et sociologie [The Celtic woman: myth and sociology]. Paris: Payot, 1972, 409 pp.

Jean Markale documents the privileged position of women in Celtic cultures when compared with women in Germanic or Mediterranean cultures. He believes that while the Celts, like other Indo-Europeans, lived under a patriarchal system, careful study of myths of Celtic origin shows that women were playing a more important role in that culture than had been suspected. Oral as well as literary traditions are surveyed to ascertain the Celtic conception of women.

There are observations on the historical and legal situation of women in Celtic societies. They practiced fosterage, or communal child care. Duties were assigned to men as well as women. The major part of the study is devoted to analysis and exploration of the myths of that culture. The author believes that these myths are relevant today. He has endeavored to "reestablish a truth that patriarchal society has tried to conceal." Markale contends that once Celtic man subjugated woman to his authority, he nevertheless continued to seek the image of that earlier period when the female was viewed as the all-powerful protector and initiator. He notes that the majority of the most celebrated French sanctuaries dedicated to the Virgin Mary--such as Notre Dame de Chartres--are built upon sites once consecrated to a female Celtic divinity.

MUHLSTEIN, ANKA. La femme soleil: les femmes et le pouvoir, une relecture de Saint-Simon [The sun woman: women and power, a re-reading of Saint-Simon]. Paris: Denoël/Gonthier, 1976, 182 pp.

The lengthy memoirs of the Duc de Saint-Simon (1675-1755) offer searching observations, brilliant descriptions, and telling details. They provide a historical fresco rich in portraits. In the past, the memoirs have been read for what they tell of Louis XIV, the Sun King, the organization of the nobility, the cabals of the court, and military history. Struck by the extraordinary importance Saint-Simon accorded women, Anka Muhlstein examines his portrayal of women.

Women have seldom been in the center of history; they were relegated to the shadows, behind the scenes. Saint-Simon puts them in center stage, in contrast to historians such as Voltaire in his Century of Louis XIV (1751).

Women were central in Saint-Simon's own life. His mother—almost half a century younger than her husband—was a preponderant influence. His wife was an ideal companion. The duke literally owed his familiarity and privileged place with the royal family to his wife's position of dame d'honneur to the Duchesse de Berry.

Saint-Simon was not content to merely describe what he saw during his many years at the court of Versailles: he sought to show motives. The many women he mentions are judged by their capacities, not their sex. The portrait of the Duchesse de Noailles, mother of twenty, concludes in an apotheosis for, "she lives still . . . at the age of eighty-seven as patriarch of her large family."

The two outstanding figures of the Mémoires are the Princesse des Ursins (1642-1722), and Mme de Maintenon (1635-1719). Together they symbolize the reign of women during this period. The former "governed" Spain, the latter, France.

The extraordinary Princesse des Ursins is praised for her "male" courage, reflection, and tenacity. Her life had international impact. She was all-powerful in Spain from 1704 to 1714 in her capacity as counselor to the very young and very malleable Marie-Louise of Savoy who, in turn, "commanded" her husband King Philip V, grandson of Louis XIV. The princess was a woman who "everywhere figured so markedly and so singularly, albeit in diverse manners;" who possessed intelligence, courage, industry, and resourcefulness. What the duke finds striking in her case was that though neither mother, wife, nor mistress, she managed to reign nevertheless.

In contrast to the highborn princess, Mme de Maintenon was the impoverished granddaughter of the ardent Protestant writer Agrippa d'Aubigné. In 1651 she married the burlesque writer Scarron, who died nine years later. Through a series of events, more "romanesques" than novels, she became governess to the children born to Louis XIV and his first mistress and grand favorite, Mme de Montespan. Through patience, adroitness, and political acumen she extended her influence. The result was that this king, "so jealous of his independence, determined never to be governed, was governed as one never had been before." All the spectators at court were aware of the reign of Mme de Maintenon except the king. Yet her power was that of influence, always a precarious power. She was unable to undertake real political decisions.

Women in French History

It is ironic that the place and role of Mme de Maintenon would have remained virtually unnoticed in history but for the duke's Memoirs. Saint-Simon could not abide her. To him she represented all that was wrong with the court of Louis XIV. Nevertheless this remarkable woman of authority, activity, and intelligence held power as the "confidant, mistress, wife, all-powerful minister." Louis XIV esteemed as well as loved women. With the freer mores of the eighteenth century, women lost respect. The century of the Enlightenment found women as protectors, mistresses, and muses. They were not politically active. The concentration of the court appears to have favored such endeavors in the preceding century.

PIETTRE, MONIQUE. La condition feminine à travers les âges [The feminine condition through the ages]. Paris: Marabout Universitaire, 1974, 315 pp. (Awarded the Broquette Cronin Prize of the French Academy.)

While this is a general historical survey of women's condition, it nevertheless possesses much material on French women. This is especially true of the historical sections. They draw upon a number of French examples. The work concludes with speculations on the portent of the International Year of Woman.

RABAUT, JEAN. Histoire des féminismes français [History of French feminisms]. Paris: Stock, 1978, 411 pp.

This history of French feminist activities was written by a man who has done works on other "oppressed" figures and groups, including those against the military, the French Left, and the Socialist Jean Jaurès. For one somewhat familiar with the general outlines of French history this is a useful survey. There is much detail and many anecdotes are recounted. Jean Rabaut presents an examination of the feminist movement with extensive documentation. He narrates the struggles French women have undertaken in their quest for emancipation.

Brief summaries cover the period from the end of the Middle Ages to the beginning of the eighteenth century. The major portion of the work is devoted to the last two centuries. Feminist movements are situated in the social context and in the working conditions of the times. Brief introductions are provided for virtually all those who participated in this movement. There is an extensive bibliography. In addition to books and studies, it includes materials from the national archives and police reports. The inclusion of reference numbers is helpful, as anyone who has worked in French archives well knows.

French, English, and American dissertations devoted to the topic are listed in a work that has been described as having the appeal of a detective novel. The reader becomes engrossed in the incredible adventures--and misadventures--travels and lives of some of the extraordinary French women who have undertaken to support the battle of their sex for justice and equality.

SAMUEL, PIERRE. Amazones, guerrières, et gaillardes [Amazons, women warriors, and determined women]. Brussels: Éditions Complexe, 1975, 319 pp. (Preface by Françoise d'Eaubonne.)

Pierre Samuel analyzes myths and folklore that tell of women whose physical exploits equal or exceed those of men. As he notes, such women have been present at every age and in every civilization.

The Amazons were self-sufficient, capable of caring for their needs and defense. Only rarely did they encounter men. The "women-warriors" equaled men in that "prestigious" occupation, while the "determined women" established their physical superiority in more pacific domains.

Most of the examples given are not well known. Samuel, a noted professor of mathematics, has accumulated evidence to contradict the claim that women are weak. He believes that such a view is the result of a cultural bias. It is not biologically tenable.

TRISTAN, ANNE, and ANNIE DE PISAN [pseuds.]. Histoires du MLF [Histories of the MLF]. Collection l'ordre des choses. Calmann-Lévy, 1977, 260 pp. (Preface by Simone de Beauvoir.)

The term MLF (Mouvement de Libération des Femmes) was first used by the press to describe a small group of women who held a demonstration at the Arch of Triumph in August 1970. They attempted to place a wreath at this shrine of French patriotism honoring "one more unknown than the soldier, his wife." This was the first in a number of similar public demonstrations held to call attention to the concerns of women.

The term "histories" in the title is deliberate; there are accounts other than those of the two young women. While they often found themselves opposed over politics and tactics, they found a common denominator in a collective revolt against women's oppressors. Anne states that every woman who will no longer accept the destiny society has imposed upon her should join the MLF. Such women are to be found in ever-increasing numbers. Their individual histories combine to form the collective history of the women's movement in France.

The perspectives of the two authors differ. Anne Tristan was involved in the MLF from the beginning. Annie de Pisan was a militant union activist. Earlier she had participated in MFA (Masculin/Féminin/Avenir), an organization that gradually assumed a radical feminist stance. The childhood and youth of the two anonymous authors, along with a growing awareness of women's oppression, all contributed to their joining in the newly emerging French women's movement.

As Simone de Beauvoir writes in the preface, this book is more than a collection of anecdotes. It places one at the heart of the problems faced in the birth and development of a revolutionary movement. The "decolonization" of women implies a radical change in society. How can this be reconciled with democracy? How can the traps of power and disorder be avoided? What

compromises are possible? Which are acceptable? These are the
dilemmas the women's movement must come to terms with. These
histories detail the struggle of those first, formative years.
　　Anne Tristan [pseud.] has since published <u>Histoires d'amour</u>
([Love stories] Paris: Calmann-Lévy, 1979, 226 pp.), the tales
of great loves past and present, tales of love in many forms.

UNIVERSITY OF POITIERS. <u>Cahiers de civilisation médiévale, Xe-XIIe
　　siècles</u> [Notebooks on medieval civilization, 10th through 12th
　　centuries]. Poitiers: University of Poitiers, 1977, 306 pp.
　　(Special issue devoted to "Women in the Middle Ages," nos. 2-3,
　　April-September 1977).
　　　　These articles employ traditional approaches and use the tra-
　　ditional sources of medieval history. This conventional scholar-
　　ship brought criticism from feminist historians attending the
　　colloquium upon which this volume is based. In general, only
　　women from the highest levels of society are studied. Further,
　　these women are described from the male perspective.
　　　　Marie-Thérèse d'Alverny presents medieval women as seen by the
　　theologians and the philosophers. Chiara Frugoni examines the
　　iconography of women from the tenth through twelfth centuries.
　　Women in French and Occitan literature of the eleventh through
　　thirteenth centuries are studied by Rita Lejeune. Jean Verdon
　　comments on the sources for the history of women in the West
　　from the tenth through thirteenth centuries. Other, more spe-
　　cialized, topics are also included.

VILLENEUVE, ROLAND. <u>Les procès de sorcellerie</u> [Witchcraft trials].
　　Paris: Payot, 1979, 246 pp. (New edition of a work published
　　in 1974.)
　　　　Roland Villeneuve provides one of the few serious studies of
　　the trial records of those unfortunates--many of them women--who,
　　until the end of the seventeenth century, were accused of witch-
　　craft. Those with physical deformities or mental troubles were
　　frequently the natural victims of such charges. Personal ven-
　　dettas also resulted in denunciations. As late as 1677, the
　　"scandalous and impure practices" of women, such as wearing low-
　　cut gowns, was thought to invite or reveal evil. Women prisoners
　　were frequently raped. This in addition to various tortures used
　　to extract confessions.
　　　　Villeneuve contends that the texts show the collusion of the
　　church in the denunciation and pursuit of presumed sorcerers and
　　sorceresses.

　　As Robert Mandrou noted, the recent literature on witchcraft is
rapidly expanding. Recent titles include:

BONCOEUR, JEAN-LOUIS. <u>Le village au sortilège: chroniques singu-
　　lières sur la magie rustique dans les pays du coeur de France</u>
　　[The village under a spell: unusual reports of rural magic in
　　the regions of central France]. Paris: Fayard, 1979, 412 pp.

Women in French History

FOURNIER, PIERRE FRANÇOIS. Magie et sorcellerie: essai historique accompagné de documents [Magic and witchcraft: historical essay accompanied by documents]. Moulins: Éditions Iponnée, 1979, 453 pp.

LEUTRAT, PAUL. La sorcellerie lyonnaise [Lyon witchcraft]. Paris: R. Laffont, 1972, 252 pp.

VILLETTE, PIERRE [Abbé]. La sorcellerie et sa répression dans le nord de la France [Witchcraft and its repression in the north of France]. Paris: Pensée Universelle, 1976, 282 pp. (A master's thesis for the licence in theology based upon 120 trials, half never before cited.)

BIOGRAPHIES AND AUTOBIOGRAPHIES

AUCLAIR, MARCELLE, and FRANÇOISE PRÉVOST. Mémoires à deux voix [Memoirs in two voices]. Paris: Seuil, 1978, 430 pp.

Although entitled two-voiced, these memoirs are mainly the reminiscences of feminist journalist and writer Marcelle Auclair, author of over thirty books, including studies of St. Theresa of Avila (whose entire work--some 2,000 pages--she translated). Brought up in an artistic and intellectual milieu, Auclair encountered many people including three women who marked her destiny: Adrienne Monnier, Colette, and the painter Marie Laurencin.

From women's columns she wrote in the 1930s, she realized that the French feminist press was then too specialized; it was also deficient. So she went to America to learn of technological advances there. France, however, was viewed as being ahead in inventiveness and style. In 1937 Auclair helped launch the popular woman's magazine Marie-Claire. By the outbreak of the war the journal had attained a circulation of almost a million and a half.

Marcelle Auclair comes from a bourgeois background. This class has been slow in accepting the idea of its women working. Her marriage was one of role reversals. As her daughter Françoise Prévost puts it, mother worked, father "received." When the war was over Auclair took up the problem of contraception, one many of her readers had written to her about. Over 600 of these letters were published in Le livre noir sur l'avortement (1972).

Though divorced, Marcelle Auclair is a practicing Catholic. She finds the church's intransigent position on contraception difficult to accept, all the more so because it accepts the death penalty, as history--with the Inquisition and the French religious wars--reveals. Her position is similar to that of a number of French women. Whatever their personal political or religious convictions, they take a larger view of women in society and work for the concerns of all women on a nonsectarian level.

BALAYÉ, SIMONE. Madame de Staël: lumières et liberté [Madame de Staël: enlightenment and liberty]. Paris: Klincksieck, 1979, 276 pp.

Many years in preparation, this is an authoritative biography of one of the most important women of her period. It encompasses many aspects of Mme de Staël's life: politics, the status of women, her concerns for liberty. Her literary accomplishments are also discussed.

Mme de Staël, née Anne-Louise Germaine Necker (1766-1817), daughter of the famous Swiss banker Jacques Necker, exercised great influence through her Parisian salon, a celebrated center for intellectual activity. Her two most important works were <u>De la littérature considerée dans ses rapports avec les institutions</u> (1800), and De <u>l'Allemagne</u> (1810). Her two novels, <u>Delphine</u> (1802) and <u>Corinne</u> (1807) reflect her concern with the solitude of the intellectual woman, a concern resulting from her own experience. She had to combat political intrigues and misogyny. As the title indicates, the work focuses on Mme de Staël's desire to propagate the ideas of the eighteenth century.

BIDAULT, SUZANNE. <u>Souvenirs de guerre et d'occupation</u> [Memories of war and occupation]. Paris: Éditions de la Table Ronde, 1973, 259 pp.

Encouraged by the reception of her previously published memoirs, Suzanne Bidault recounts her experiences during the Second World War and the Resistance. To do so after an interval of some thirty-odd years, she explains, is not an effort to acquire merit for her particular contribution to France during those troubled times but to respond to those who claimed that it was only the Communists and those of modest means, <u>les petites gens</u>, who risked their lives for liberty.

The author acknowledges that she was not initially fully aware of what was happening. She did not immediately join the underground. Her first Resistance was verbal. Then when approached about joining a group, she did so. Since she was in a position in a Vichy ministry, she could and did play a very important role. The activities she details compare favorably with the best spy thrillers and espionage films.

CABANIS, JOSÉ. <u>Michelet, le prêtre, et la femme</u> [Michelet, the priest, and the woman]. Paris: Gallimard, 1978, 243 pp.

Jose Cabanis, a prize-winning novelist, turns his attention to the historian Michelet, a man more honored than read today. Jules Michelet (1798-1874), professor at the Collège de France and Keeper of the National Archives, left an immense opus. In addition to personal reminiscences, he wrote on natural science, and above all on history. Titles range from <u>Jeanne d'Arc</u> to <u>Les femmes dans la Révolution</u> and <u>La femme</u>. He is best known for his romantic narrative history, <u>L'histoire de France</u>. Some of his journals are just now being published for the first time. These documents offer insights into the man, not just the historical figure.

The title of this study is abridged from <u>Du prêtre, de la femme, et de la famille</u> (1845). This work must be understood not just in terms of the historical context of the battle then being waged between advocates of lay versus religious education. It must be viewed in terms of Michelet's personal life. At this point the professor and scholar gives way to the public man. Michelet becomes the prophet and priest of a new religion, a religion that worships France.

This work expresses a theme central to Michelet's work: the opposition between clericalism and feminism, a feminism that approaches the mystical, like that of the poets Musset, Hugo, and Vigny who celebrated women. For Michelet, women were all that men could not be. They were the counterweights of men. They were History. Witches were victims of patriarchy, vessels of original knowledge.

Michelet had firsthand experience of the clergy intervening in personal affairs where women were concerned. This led him to claim that "our wives and daughters are instructed by our enemies. The priest becomes the intimate, soon the indispensable confidant of women."

With renewed interest in French women's past, his work is being reviewed and reissued. He was in several ways a man ahead of his time. Several recent studies on Michelet include:

BARTHES, ROLAND. Michelet. Écrivain de toujours. Paris: Seuil, 1965. Reprint. 1974.

CHALON, MARIE-THÉRÈSE. Une vie comme un jour [A life like a day]. Paris: Stock, 1976, 174 pp.

Marie-Thérèse Chalon was born at the beginning of this century into a hard-working peasant family in Provence. Life was dictated by the rhythms of nature. Both sexes shared in the arduous work. Family reunions to mark national and religious events were virtually the only distractions. "One learned to economize as one learned to breathe."

It was only later in life that she came to recognize that she, like her mother and other women of her class, had the temperament of a "slave," full of devotion and humility. As women they felt inferior. They would never dare to say that a task was too difficult. Though her free time was extremely limited, Marie-Thérèse Chalon secretly purchased and read a feminist weekly, Le Journal de la femme. Her daughter had to abandon schooling for domestic responsibilities, just as she had had to. Now the pattern is broken. A granddaughter is at the university, still a notable accomplishment for a French woman (or even man) from a peasant or working-class background.

These memoirs chronicle a woman's life in a period now gone, like the language of her childhood, Provençal.

CHOFFEL, JEAN. Seule une femme . . . [Only/alone, a woman]. Paris: Flammarion, 1979, 149 pp. (A biography of Alice Saunier-Seïté.)

Alice Saunier-Seïté was the first--and thus far the only-- woman to become Minister of National Education in France

(1976-81). She undertook sweeping reforms of the French educational system under strong opposition from faculty, students, and the public.

Alice Saunier-Seïté is indeed a militant, although not necessarily a militant feminist. She rose to prominence--professor of science, later provost, the first woman to head a French higher educational establishment--through her merits and achievements. This biography details her career. It also provides information about education in France during the last decade. The list of her accomplishments leaves no doubt that it was talent combined with hard work that brought these honors in an almost exclusively masculine domain, namely university academic administration.

The years of her ministry were marked by acrimonious debates and difficult decisions. The French national system is vast. It has serious problems. Student strikes and teacher walkouts were the response to some of the reforms she undertook to help change what sociologist Michel Crozier has termed the "stalled society." The second part of the book contains detailed analyses of her various measures and the tactics and politics involved.

CLOULAS, YVAN. Catherine de Médicis. Paris: Fayard, 1979, 704 pp.
Catherine de Médicis (1519-89) is one of those extraordinary women whose lives have marked French history. For 400 years she has held an important place in French national mythology as the troubling and fascinating widowed queen. She became the archetype of the providential queen mother and great sovereign, widow and exemplary mother, protectress of the arts. Successive regents endeavored to continue this tradition. At the same time, Catherine has been the subject of much criticism for her political machinations. The ten volumes of her correspondence that were published at the turn of the last century amply document her role in many areas of French history.

For half a century Catherine was linked to France's destiny. Wife of Henri II, three of her sons became kings of France. During the minority of Charles IX she ruled officially as Gouvernante; at other times she ruled unofficially.

This biography by the head of France's national archives is rich in detail, like a tapestry of the complex period of the French Renaissance, a time of conflict and civil strife. It is based upon primary sources as well as extensive printed documentation.

DÉMAR, CLAIRE. L'affranchissement des femmes [The emancipation of women]. Paris: Payot, 1976, 233 pp.
The reissue of these texts for the first time since 1834 should continue the much needed reassessment and rehabilitation of Claire Démar (c. 1800-1833), a Saint-Simonien for whom little biographical information exists. Démar linked the liberation of women and the emancipation of the proletariat. She denounced the tyrannical exploitation of women for the profit of men. True

republicans, she insisted, were those who refused to tolerate the oppression of any member of society.

The two pamphlets reproduced here are accompanied by Ma loi d'avenir, which Suzanne Voilquin, editor of La Tribune des femmes, published after Claire Démar's suicide. There are also seventeen unpublished letters. These texts should help to mitigate the notoriety she held on two accounts: her suicide and her equation of arranged marriages as legal prostitution. Heretofore this lucid woman had been assigned to a literary limbo between creativity and madness. The substantial postface by Valentine Pelosse places Claire Démar in the Saint-Simonien current and in the feminist movement of the early 1800s.

DERAISMES, MARIA. Ce que veulent les femmes: articles et discours de 1869 à 1894 [What women want: articles and speeches from 1869 to 1894]. Paris: Syros, 1979, 143 pp. (Preface, notes, and commentary by Odile Krakovitch.)

Maria Deraismes (1828-94) was one of a number of strong, independently wealthy upper-bourgeois women who contributed to the feminist movement of the late Second Empire and the early Third Republic. In the feminist daily she founded in 1869 with Léon Richer, Le Droit des femmes (which lasted until 1891, making it one of the longest lived of these earlier feminist periodicals), Deraismes affirmed her anticlerical and republican convictions, convictions inseparable from her feminism.

In an early pamphlet addressed "To Rich Women," she accused the wealthy of having made prostitutes their victims. One of her key ideas was the responsibility of women in public as well as private life. In another pamphlet, "Ève contre Dumas fils," she answers the misogynist author Dumas's "L'homme-femme" (1872), a pamphlet issued in over forty editions.

Like most feminists of the Second Empire, Deraismes was a partisan of reforms, not revolution. Her aim was to gain wider entry for women into the world, not necessarily to change the socioeconomic system. Further, she parted company with feminists like Hubertine Auclert over suffrage. The vote, she believed, was secondary to the pressing concerns of sustaining the republic and democracy. With Richer she helped organize the First French International Congress on the Rights of Women in 1878, as well as one for the Rights of Women in 1889. Although too ill to attend the 1889 Chicago International Exposition, she sent a written contribution.

Deraismes fought to end the exclusion of women from all domains and was responsible for creating a mixed Masonic lodge after having been rejected by the Grand Lodge from one she had succeeded in joining. Masonry she saw as a source of potential assistance to women in their intellectual and professional progress.

The excellent education Deraismes had received--in contrast to most women of her time--served her well in her writing and in the very popular lectures she gave. As this collection reveals,

Maria Deraismes was a woman of strong, advanced convictions. Her life was characterized by struggle and intense activity for many causes.

DESANTI, DOMINIQUE. <u>Flora Tristan: oeuvres et vie mêlées, évoquées, commentées, et choisies</u> [Flora Tristan: her life and works together, evoked, commented upon, and selected]. Paris: Union Générale d'Éditions, (10/18), 1973, 446 pp.

Flora Tristan (1803-44) stands out in an already outstanding group of women who worked for women's causes in nineteenth-century France. She saw woman as a pariah through birth, serflike in her status, of necessity unhappy. Her theoretical work <u>Union ouvrière</u> (1843), partially reproduced here, expressed views that Marx and Engels were to elaborate subsequently. Woman is the proletariat of the proletariat: even the most oppressed man can oppress another human, his wife.

Dominique Desanti uses Tristan's works as far as possible in this rich portrait of a remarkable woman. The last chapter, "After Flora," shows the many ways in which Flora Tristan was ahead of her time.

FRANCIS, CLAUDE, ed. <u>Simone de Beauvoir et le cours du monde</u> [Simone de Beauvoir and the way of the world]. Paris: Klincksieck, 1978, 170 pp. (Includes a large number of photos assembled by Janine Niepce.)

The global dimensions implied by the title are appropriate to a woman whose activities have been on an international scale and whose life and work have had an impact on world history. Throughout her life Simone de Beauvoir has struggled against subjugation, injustice, and poverty for all the oppressed, not just women. This album-anthology brings together the principal stages of her extensive travels in the pursuit of justice.

GASCARD, FRANÇOISE. <u>Madame le . . .</u> [Madame the . . .]. Paris: Grasset, 1979.

The difficulties of French women who are just recently assuming prominent positions such as minister, state secretary and mayor, is underscored by the problem of how to designate them officially. There is no feminine <u>la</u> for the titles, only the masculine <u>le</u>. Françoise Gascard surprised her own party, the Socialists, by being elected mayor of the town of Dreux in 1977, with the support of the United Left Front. Now there was a young woman of thirty-four in an office that had always been held by older, managerial men. The mayor maintains that she will not be passive or decorative in her position. She outlines concrete proposals she plans to undertake on behalf of women, proposals she hopes will be implemented elsewhere in France.

GENNARI, GENEVIÈVE. La robe rouge [The red dress]. Paris: Éditions Tchou, 1978, 265 pp.

Geneviève Gennari is the author of eleven volumes, including novels, tales, and autobiographical works such as Journal d'une bourgeoise (1959). Here she continues relating the life of a French woman of today. She recounts the first thirty years of her life. One of her problems was trying to reconcile her heritage: her mother was from a very religious French milieu, her father was from a more modern Italian background. Gennari's itinerary is summarized in the chapter headings: not from the [fashionable] XVIe district of Paris; a very Catholic childhood; the war; literature; psychoanalysis and freedom. The major themes developed are the bourgeoisie, Catholicism, psychoanalysis, and above all, the difficulty of being a woman writer. She had to take off "the red dress," symbol for the author of female passivity.

Her Dossier de la femme (1965) was one of the first of many recent works on women. It narrates the evolution of the feminine condition from the end of the nineteenth century to the present, a present where polemics must give way to practice. The dossier includes a number of interesting period photographs.

GONTIER, FERNANDE. Benoîte Groult. Paris: Klincksieck, 1979, 236 pp.

This book is part literary citicism, part biography, based upon several interviews with the well-known author, feminist, and journalist. Benoîte Groult has written several works with her sister Flora, including: Journal à quatre mains (1962); Le féminin pluriel (1965); and Il était deux fois (1968), all published by Denoël/Gonthier, as well as a children's book published by éditions des femmes (1976). Groult's own works include the best-selling novel La part des choses (1972), Le féminisme au masculin (q.v.), (1977), and the very successful feminist manifesto, Ainsi soit-elle (q.v.).

Groult's writings are characterized by a call for action and times, a cold anger. Groult acknowledges that she came to feminism belatedly--and with great difficulty. Once there, however, she has utilized her considerable energies and talents for the cause.

Her family came from a milieu that she describes as "proustien." It was part of the artistic world of Paris in the early decades of the century. Both her mother and her grandmother were imposing figures. In contrast her father, a decorator and artist, had a more retiring temperament. Widowed less than a year after an early marriage, she was "liberated" from her family. At this time Groult became acquainted with America through the GIs then in France. Her first published work was a translation of Dorothy Parker's short stories, published as Comme ils sont (1960). After the Liberation she entered into the world of radio and journalism, and embarked upon a career of writing. Photos from the author's personal collection enhance this volume in a series devoted to notable contemporary French women.

GRÉGOIRE, MENIE. Le métier de femme [Profession, woman]. Paris: Plon, 1965, 315 pp.

This study written in the mid-sixties offers a basis for comparison with works of the seventies. It reveals how much French women have achieved and accomplished in a scant fifteen years. For the first time concerns about contraception, career, and re-entry problems are discussed openly. In contrast to the "intellectually oriented" Second Sex, Menie Grégoire, a writer and journalist, proposed to examine the everyday problems women face. She stresses the importance of Simone de Beauvoir and Margaret Mead in her own development. Freudian analysis, then just becoming well known in France, was also influential.

Menie Grégoire admires American women. She finds them ahead of their French counterparts in many areas. (They, however, criticized her for not being militant enough.) American women have a tradition of working in groups; French women are too independent and individual. They speak in the singular. They will have to learn to work together, she contends. To America goes the credit of developing the pill.

To undertake her book, Grégoire sent out several thousand questionnaires. The sociological data received provides a composite picture of the 1963 woman, French model: a slightly romantic but strong woman with her eyes firmly fixed upon reality. She will be replaced, the author accurately predicts, by a more up-to-date model.

_____. Telle que je suis [Such as I am]. Paris: Éditions J'ai lu, 1976, 412 pp.

The name of Menie Grégoire is known to French millions through the national radio program she started in 1967. This talk show made her the lay confessor or analyst of many average citizens. They asked questions and raised issues such as women's rights, abortion, and sexual problems, problems that had not been discussed openly before. (A selection of her voluminous correspondence on these and other topics was published as Les cris de la vie (1971).

Grégoire says that her belated awareness of the implications of the feminist movement and of the world around her--after marriage and three children--is typical of her entire generation of bourgeois women. Their revolution consisted in obtaining the right to work, receive an equal education, be free in one's actions. At heart her generation was closer to the world of their mothers than it would ever be to the next generation of daughters.

Anyone familiar with France will be charmed by her description of a childhood spent in the Loire region. But the main subject is her development as a feminist and her many activities. Through working with Allied troops she first learned of the demands being voiced by Anglo-Saxon women. Then came the Second Sex, a work which counted more for women of her generation than historians realize.

Menie Grégoire's long involvement and reflection upon the issues relating to women have been motivated in part by the desire to construct a feminism à la française, one different from American feminism. She insists that there should not be revenge against men, nor a rivalry or emulation of the other sex. The aim is the equality of women--perhaps even recognition of a certain superiority. The emphasis should be on the right to be oneself without being compared.

LAGUILLER, ARLETTE. Moi, une militante [Me, a militant]. Paris: Stock, 1974, 164 pp. (Discussions with Max Chaleil.)

Most of the recent writing by contemporary French feminists has been done by women from middle-class or intellectual background, well-educated women. In contrast, Arlette Laguiller is very much a woman of the people. She grew up in Lilas; her family received social assistance and she had to leave school at an early age to work. Books provided her main education, in particular the works of Zola.

In 1974 Laguiller became involved in the strike at the large national bank, Crédit Lyonnais, where she had worked as a secretary since 1956. She worked with the Trotskyite party Lutte Ouvrière and, in 1974, found herself standing as the first woman candidate in a French presidential election. She won close to 600,000 votes.

Her story is that of a young (b. 1940) working girl's awakening consciousness. There are inside observations on union intrigues during the troubled times of 1968 and the strike against the bank. Lutte Ouvrière was founded because the older union was not supportive of women's claims. It is more radical than "Nine to Five." For some years the women met to discuss not just professional demands, but also feminist concerns. They organized a lending library and theater visits. Self-education was deemed essential to the working class to improve and extend its horizon and participate in France's bourgeois-dominated culture. The tone becomes more militant as the women see the effectiveness of their work. Lutte Ouvrière develops into a national party of the working class.

Arlette Laguiller's credo is: "I believe that one can neither be socialist nor militant without the desire to link oneself, including through reading, with humanity and history."

LAOT, JEANETTE. Stratégie pour les femmes [Strategy for women]. Collection les grands leaders. Paris: Stock, 1977, 243 pp.

Like Arlette Laguiller, Jeanette Laot comes from the working class. She also worked her way to prominence through union activity, at the same time extending her feminine consciousness. First there is an account of a short, difficult childhood in

Brittany--a region with a different language and a separatist movement. The only future envisioned for young girls in that poor region was of becoming wives and mothers.

Jeanette Laot started work as a dressmaker, one of the most traditional occupations for women, one that has long depended on an underpaid female work force. Then she entered a tobacco factory, a nationalized industry, "the way one enters teaching or administration." The work was difficult but there was solidarity among the women who were virtually all union members. Laot joined the CFTC (Confédération Française des Travailleurs Chrétiens), rose rapidly in the organization, and was sent to the Paris headquarters. Her explanation for these events is that the salaries were insufficient for a man.

The remainder of the book deals with national problems. Women's problems she views as distinct from those of workers in general. To be a woman and salaried worker she finds a "privileged" position from which to analyze the mechanics of society. The conclusion suggests strategies for women. They must work, organize, and fight together. The causes of work and women are inextricably linked.

The long index deals with the CFDT, a union formally constituted as the CFTC in 1919, from Christian labor unions started in the 1880s. A debate ensued over whether to call it Catholic or Christian. In 1947 the statute was modified; the union's aims became those of more general Christian concerns. All religious references were withdrawn in 1964 when it became the CFDT, the Confédération Française Démocratique du Travail. The 1974 CFDT demands for women's workers are included along with those of the Communist dominated CGT, Confédération Générale du Travail. With almost two million members in 1981 the CGT is France's largest union. The CFDT is second with not quite a million members.

LEJEUNE, PAULE. Louise Michel l'indomptable [Louise Michel the unconquerable]. Paris: Éditions des femmes, 1978, 336 pp.

Louise Michel (1830-1905) is not unknown. Her role as the "Red Virgin" in the development of the international anarchist movement has long been recognized and documented. It is only now, however, that her place in the history of women's achievements is being recognized. For too long the emphasis was placed upon Louise Michel the exalted and messianic woman, one of the "pétroleuses," incendiary women, and for some, the antiwoman.

This biography traces Louise Michel's life from her childhood in Haute Marne to deportation to New Caledonia and thence to international prominence, from witness to participant. Paule Lejeune has let Louise Michel tell much of her story through her own writings, for she wrote a great deal--including poems--throughout her life. Michel chose Victor Hugo for her "spiritual mentor." One of the more interesting aspects of this book is the material it provides on women's education in modest milieus in nineteenth-century France. For Louise Michel, as for many women, teaching provided both a profession and an opportunity to cultivate herself and make a contribution to society.

Louise Michel was illegitimate. Her mother was a servant in a rather unorthodox liberal family influenced by Voltaire and Rousseau. The family's son was presumably her father. She was brought up by the grandparents in the semiruined chateau of Vroncourt in the Haute-Marne. When the presumed grandparents died, she was forced to move in with her mother's relatives, an extended family. Unusual though it was for one of her sex and modest background, her schooling continued. She prepared and obtained a teaching certificate.

In 1856 Louise Michel went to Paris to find her way, alone if need be, "to the call of destiny," as a poem written at this time puts it. In spite of long hours and little money, she found time to become active in politics. She participated in the uprising of the Commune. She dressed as a soldier to facilitate movement and carried a rifle on her shoulder. Her memoirs vividly describe this period when she found herself in the thick of things, yet always concerned with others.

When the uprising was defeated, Michel was tried with other Communards and sentenced to deportation to New Caledonia. She viewed the trip as a great adventure and prior to her departure wrote from prison for books and scientific data. Once there her conduct was exemplary. An 1884 police report describes her as a "saint." With a scientist's eye the indefatiguable Louise observed the new world. She tried to introduce new plants and took notes on the language. After great difficulty she was allowed to teach the children of the other déportés and later, the forest dwellers for whom she developed new pedagogical methods. Above all, she saw the wretched of the earth exploited by the colonists. The brutal repression of an abortive native uprising left an indelible mark.

When general amnesty was declared in 1880, Louise Michel and the other déportés returned after a very long voyage to a triumphal homecoming, first in London, then in Paris. Released from ten years of prison and exile, she plunged into political activity. Women and workers, she insisted, are engaged in the same struggle.

Her new activities did not go unheeded by the government. On a trumped-up charge she was sentenced to six years solitary confinement, time she used to write both serialized popular novels and rework her memoirs. She also continued her education, teaching herself English and Russian.

When she was pardoned three years later, Louise Michel had to be physically expelled from prison. There, as in New Caledonia, she refused special treatment as a woman. Lecture tours were resumed. She was shot during a speaking engagement. Characteristically, she mobilized all her efforts to free her would-be assassin.

Louise Michel then entered the period of her life best known to history. She settled in London where, free from surveillance, she wrote The Commune (1898) and undertook speaking engagements in towns large and small. She died in Marseilles on January 5, 1905. Three battalions of infantry and six cavalry squadrons were deployed to control the massive crowds at her funeral cortège. In Paris, hundreds of thousands of working-class men and women paid homage to Louise Michel and the spirit of the Commune on the very day of the uprising at the Winter Palace. See also:

THOMAS, EDITH. Louise Michel: ou la Valléda de l'anarchie [Louise Michel: or the Valleda of anarchy]. Paris: Gallimard, 1971, 475 pp.

Le TRIUDIC, DOMINIQUE-MARTIN, ed. Une femme du réseau Shelburn: l'histoire de Marie-Thérèse Le Calvez de Phouha en Bretagne [A woman of the Shelburn network: the story of Marie-Thérèse Le Calvez of Phouha in Brittany]. Les Sables d'Olonne: Cercle d'Or, 1979, 110 pp.

Two Breton women collaborate to detail the heroic actions and subsequent reflections of a young woman Resistant. Marie-Thérèse Le Calvez (b. 1924) recounts her activities as the only woman member of the famous underground network Shelburn, a network that rescued and sheltered 128 aviators, mainly Americans, who were picked up on the rocky Breton beach.

Securing food for these hidden guests during a period of scarcity was but the most obvious of the many tasks this intrepid, courageous young woman performed. Taking aviators down steep, mined cliffs under German guard posts and then carrying up supplies, arms, and transmitters were among the hazardous occupations the clandestine unit undertook. There were long trips by bike or foot on out-of-the-way roads, dangerous moments all shared by the young Marie-Thérèse. Three grateful governments recognized the young girl's activities and the contribution of her mother, who cooked and shared the daily danger of harboring enemy agents under the eyes of their small community and the Gestapo.

MALLET-JORIS, FRANÇOISE. Jeanne Guyon: le siècle des femmes savantes [Jeanne Guyon: the century of learned ladies]. Paris: Flammarion, 1978, 586 pp.

The well-known novelist Françoise Mallet-Joris (b. 1930), is author of La rempart des béguines (1951), La maison de papier (1970) and other works that deal with tensions in the family. Here she describes with passion and erudition the result of ten years' research into the situation of women in France's Enlightenment. Mallet-Joris details women's efforts to improve their marginal status and the ruses they were sometimes forced to employ.

The study focuses on the life of Mme Guyon (Jeanne Marie Bouvier de la Motte, 1648-1717), the advocate of a religious doctrine known as Quietism. Mme Guyon became involved in a struggle with Bossuet, one of the most powerful religious figures of the time. Famed for his educational works, sermons, and funeral orations, Bossuet was also tutor to Louis XIV's sons. Here, as in her earlier conflicts with authority, during every effort made to repress her, Jeanne Guyon refused to conform or renounce her strongly held views. She emerged from each struggle reinforced in her beliefs.

MALRAUX, CLARA. Et pourtant j'étais libre [And yet I was free]. Paris: Grasset, 1979, 264 pp.

Clara Malraux (1897-1982), the former wife of André Malraux, writer, critic, and minister, was an extremely talented and accomplished woman in her own right. This latest volume of her memoirs covers the period from the Occupation to the 1960s and the uprising of May 1968.

Prior to and during the war, Clara Malraux organized a network to help German Jews escape Nazi persecution. And this, in spite of what she risked as a Jew herself. Witness to many of the political and cultural events that have shaped France's history in the past decades, she wrote of these in her memoirs published under the collective title Le bruit de nos pas.

Other titles in the series include: Apprendre à vivre (1963); Nos 20 ans (1966); Les combats et les jeux (1969); Voici que vient l'été (1973). All have been published by Grasset in Paris. An abridged selection has appeared in English, published by Farrar, Straus & Giroux in 1967.

MONESTIER, MARIANNE. Elles étaient cent et mille [They were a hundred and a thousand (women)]. Paris: Fayard, 1972, 256 pp.

This is an account of the important role played by French women in the Resistance by a writer and journalist with the popular women's magazine Marie-Claire. Through following the destinies of a few of the many heroines who participated in the clandestine underground organizations, Marianne Monestier renders homage to all.

In some cases it is the former Resistant herself who recounts her experiences. In others, the surviving family and friends reveal personal dramas in their accounts. The backgrounds of the women differed. For example, Gilberte Arcambal was a Freemason while Marie-Magdeleine Davy was a philosopher and religious mystic. Simone Saint-Clair--who headed the Paris sector of the Mithridate network--was a journalist. The martyred France Bloch-Sérazin was an intellectual committed to political activism. At nineteen, Madeleine Riffaut became a Resistance officer. For all these women, however, the period of the Resistance served as an opportunity to use hitherto unsuspected capabilities: courage, organizational skills, and even acceptance of the unthinkable-- torture and death. This experience proved in every sense a revelation. Women shared all the activities and responsibilities of men. Some even commanded men. In each instance these women undertook activities that women were presumed not to engage in.

PICQUERAY, MAY. May la réfractaire: pour mes 81 ans d'anarchie [Refractory May: for my 81 years of anarchy]. Paris: Atelier Marcel Jullian, 1979, 260 pp.

After 60 years of struggle, May Picqueray accepts the label of "refractory." Since 1920 she has participated in all the major rendez-vous of history. After a Breton childhood, she spent several years in Quebec as a mother's helper. There was a short marriage at eighteen. Then May went to Paris where she came in contact with the international anarcho-syndicalist movement. Finding that she shared their views, May decided to join their movement.

Her life-long activities for the anarchist cause included a trip to Russia and a stormy interview with Trotsky in the Kremlin in 1922. During the Second World War she worked with various Resistance groups. Emma Goldman was one of her many friends.

May's rich and full life included imprisonment, many jobs, a number of romantic attachments and three children born out of wedlock. Hers has been a long, full, passionate life devoted to improving the situation of others.

RENAUDIN, EDMÉE. Edmée au bout de la table [Edmée at the end of the table]. Collection elles-mêmes. Paris: Stock, 1973, 265 pp.

These recollections offer some idea of the training and education of jeunes filles bien élevées, well brought up young ladies, prior to the First World War. The subtitle might well be "Life and customs of a bourgeois family at the beginning of the century."

Conceived as a memoir for her grandchildren, this volume describes Edmée Renaudin's family, servants, schooling, and vacations, in short, daily life during the "belle époque." There are many small but revealing details. She notes that Paris at that time was filled with virtuous young ladies who, not having found a husband, gave private lessons. This was a "respectable" way to earn a living, even if there was often little inclination or vocation.

_____. Sans fleur au fusil [Without a flower in the gun barrel]. Paris: Stock, 1979, 340 pp.

This continuation of Edmée Renaudin's journal recounts events during the last war. International events mingle with everyday incidents. The author, mother of five, tells how the family—particularly the women—coped with difficulties, providing schooling and giving assistance to those involved in the Resistance.

RICHARD, MARTHE. Mon destin de femme [My destiny as a woman]. Collection vécu. Paris: Robert Laffont, 1974, 377 pp.

Her difficult birth and survival over her twin sister prefigured Marthe Betenfeld's (1887-1982) survival through an extraordinary destiny. She became the double agent Marthe

Richard, a spy in the service of France in the First World War, a woman both admired and detested.

Prior to playing that role, Marthe went through a troubled adolescence. She lost two husbands, both deeply loved. To serve her country she became the mistress of the head of German Naval Intelligence in Madrid. Her activities and adventures are the stuff spy thrillers are made of. Here, reality exceeded fiction. Again and again her presence of mind and her ingenuity helped rescue her from dangerous situations.

In the Second World War Richard organized a network to help downed aviators escape. After the war she was one of the first women municipal counselors, serving on the council for Paris. She was largely instrumental in passing a national law which closed houses of legalized prostitution. She found her own experience of having made love to a man she detested helped her to better understand prostitutes. For her work as a spy a grateful government awarded her the Legion of Honor for military activities, the only women so honored thus far in France.

ROCHEFORT, CHRISTIANE. Ma vie revue et corrigée par l'auteur [My life reviewed and corrected by the author]. Paris: Stock, 1978, 355 pp.

Christiane Rochefort (b. 1917) is another well-known French writer and feminist activist. Her Le repos du guerrier (1958) has been translated into fourteen languages thus far. In Les petits enfants du siècle (1961) Rochefort evokes a childhood in one of the many recently built low-cost, impersonal housing complexes that now encircle Paris and other major French cities, the HLM (Habitation de Loyer Moderé).

Originally Rochefort had granted a series of interview to Maurice Chavardès for an eventual biography. Midway into the project the author decided to take charge of a life which is, after all, her own. Her "autobiography" is deliberately uneven and varied--as is life itself. Different periods are left out: whole years are not remembered. A single event can produce long meanderings. There are poems, proverbs, and cartoons. Alternative titles and "found" feminine forms for words which have none are offered in the playful spirit that marks this work.

ROUSSEL, NELLY. L'éternelle sacrifiée [The eternally sacrificed (woman)]. Collection les points chauds. Paris: Syros, 1979, 112 pp. (Preface, notes, commentary, and bibliography of Roussel's works by Daniel Armogathe and Maïté Albistur.)

L'éternelle sacrifiée is the text of a speech given at Lille on January 28, 1906. Nelly Roussel (pseudonym of Mireille Godet, 1878-1922) broke at twenty with her traditional Catholic family and became involved in activities she felt would help women. She campaigned for Maternité Consciente and was active with other feminists such as Marguerite Durand and Madeleine Vernet in the major feminist battles at the beginning of the century.

Roussel's speaking engagements led to La Voix des Femmes, a group she founded in 1920 to make available women speakers. The same name was given to their monthly publication. They were militant women, informed and experienced, who were prepared to set forth the group's program and ideals whenever called upon.

No one exemplified the group better than Nelly Roussel. She lectured in France, Europe, and the Orient. At one point she proposed a "grève des ventres" (1919) to protest the government's militant postwar natalist policy. She felt there should be no more children for capitalism and the military to exploit and destroy.

Nelly Roussel's commitment and lucid analyses of women's problems are seen more fully in her collected works, Derniers combats, published posthumously in 1932. Her proposals and their expression anticipate many of the concerns of French feminists today.

TRISTAN, FLORA. Les pérégrinations d'une paria, 1833-1834 [The peregrinations of a pariah, 1833-1834]. Paris: Maspero, 1979, 377 pp.

This work combines the appeal of a travel book with an exceptional woman's perceptions. It evokes the contrasts of postcolonial Hispanic-American society. Overwhelming opulence contrasts starkly with dire poverty and oppression. The term "pariah" designates the world's judgment of this foreigner, this outsider, this woman.

Flora Tristan (1803-44) was the daughter of a distinguished Peruvian general who had married in a church ceremony. Unfortunately this wedding was not recognized by civil authorities when the father died shortly thereafter. Forced into an early and unhappy marriage, Flora Tristan undertook an arduous 130-day long sea journey to Peru to meet her father's family and to attempt to claim his considerable wealth as the sole heir. During a stopover in the Caribbean the young woman witnessed slavery for the first time. She revolted inwardly against such an institution and placed herself in league with the American abolitionists.

One is not surprised that her father's younger brother--who owed much to him--provided generous hospitality in spite of the fact that she was technically "illegitimate" but cheated her out of her inheritance. Paradoxically, Tristan found her female relatives envied her the freedom her presumed illegitimacy brought.

During her extended stay in Peru she traveled a great deal. She visited sugar plantations and again saw the appalling sight of slaves. She noted that women were oppressed whatever their class. The Indian women ravinas or camp followers were praised. While Indian men would often kill themselves rather than serve in the army, Indian women voluntarily took up servitude to support the army. The women of Lima impressed her. They were free to move about, a trust their superior intelligence and moral strength "merited." While the women of Lima were free, European women were the slaves of laws, mores, customs, prejudices, and fashions—in virtually every respect.

The lengthy account ends with Flora Tristan's conviction not to succomb to personal misfortunes but to take up the fight of all the oppressed. The quest for fortune proved to be a journey of self-discovery. Like Fourier, this woman (a heroine worthy of Stendhal) maintained that the degree of civilization which societies have attained is always proportional to the degree of independence their women have achieved.

_____. Promenades dans Londres: ou, l'aristocracie et les prolétaires anglais [Promenades in London: or, the English aristocracy and proletariat]. Edited by François Bédarida. Paris: Maspero, 1978, 356 pp.

In her promenades about London Flora Tristan saw what she describes in detail, the capital of the first industrial nation. As her friend and disciple Eleanor Blanc wrote, Tristan wanted to know everything, to observe all. What she saw was the gulf between rich and poor, between an all-powerful aristocracy and a population of "slaves." The very existence of the worker, as well as that of his wife and children, was at the mercy of the capitalist system.

English women were treated like slaves, slaves who she felt were more miserable than the blacks. Education, the work force, social pressures, and the laws all conspired to leave women with a choice between oppression or infamy, marriage or prostitution. In the last chapter, devoted to English women, she notes the deplorable contrast between the extreme subjugation of English women and the intellectual superiority of English women authors.

The title, which recalls Stendhal's Promenades dans Rome (1829), is misleading. These are not the leisurely meanderings but the march, in the militant sense, of an intrepid researcher across a city teeming with the oppressed in the manner evoked by William Morris's "Tis the People Marching On." But, as Flora Tristan proclaimed in Paria, "my role as enlightened traveller with a conscience obliged me to tell the whole truth." What she depicts is worthy of Goya or Daumier, the writing recalls Dickens.

In her biography, translated as Flora Tristan, a Woman in Revolt (1976), Dominique Desanti notes, as have others such as Hélène Brion, that Engels used Promenades without acknowledging his debt. Their dedications are very similar. There is also the same call for international action. And, eight years before the Communist Manifesto, Flora Tristan clearly sets forth the idea of a class struggle.

This is a fine critical edition by Bédarida, the author of three scholarly works on nineteenth-century England. Flora Tristan's observations are placed in the political and historical context of that century. Several recent biographies have appeared indicating that, with the advent of socialism and new feminist activities in France today, this "prophet'"'s time has come. These works are:

BAELEN, JEAN. <u>La vie de Flora Tristan</u> [The life of Flora Tristan]. Paris: Seuil, 1972, 256 pp.

LEPROHON, PIERRE. <u>Flora Tristan</u>. Paris: Corymb, 1979, 270 pp.

——. <u>Le Tour de France: journal, 1843-44</u> [The tour of France: journal, 1843-44]. Maspero, 1980, 1:233 pp.; 2:238 pp.
    The manuscript of the <u>Tour de France</u>, part journal, part sociological inquiry, is incomplete. Death interrupted Flora Tristan's pilgrimage. In 1843 she published <u>L'Union ouvrière</u>. Influenced by the ideas of the Saint-Simoniens, she undertook a tour of France in the manner of the <u>compagnons</u>, apprentices who traveled across France perfecting their craft and becoming affiliated with one of the trade guilds that still existed at that time. (George Sand's novel <u>Compagnon du Tour de France</u> [1840] describes the origin and customs of these journeys.) In the middle of her tour, Flora Tristan died of exhaustion at Bordeaux.
    Earlier in this ill-fated trip the authorities of Lyon confiscated part of this work. Her admirers put the rest away for safekeeping--which turned into oblivion. J.L. Puech, who devoted his life to working on Flora Tristan (his thesis, <u>La vie et l'oeuvre de Flora Tristan, 1803-1844</u> [1925], is still the basic reference work), found the manuscript in the course of his research but it was lost again during World War II. The work was not published until 1973--a hundred and thirty years after its completion.
    The passionate commitment of Flora Tristan is still felt in her vivid, spontaneous reactions to the misery of the working classes in France in the years preceding the revolution of 1848. She gave her life for two causes she saw as inextricably linked: the rights of women and the rights of the working class. Death interrupted Flora Tristan, but as she foresaw, "work is unfinished but ideas germinate, they do not die."
    A critical edition of her unpublished correspondence edited by Stéphane Michaud was published by Seuil in 1980.

VAILLOT, RENÉ. <u>Madame du Châtelet</u>. Paris: Albin Michel, 1978, 352 pp. (Preface by René Pomeau.)
    This biography encompasses not just a life, but a period, that of the first half of the eighteenth century, the age of the Enlightenment. If Mme du Châtelet (1706-49) was previously known, it was because of her long liaison with Voltaire, <u>l'amant de neige</u>. This works shows that she was a remarkable, intellectual woman, as well as a passionate one.
    She spoke several languages and was well versed in mathematics, philosophy, and science. When she translated Newton's <u>Principia</u> from Latin into French (in a translation still used in

France today), she added a commentary. Unfashionable in a worldly period, with the new interest in feminism she is receiving the recognition she richly deserves. A feminist ahead of her time, she wrote "For my part, if I were king I would correct an abuse that cuts off one half of humanity. I would have woman participate in all the rights of humanity, and especially those of the intellect."

Like many women of earlier periods, she died in childbirth. Unlike the majority of women writers of her age who wrote poems or prose, she wrote intellectual treatises and works on metaphysics for which she was particularly gifted. In the author's view passion killed her, but she lives on through her intelligence.

VOILQUIN, SUZANNE. Suzanne Voilquin: mémoires d'une Saint-Simonienne en Russie, 1839-1846 [Suzanne Voilquin: the recollections of a Saint-Simonien in Russia, 1839-1846]. Paris: Éditions des femmes, 1977, 316 pp. (Text established by Maïté Albistur and Daniel Armogathe from the manuscript at the Bibliothèque Marguerite Durand.)

The century was but a year old when Suzanne Monnier was born (1801-76 or 77). Very much ahead of her time, she has been the subject of legend and myth. The brief summary of her life included in this volume helps explain why. Frequently ill and often suffering, she persisted nevertheless in helping others.

Voilquin was a seamstress from a poor working family. She separated from her husband soon after marriage. An unmarried mother, she became involved in the Saint-Simonien movement. She was also a militant journalist for the feminist paper La Tribune des femmes and helped found La Femme libre (1832). When Voilquin returned to France from the trip to Egypt (described below), she participated in various strikes. She also spent eleven years in Louisiana. Unfortunately no account of her activities during these years appears to have survived.

This is the first time that Suzanne Voilquin's impressions of the Russia of Nicolas I have been published, something for which they were not intended. She confides her thoughts on the difficulties of being in exile, her apprehensions as a woman, and the problems she had in exercising her profession of midwife. There are also views on the Russia of that time. Some years before her death, Suzanne Voilquin prepared a box of personal effects. They were to be used "when women will have their own archives" (des archives à elles). That time has come.

_____. Suzanne Voilquin ou la Saint-Simonienne en Egypte [Suzanne Voilquin or the Saint-Simonien in Egypt]. Paris: Maspero, 1979, 408 pp. (Introduction by Lydia Elhadad.)

This is a reissue of Suzanne Voilquin's 1866 account--part tourist observations, part social commentary--of her travels in Egypt with the Saint-Simoniens in search of the female Messiah.

She accompanied the band in spite of reservations about the group and its quest, a quest she felt would benefit the men but not the women.

In Egypt she donned male attire to attend courses at the Cairo medical hospital. A midwife devoted to homeopathic medicine, through her profession she gained entry into Moslem harems where she could observe the women. Her adventures in Egypt included a narrow escape from the plague.

Here, as in all her writings, one sees a love of independence and an exemplary dignity. Voilquin tried in Egypt, as elsewhere, to implement her view that all classes must unite to help one another. To be free, she held, women must first be free from material concerns.

WEISS, LOUISE. Combats pour les femmes [Struggles for women]. Paris: Albin Michel, 1979, 270 pp.

The third volume of Louise Weiss's Mémoires d'une européenne, covering the years 1934-39, has been republished. No doubt this is because it covers an important period in the history of French feminism. It details the efforts to obtain suffrage during the 1930s.

Louise Weiss (1893-1983) was a brilliant, active woman. Turning from earlier "combats" on behalf of disarmament and world peace, Weiss became involved in the French feminist movement's efforts to obtain suffrage and revolt against the injustices of the Napoleonic Code. Solicited by friends who were concerned about the stagnation of the movement, she wondered about the apparent lack of aggressiveness of her fellow countrywomen when compared with Anglo-Saxon "tigresses." They had been indoctrinated by Catholicism, which teaches resignation, and by Napoleon's establishment of male authority.

In 1934 she entered the feminist ranks with figures such as Edmée de la Rochefoucauld (b. 1893) and Cécile Brunschvicg (1877-1946). Following Anglo-Saxon tactics she recommended an offensive strategy. Public opinion was to be mobilized through press, radio, and cinema. The demonstrations did attract attention, though it was not always favorable. Their efforts provoked hostility, some from shocked bourgeoises or indifferent working women. One senator proposed in the august chambers, "Let these ladies who would be deputies remain what they are, whores." Weiss and her group led a successful campaign to defeat his reelection bid. Their tactics included passive resistance and chaining themselves to locations to halt traffic. Weiss was helped by women in the news, like three early flyers: Adrienne Bolland, Maryse Bastie, and Hélène Boucher.

The Popular Front (1936) initiated the extensive social services that the French enjoy today. It did little, however, for women's rights. Three women were appointed under secretaries of state (even though they could not yet vote) but, as Weiss observes, three swallows do not make a spring. Louise Weiss, one of the first women agrégées, provides an engrossing account of a period that is not generally well known.

*FRIANG, BRIGITTE. Regarde-toi qui meurs [Look thou who art dying]. Paris: Robert Laffont, 1970, 451 pp.
    The account of a war correspondent in the Second World War.

*JACOB, MADELEINE. 40 ans de journalisme [Forty years of journalism]. Paris: Julliard, 1970, 348 pp.

*La TOUR Du PIN, Marquise de. Mémoires [Memoirs]. Paris: Mercure de France, 1979, 496 pp.
    This titled woman's observations cover a dense period in French history, from 1778 to 1813.

*MONESTIER, MARIANNE. Les initiées: les femmes, l'esotérisme, et les sociétés secrètes [The initiated: women, esoterism, and secret societies]. Paris: Denoël/Gonthier, 1971, 317 pp.

*TEYSSIER-JORE, RAYMONDE. Le "corps féminin" [The "feminine corps"]. Paris: Éditions France-Empire, 1975, 320 pp.
    The personal narratives of women who participated in World War II.

French Views on American Women

BALLORAIN, ROLANDE. Le nouveau féminisme américain: étude historique du Women's Liberation Movement [The new American feminism: historical study of the WLM]. Paris: Denoël/Gonthier, 1972, 472 pp.

Many comparisons are to be found--either explicit or implicit--in this study of the American Women's Liberation Movement by a young French woman. Rolande Ballorain came to Smith College to pursue studies of the American novel. Within a short time of her arrival there, she first heard of women's liberation. Further, she heard women saying things out loud that she had never heard expressed before. This experience in America proved to be her liberation as well. There was a "living thought" (pensée vivante) she had not yet found in France.

Aware of her privileged position as a foreign observer of this newly emerging movement, Ballorain collected documents and attended lectures and meetings. When she realized that the French press did not seem to portray the situation here accurately, she decided to write an as objective and fully documented account as possible of the WLM. Fortunately Rolande Ballorain had access to both French and American academics, theorists, and participants. Simone de Beauvoir reviewed her manuscript.

The work traces the historical development of the American movement, follows the dialectic of the groups, and presents portraits and interviews of the militants. There is also a section on the expression of the new American feminism in the press and literature. The young French woman was impressed by the dynamism, vitality, and imagination of these early militant feminist texts and their authors.

CARLANDER, INGRID. Les Américaines [American women]. Paris: Grasset, 1973, 309 pp.

Ingrid Carlander arrived at her views and understanding of American women through study of a culture she loves, that of her second country. As she notes, American women have long exercised a fascination upon the French, from De Tocqueville to de Gaulle. Psychologically, physically, and socially--from the pioneers to the "ladies"--they are different. Therefore the French must see them as they are and dispense with clichés and contradictions. American women are neither despots nor "domesticated" slaves.

The differences between women in the two countries are due to factors such as: the Protestant heritage that permitted women to play a significant role and exercise considerable influence in religious communities; the impact of the Abolition movement, a unique undertaking in which women participated; and civic passion such as that found in movements like the League of Women Voters. In a land of "self-made" men it is more difficult for women to move, to change, to attain self-fulfillment. Women, she finds, are absent from American folklore as they are absent from American history.

The American trait of competition is not without its dangers; it leads to narcissism in some cases. She notes that there is no counterpart in France for the practice of dating. And French parents have little opportunity to contribute to school policies. The author detects a consumer mentality to many things in the States, including sex. Women's true situation exemplifies the death of the American dream. American feminism is but part of the daily struggle for human dignity against the intrusions of technology. While one may not always subscribe to Ingrid Carlander's views, her evaluation does force reflection and analysis.

MASNATA, CLAIRE RUBATTEL. La révolte des Américaines [The revolt of American women]. Paris: Aubier-Montaigne, 1972, 189 pp.

Claire Masnata examines the American Women's Liberation Movement in the political, legal, and social spheres. Her study follows earlier works on America: L'Amérique blanche et les droits des noirs: contribution à l'étude du processus de décision aux États-Unis (1969) and Pouvoir, société, et politique aux États-Unis (1970), a collaborative work.

American women are portrayed as invisible through much of the country's history. The French incorrectly consider America to be the land of matriarchy. According to the author, the three major factors that distinguish the two countries and the respective position of women are: the Puritan ideology; the shortage of women in pioneer days; and the risks of frontier life, where women assumed many activities. The revolt of the early 1970s is placed in the context of earlier feminist activities. The volume concludes with a number of documents in English ranging from Lucy Stone's marriage contract of 1858 to Alix Shulman's "Marriage Agreement."

French Feminisms

GENERAL AND THEORETICAL STUDIES

These studies best fit the description of the "essay" given in the Introduction. They present views and observations on a wide range of topics and issues related to women and their concerns. Some have an ideological thrust; others present a more personal view. Some have a reformist approach; others are more radical.

Over the years the term feminism has been assigned various meanings, a fact attested to by the plural used in the titles of Jean Rabaut's Histoire des féminismes français and New French Feminisms, edited by Elaine Marks and Isabelle de Courtivron. In 1905 Gabrielle Petit protested that feminism is not feminine but human. Françoise Parturier views feminism as a study, an investigation, an erudition, a teaching. Simone de Beauvoir described feminism in a 1967 interview as a manner of living individually and a manner of fighting collectively. Women, she stated elsewhere, were tired of always being right but never having their rights.

Some of today's French women no longer wish to be glorified or placed upon a pedestal. They want justice at last. The problem thus far has been that women make the mores and men make the laws. The right to life has taken on a larger meaning, that of freedom for all from hunger, poverty, illiteracy, and oppression. While there is still considerable disagreement among French feminists on how to attain those goals, there is general consensus on these larger aims.

Within French society itself there is diversity. In the feminist camps there is a division between bourgeois intellectuals and the working class, between focus on theory or praxis in feminist activities. This diversity and disagreement over tactics among French women's groups is reflected in the proliferation of feminist reviews and journals. Further, the French national trait of individualism appears to be reinforced for both sexes by recent trends toward self-concern, the advent of the "me" generation. Difficulty in organizing is also impeded by the fact that, unlike American women, they have had little experience in joining clubs. Nevertheless, there is a strength and an openness in feminist endeavors despite the tendency toward chapelles, small coteries and interest groups.

The militant French feminist lawyer Gisèle Halimi describes the French women's movement as being a little like the proverbial Spanish inn. Each woman finds in it what she herself brings. Between the Freudians on the one hand, and the Marxists on the other, there are many nuances and degrees, represented by many groups. These groups open, change, and close access according to the personality of this or that woman and also according to the political context. The French women's movement is not one large association nor is it a homogeneous group. And while the majority of French women today are convinced and concerned about obtaining their rights, many would reject the term feminist for it tends to retain a restricted, at times perjorative, meaning equated with militant feminist activities.[1]

Any assessment of contemporary French feminism must be put into the larger context of contemporary France, a society that has been undergoing profound political, economic, and social changes. The country has moved to the left with the Socialists now in power. Historically, the Socialists have been the most active in supporting women's concerns. They were the only party to oppose the 1920 law against abortion and propaganda on behalf of certain contraceptive measures, for example. Beyond that, in the economic sphere industry has been modernized, foreign trade increased, and the tertiary sector expanded. The exodus to the cities continues. The population is now younger. At the same time, there is still a strong residue of the past. Traditional institutions have adapted but remain. Both within and without the family--still the central social unit--these changes have all affected women's lives.

French women have had to contend with the heritage of a Latin country. The Catholic church and the Napoleonic civil code have long encouraged women to be submissive and subordinate their lives to men. Andrée Michel and Geneviève Texier, two distinguished sociologists, maintain that in no other Protestant or Socialist country of comparable industrial level have efforts to limit women within the family and within society itself been as concerted as they have been in France. To the exterior obstacles, the pressure groups, must be added internal ones, the psychological dimension. Contemporary French feminism is trying to set the record straight, to free women from the burden of the past, to permit them to realize their potential.

French Feminisms

CREATIVITY

French women are finally receiving official recognition for their many contributions to French culture; in the past official criteria were male-dominated. Within the past few years they have been elected--in some cases for the first time--to the official French Academies; prestigious institutions, some founded several centuries ago. Feminists contend that there has been a misplaced emphasis on these many "firsts." These are not victories but recognition long overdue.

Critical to any assessment of women's creativity is the fact that in the past masculine norms determined what was art, what constituted creative activities. Women suffered in comparison with men's "accomplishments." Now the whole range of women's creative endeavors, from the individual to the collective, is being examined. Women's contribution to the arts is being noted at last. The feminist filmmakers group Musidora, to cite but one example, succeeded in bringing public attention to the pioneering role played in filmmaking by Alice Guy (1873-1968), the first woman cinéaste.

Artistic activities are related to the larger concern of French women to find their own mode of expression. The search for women's language is a theme central to a number of recent literary works. A link is discerned between silence, solitude, and suffering. Many feminists hold that women must break out of their solitude and, through collective efforts and common speech, find solidarity.

While literary works are beyond the scope of this volume, their role in French feminist activities is such that they merit brief mention. France has a rich tradition of eight centuries of women writers, starting with Marie de France in the twelfth century, then Christine de Pizan, the first woman to live by her pen. This tradition is unique in Western culture. Apart from the "exceptions"-- women such as Jeanne d'Arc and Catherine de Médicis--who played an important part in their country's history, French women have always voiced their concerns, aspirations, and thoughts in writing. The written text occupies a privileged place in France. That is particularly true today given the current concern with theoretical discourse in structuralism and semiotics. Many of the recent French feminist texts are a product of this interest in discourse, which has produced innovative theoretical works on l'écriture féminine, feminine writing.

In 1972 writer Catherine Valabrègue founded the group Spiral. Its aim was to study women and creativity and what was to be called the problem of "stifled creativity." The following year, an association of women filmmakers and actresses, Musidora, organized the first French Women's Film Festival. More women artists joined together to exhibit, enlarging a tradition started with the first group of women artists in France, now celebrating its centenary. Related women's activities in the arts continue. In a country where culture plays such an important role, where intellectuals and artists are accorded the status of stars, the question of women's artistic expression assumes particular importance.

JOURNALISM, THE FEMINIST PRESS, AND ADVERTISING

Throughout the nineteenth and twentieth centuries, journals and papers have played an important part in publicizing and disseminating the demands and aspirations of French women. The appearance and proliferation of these papers closely parallels the nation's uprisings and upheavals, from the revolution of 1789 to that of 1968.

In the early 1830s, several feminist journals appeared. Their founders included women workers who had participated in the 1830 revolution, only to find their hopes and expectations were not shared by their male colleagues. Many of the early women journalists were involved in the Saint-Simonien movement. They included Suzanne Voilquin, who directed La Tribune des femmes (1832), the voice of working-class women. The Journal des femmes (1832) aimed primarily at making women better wives and mothers, La Gazette des femmes (1836) was more politically oriented. In 1848 Eugénie Niboyet founded the first feminist daily, La Voix des femmes, a journal that proudly proclaimed itself to be the organ of all interests. Niboyet was assisted by committed feminists including Désirée Gay, Elisa Lemonnier, Suzanne Voilquin, and the indefatiguable Jeanne Deroin.

These feminist publications, while generally short-lived, continued to appear throughout the century. Their number increased dramatically toward the end of the century. The most important was La Fronde, named after two seventeenth-century uprisings against the power of monarchy, in which aristocratic women played a central role (fronde means slingshot). Prominent feminist and journalist Marguerite Durand directed La Fronde. Her good friend and colleage were involved in these revolts. Prominent feminist and journalist Marguerite Durand directed La Fronde. Her good friend and colleague Séverine (the pen name of Caroline Rémy Guebhard [1855–1929]; Evelyne Le Garrec's biography, Séverine: une rebelle, was published by Seuil in 1982) who supported herself entirely through her work, is considered the first professional woman journalist. Séverine dedicated her life to liberty in thought and writing. With the Socialist Jules Vallès she founded Le Cri du peuple in 1883. She defended Dreyfus, supported peace in 1914, condemned totalitarian ideologies in the 1920s. Above all, she advocated women's rights through her example. Séverine was but one of many French feminists who were journalists. The press provides a forum for ideas. And for a number, journalism also provides the necessary salaried work.

French Feminisms

The most recent French feminist movement has also been accompanied by yet another outpouring of feminist papers and reviews.[2] Many have a limited printing or appear at erratic intervals. Some are ephemeral for lack of financing or sustained commitment. All work under difficulties for they are outside the traditional mass circulation French women's press represented by magazines such as Elle, Marie-Claire, and Cosmopolitan. These feminist journals span the entire range of feminist positions: reformist and radical, Catholic and Communist, heterosexual and lesbian, homemaker, intellectual, and worker. They include the elegant review of women in publicity, Visuelle, and the review of the prostitutes, L'Écho du macadam. These reviews attest to the breadth and diversity of the contemporary French feminist movement.

NOTES

1. Three recent works on French feminism are: Naty Garcia Gaudilla, Libération des femmes: le MLF (Paris: P.U.F., 1982); Danièle Léger, Le féminisme en France (Paris: Sycamore, 1982); and Les femmes en France dans une société d'inégalités (Paris: Documentation Française, 1982), a report issued by the Ministère des Droits de la Femme. See also Claire Goldberg Moses's forthcoming Feminist Thought in Nineteenth-Century France (Albany: State University of New York Press, 1984).
2. For further information on this recent French feminist press see Liliane Kandel's article in Pénélope, no. 1 (June 1979); reprinted in Questions féministes, no. 7 (February 1980), and in Débat, no. 1 (May 1980). A listing of these journals, with references to their affiliation, orientation, and publisher's address will be found in my article, "An Annotated Bibliography of Recent Studies on French Women," Contemporary French Civilization 3, no. 3 (Spring 1979).

French Feminisms

GENERAL AND THEORETICAL STUDIES

ALZON, CLAUDE. Femme mythifiée, femme mystifiée [Woman mythified, woman mystified]. Paris: P.U.F., 1978, 422 pp.

The cover of this long, well-documented work illustrates the ambiguity of its content: it features Magritte's Les cornes du désir, which depicts two headless women.

A professor of political science specializing in the family, Claude Alzon does not always succeed in maintaining scholarly objectivity when he discusses certain women, such as Simone de Beauvoir and "Saint" Luce Irigaray. Critics, in fact, have questioned why he devoted so many pages to the subject of feminism when he feels that it has already been overemphasized and is now on the wane.

In any event there is much to consider in this critical exposé of major contemporary themes involved in the rapports between the sexes. The author notes how certain political groups--like the Socialists and the Communists in particular--have changed their positions in order to take advantage of the popularity of women's issues now that feminism is à la mode.

———. La femme potiche et la femme bonniche: pouvoir bourgeois et pouvoir mâle [The decorative woman and the devoted woman: bourgeois power and male power]. Paris: Maspero, 1977, 112 pp.

The contemporary French feminist movement agonizes over the central question: Who is the principal enemy of women? Men who have oppressed them for milennia, or capitalism, an answer that relieves male guilts. The problem is analyzed in an essay that is both vigorous and ironic.

Women Alzon views as oppressed by both male and bourgeois politics. Their lives are either decorative (potiches) and vacuous, lived in golden cages, or devoted (bonniches) to work as slaves of capitalism and husbands. The extensive documentation--political documents, surveys, etc.--takes up almost half the text. It is printed on the left page, facing the text. The reader is thus drawn into a dialectic.

ANGENOT, MARC. Les champions des femmes: examen des discours de la superiorité des femmes, 1400-1800 [The champions of women: examination of discourses on the superiority of women, 1400-1800]. Québec: Presses de l'Université de Québec, 1977, 208 pp.

Although published in Québec, this study has been included because the entries are European. Further, it is one of the few works that present the history--or possibly the prehistory--of feminism. The ideological and literary tradition it describes is little known. From the fifteenth to the eighteenth centuries more than eighty moralists and essayists voiced feminist demands, accomplishments, and aspirations. The moral, intellectual, and biological superiority of women has been set forth in essays and tracts. Thus to some extent, these discourses on women's superiority provide a corrective to the prevailing views--in male-dominated societies--of women's presumed inferiority. Some of these discourses are rhetorical exercises, the close arguing of a controversial position. The panegyris was by nature paradoxical. It presented an opinion contrary to current acceptance, here, that women were superior.

The first section of the study includes selections from some of these tracts. Misogynist and "sexist" texts are included for comparison. The second part and the conclusion speculate upon the prevalence of this oldest, most widespread, and most universal of prejudices, that against women. A comprehensive bibliography, including a list of all the manuscripts studied, completes the volume.

BENOÎT, NICOLE, EDGAR MORIN, and BERNARD PAILLARD. La femme majeure: nouvelle feminité, nouveau féminisme [Woman comes of age: new femininity, new feminism]. Paris: Club de l'Obs/Éditions du Seuil, 1973, 162 pp.

This collection of essays was written shortly after the development of the new feminist movement of the 1970s. It presents some of the factors that contributed to this movement.

Several psychosociologists attempted to follow the direction of women's activities in France and assess the status of women's emancipation. They saw that socialist feminism was becoming organized, becoming integrated into women's groups in the unions. It was influencing a growing number of salaried women.

These researchers endeavored to ascertain the goals women sought and the strategies then being employed, along with what the errors and uncertainties of women were. Two main themes emerged and asserted themselves: a new freedom for one's body and the freedom for self-realization. These themes, it is held, reveal a crisis in feminine identity.

The initial section on femininity and feminism, from utopias to crises, sketches a short historical survey of French feminisms from the period of the Saint-Simoniens and utopian movements of the nineteenth century to post-May 1968. Two crises are discerned in this last period. One encompasses all the problems of the "feminine condition"; the other, seen as more restrictive, concerns feminine nature itself, the nature of the couple, sexuality, and feminine realization.

The next section, the new feminism, offers a detailed study in the changes of the feminist weekly Elle (comparable to Seventeen and Mademoiselle) underwent from 1945 to 1966. These changes are viewed in the context of Edgar Morin and Roland Barthes's more general studies relating to mass culture.

The last section concentrates on the struggle for family planning after the neo-Malthusian years of the 1930s. It goes from the founding of Maternité Heureuse to the passage of the Neuwirth law.

French Feminisms

BRIAC, AURÉLIA. De la drague [On pickups]. Paris: Grasset, 1978.
   Words serve as bait in "fishing" for pickups. But women are not fish. Briac decided it was time for someone to analyze this "amorous discourse": "Haven't I met you somewhere before?", etc. The lexicography drawn up shows how the vocabulary varies with the character assumed: soldier, boss, policeman, student, etc. These revealing—at times humorous—observations are presented without explicit criticism or condemnation. They speak for themselves.

CARISSE, COLETTE, and JOFFRE DUMAZEDIER. Les femmes innovatrices [Innovative women]. Paris: Seuil, 1975, 282 pp. (With the collaboration of Mireille Gagnon, Marguerite Langlois, and Serge Proulx.)
   The subtitle of this work is "Post-Industrial Problems of Francophone America, Québec." Québec is an area where French and American feminist ideas intersect. Thus it offers a unique observation point from which to analyze the situation of women as they are affected by the development of postindustrial society. In spite of some delays and contradictions, Québec is the most advanced of Francophone societies. The dialectic of the two influences, French and Anglo-Saxon, is examined by tracing the changing image of women in both the French and English papers of the province. Statistical data is included.
   Two-thirds of the women designated as "innovative" are found to have a highly developed social conscience. This would seem to indicate that society is not providing the time and material resources which permit women to make positive choices. Québec women must also contend with the Québec male. He is held to be full of complexes and intimidated by women's intelligence. He has yet to come to terms with the defeat of 1767, the defeat that gave England New France. This work also features the views of some well-known French-Canadian feminists.

CHEVERNY, JULIEN. Les matriarches: essai sur la fin du pouvoir mâle [The matriarchies: essay on the end of male power]. Paris: Copernic, 1978, 160 pp.
   Julien Cheverny's wide-ranging essay is written with a mixture of seriousness and wit that characterizes his monumental Sexologies de l'occident (1976). He discourses on paleofeminism, abortion, eugenics, the priesthood of women, and the marriage of priests.
   The title indicates Cheverny's perspective. Women aspire to remain aloof from the crises of civilization. They "presume" to consider themselves alone capable of giving the world a new order. The myth of the modern couple is denounced. Its only function would appear to be to aid the individual, of male sex, to better support his decline. Cheverny is also critical of Simone de Beauvoir for a life and works that bear the mark of masculinity. It is held that her writings are but the projections and development of those works Sartre had neither the time nor the inclination to write.

French Feminisms

CHOISY, MARYSE. La guerre des sexes [The battle of the sexes].
  Paris: Éditions Publications Premières, 1970, 279 pp.
  A prolific author, Maryse Choisy is known to English readers for two essays she wrote in English (but never translated into French), "Sigmund Freud: A New Appraisal" and "The Psychoanalysis of the Prostitute." Long engaged in women's issues, she concentrated on the problem of prostitution and undertook a campaign to close the legalized brothels. The powers behind this organized exploitation of women, this "institution," orchestrated a scandal in 1930 when her book, Un mois chez les filles, appeared. It was translated into thirty-two languages.
  The first section considers the existence of the feminine: the biology and physiology of women and feminine sexuality. In the second part, "The History of Mother," a study of matriarchies and the religion of the "Great Mother" (Magna Mater) endeavors to restore authentic feminine values and provide solid, historical bases for today's feminist movement.
  Maryse Choisy reproduces a letter received from the eminent theologian Teilhard de Chardin. In it he disagrees with Jung and notes that those with the greatest devotion to Mary were men, while those with the great devotion to the "human" Christ were women such as Saint Theresa. This, the theologian feels, reveals an irresistible Christian need to "feminize" a terribly masculine God.

CLÉMENT, CATHERINE. Les fils de Freud sont fatigués [The sons of
  Freud are tired]. Paris: Grasset, 1978, 185 pp.
  Catherine Clément has participated in feminist journals and debates in addition to publishing a number of books, including Le pouvoir des mots (1974). Her contention that the class struggle must take precedence over the stuggle between the sexes provoked violent discussion at the session devoted to "Women and Sexuality" during the week of Marxist Thought on Women. Clément coauthored La jeune née (q.v.).
  Note: The most recent works of this author are listed under Backès-Clément, Catherine.

COLLANGE, CHRISTIANE. Je veux rentrer à la maison [I want to go back
  home]. Collection humeurs. Paris: Grasset, 1979, 188 pp.
  This book evoked much comment—not all of it favorable—when it was published. The author, a well-known writer, seemed to have done a volteface and joined those who would oblige women to return to their homes (la femme au foyer) and leave their work and outside activities. No longer should they be "cut in two" trying to maintain a precarious equilibrium. What the author advocates is that society reorganize itself so that women can reconcile professional and personal responsibilities.
  Christiane Collange herself will not accept either professional fatigue or domestic boredom. She does not believe in the concept of "liberating" work or in unlimited feminine sacrifice. The main solution proposed is to give motherhood the recognition it does not yet receive in our materialistic culture.

French Feminisms

_____. Madame et le management: une femme organisée en vaut deux [Madame and management: an organized woman is worth two]. Paris: Tchou, 1969, 206 pp. (Preface by Françoise Giroud.)

Christine Collange, journalist, wife of a journalist, and mother of four boys, tells how she puts into practice "at home," modern techniques of organization known as management. Thanks to management all women should be able to come to terms with their "profession" of housewife and become truly heads of the house instead of being devoured by domestic tasks. Unfortunately it is not always easy to put this theory into practice, particularly in many lower-class homes.

La condition féminine [The feminine condition]. Paris: Éditions Sociales, 1978, 386 pp. (A collective work under the direction of CERM [Centre d'Études et de Recherches Marxistes].)

The unity of this collection of essays resides in the subject, women, and in the party perspective of French Communist scholars and researchers. Beyond that, there is considerable variety in the offerings that range from a scholarly article on "The Literary Images of Women in the Middle Ages" to more popular and political works such as "Sexist Ideology Exists, I Know, I Have Encountered It."

A long article on male-female rapports and the problem of masculine domination shows that anthropological studies reveal that masculine domination existed in early societies. These findings contradict long-held party views (based upon Engels) that made capitalism the sole oppressor of women. There are several studies on women's portrayal in the feminist press and in school textbooks, and on the party's dealings with the growing feminist movement in France. Finally, there are several articles dealing with working women in France in 1978.

DUCHÉ, JEAN. Le premier sexe [The first sex]. Paris: Robert Laffont, 1972, 490 pp.

Drawing upon his experience as a popular writer and journalist for the women's magazine Elle, Jean Duché presents an extensive compendium of materials on women, in his view, the "first sex." Much of this material, he contends, shows the primacy of women and women's sexual freedom. And this, in spite of appearances or preconceived notions. Starting with antiquity, all men's efforts to reduce women's powers have proved unsuccessful.

The American woman is viewed as sexually demanding and consumer oriented. Her life is a total of material possessions and fragments of existence: three husbands, six washing machines, four children, seventeen autos, fourteen lovers, etc.

The nineteenth century is seen as "the worst moment in the history of women." Working women were exploited. For bourgeois women the emphasis on virginity, which started in the Renaissance with the reign of financial concerns, became a virtual obsession. To lose one's honor was a veritable bourgeois banqueroute.

d'EAUBONNE, FRANÇOISE. Écologie, féminisme: révolution ou mutation? [Ecology, feminism: revolution or change?] Paris: Éditions A.T.P., 1978, 233 pp.

D'Eaubonne stresses her ongoing argument, namely that the two major concerns of the modern world, ecology and feminism, are interlinked. Fearful that it has done a poor job in managing the world's resources, capitalism—the latest stage of patriarchy—is beginning to return to the values once held to be "feminine": peace, tranquility, enjoyment (jouissance), spontaneity, and so forth.

The first part of the book analyzes the ways in which nature is being destroyed. The author rejects the idea of "growth," or at least the myth of economic growth. The second part focuses on capitalism. D'Eaubonne maintains that the history of the patriarchal family began with the concept of inheritance. Recent studies, in particular those of Lévi-Strauss, posit that women were "put into circulation" as a commodity. They were also exchanged as the "words" of men, even though the women themselves had no voice. She again emphasizes that the current ecological "disaster" is due to the two principal founding factors of patriarchy: the male system that appropriated agriculture, and the discovery of the true process of paternity.

_____. Le féminisme ou la mort: ou la subjectivité radicale [Feminism or death: or radical subjectivity]. Collection femmes en mouvement. Paris: Pierre Horay, 1974, 274 pp.

One of France's most prolific feminists analyzes the feminist movement there. In 1974 she felt it imperative to investigate the historical origins and consequences of the feminist movement; it proved to be a larger project than first envisioned. In a few short years there had been a number of events, such as the founding of the MLF and work with the Ligue Française pour le Droit des Femmes (dating from the 1870s), as well as the evolution of American feminism.

The battle of the sexes is linked to larger social changes. For the author the only possible positive outcome of the new feminism is a new humanism, a theme developed in the 1890s. Socialism is charged with maintaining sexism just as does the capitalist block. It is only the forms that have changed. In all cultures women are viewed as property, as the proverbs culled from many lands amply demonstrate. It is d'Eaubonne's view that ultimately the struggle between the sexes must be reconciled if there are to be positive and viable results for society as a whole.

_____. Les femmes avant le patriarcat [Women before the patriarchy]. Paris: Payot, 1976, 239 pp.

This volume offers a sociological/anthropological assessment of the legends and myths that point to the two major events in men's ongoing oppression of women: their taking over of agriculture from women and the discovery of the true process of paternity.

French Feminisms

D'Eaubonne is particularly concerned with the impending double ecological catastrophes--overpopulation and exploitation. Both of these problems are intrinsically linked to women's concerns.

_____. Histoire et actualité du féminisme [History and actuality of feminism]. Paris: Alain Moreau, 1972, 398 pp.

Here are views of a woman who pioneered in writing on feminism in France during the recent resurgence of that movement. She feels the views found in her early work, Le complexe de Diane (1951), only retain historical validity now. D'Eaubonne admits to sharing in many of the prejudices against America of the French Left of that period.

The author believes that the books that have had the most influence on French women have been: A Room of One's Own (translated by Clara Malraux earlier, but not published until 1951), The Second Sex, and The Feminine Mystique. Several chapters outline the Radical-Feminist movement in America. The work closes on an optimistic note, for it was written after the pivotal year of 1971 when the current French feminist movement was getting under way. An appendix includes some of the pamphlets and manifestos published in 1971.

LES FEMMES DE NICE. Les babarotes. Paris: Éditions des femmes, 1978, 134 pp.

Between 1974 and 1976 a group of women met regularly in what Americans would call a consciousness-raising group. They took their name from their local dialect, that of Nice, a region they love. In the south of France, the Midi, babarote means "to be blue," to have bizarre ideas, to be a bit crazy. The term also designates the black-winged insects that frequent kitchens and go out at night. The women of Nice have brought together their views in a collection of ideas that are contradictory at times. They offer comments from a group not based in Paris.

Les femmes s'entêtent. Collection idées. (The title defies translation. It is taken from the surrealist Max Ernst's work, La femme 100 têtes. There are multiple puns on the homonyms of s'entêter: women are becoming stubborn, s'entêter; they are without heads, sans têtes; they are numerous, cent têtes; they nurse and support, téter.) Paris: Gallimard, 1975, 478 pp.

The volume, essentially a reissue of Les Temps Modernes (April-May 1974) bearing the same title, is a collection of texts presented without any preconceived plan. The aim was to preserve liberty. It is an important expression of French women's concerns in the early 1970s. The volume is placed under the sign of "pertubation, ma soeur." The women--some of whom preferred to remain anonymous--speak of the subjects that most interest them. While this is not an explicit exposé of the feminine condition, a common theme does emerge, the radical oppression of women. There are women who accept masculine culture, but appropriate it to their use. Other contributors see culture as one of the forms of their oppression. All refuse oppression in any form.

The general divisions of the volume are: I, Encirclement; II, Rupture of the Circle; III, Desires/Deliriums. Of particular interest is an article on schools for women and science courses on the "sciences of man." It is based upon a rereading of several classic treatises of education. Throughout the work there are examples of contemporary French feminists play with language, reappropriating the "father" tongue. For example, there is an article on femmage (untranslatable).

Simone de Beauvoir states in her preface that each woman engaged in struggle has her own motivations, her own views, her own unique perspectives. She acknowledges that she, de Beauvoir, has more or less played the role of alibi woman. She urges vigilance as the order of the day.

GELLY, JACQUELINE. Moi, Claire [Me, Claire]. Paris: Stock, 1975, 233 pp. (Reprint. Paris: Union des Femmes Françaises, 1977.)

Secretary general of the Union des Femmes Françaises Jacqueline Gelly recounts her background and that of other UFF members including Claire, who no longer wishes to be defined by parents, husband, or children, but by her autonomous self. Gelly, from Nimes in the south of France, had to start work at fourteen. Like many of the UFF members, she has not had an easy life. Yet adversity seems to have brought out the best in these women. They commend the support and solidarity they receive from the Communist-dominated organization formed from Resistance and women's groups after the last war.

GROULT, BENOÎTE. Ainsi soit-elle [And thus may she be]. Paris: Grasset, 1975, 220 pp. (Elle is the feminine form of it; normal usage calls for il, the masculine form.)

Feminism, Groult insists, is neither a neurosis nor a mode; it is a vital necessity in today's world. Women must "cure" themselves of being women, that is, from having been brought up female in a male universe. She points out how women have lived for centuries in a blissful daze. Lived, that is, as they were instructed to live, think as they were taught to think, and enjoy life in the manner permitted. It is not surprising, then, that women have remained in their "place" for so long. Men have been astonished to see French women's recent revolt, to see the indignation and hear the protests of so many women, women they had always assumed were capricious, coquettish, jealous, and possessive. The "unpardonable" sin was to step out of the "place" to which men had assigned them for so long.

This exposé of women's subjugation from biblical times on--for the pleasure and benefit of men--is also humorous. The humor is at times corrosive as well as ironic, a necessary corrective element. The work is rich in anecdotes, details, and telling citations about women writers, politicians, and public figures. They are judged by different standards from those of their male counterparts. Rarely are they shown in anything other than traditional "women's activities." Indiscretions in public women's lives are more published than their accomplishments.

France is generally referred to as the oldest daughter of the Catholic church. America is seen as the oldest daughter of Freud. There is some material on American women. The title of one of the chapters of this very successful work comes from Nixon's statement: "My mother, she was a saint."

Thanks to the women's movement, Groult holds, humanity need no longer be deprived of women's contribution. They are the ones who have sustained humanistic values through the violence, oppression, and egotism that have marked history. Together women must proclaim their opposition a thing of the past. But they must do so in unison. Solidarity is new to French women. It will require effort to attain.

_____. Le féminisme au masculin [Feminism in the masculine]. Paris: Denoël/Gonthier, 1978, 196 pp.

For centuries women have been reduced to virtual silence. During this time a few courageous men have tried to present and promote women in something other than their traditional image of devoted wife, guardian of the foyer. They have seen women as independent human beings who were entitled to the same rights as men.

These enlightened men saw maternity as an additional contribution women brought to life in society, not as a handicap. To express such views, these men--Poullain de la Barre, Condorcet, Enfantin, Fourier, and Stuart Mill--risked irony and mockery. But they were endowed with freedom of thought and qualities such as courage which the well-known feminist novelist and journalist Benoîte Groult details. These brave men were taken for mad. A sense of justice enabled them to brave public opinion and demand the end to male abuse of power.

GUELAUD-LERIDON, FRANÇOISE. Recherches sur la condition féminine dans la société d'aujourd'hui [Research on the feminine condition in today's society]. Institut National d'Études Démographiques, Commissariat Général du Plan d'Équipement et de la Productivité, Travaux et Documents no. 48. Paris: P.U.F., 1967, 123 pp. (Preface by Jean Fourastié.)

This early work is serious, scholarly, and well documented. The report is divided into demographic characteristics: the state of the feminine population; demographic changes such as marriage, divorce, and birth; and schooling and professional activities. There is a lengthy appendix summarizing the legal status of French women in 1966 and another detailing the facilities offered for the care of preschool age children, most of who are in the government run écoles maternelles.

LAINÉ, PASCAL. La femme et ses images [Woman and her images]. Paris: Stock, 1974, 286 pp.

    A philosopher who teaches at the University of Paris XIII, Pascal Lainé has published philosophical and sociological analyses. In early 1972 she and twenty colleagues surveyed women throughout France. Their findings raised a number of questions about the problem of womanhood, femininity: Is it inherent in woman's nature? Is it not rather the indication of social constraints upon women?, etc.

    The opening section discusses feminist discourse. Then the problem of French women, marked as they are by notions of the "eternal feminine," is studied. The fundamental dichotomy (discussed at length in The Second Sex) of the masculine "exterior" and the feminine "interior" persists. Woman's body is seen as the guardian of "femininity." The emphasis on physical attributes, more prominent in Latin countries, makes the problem of aging particularly traumatic.

    Emancipation must not become yet another way in which the consumer society subjugates the young girl, the wife, the mother. The presumed "permissiveness" of today's mores has not transformed the intrinsic relationships among individuals, among the classes, among the sexes.

    Pascal Lainé maintains that the supposed modernism of today's sexual liberation is but another manifestation of the differences between the sexes. Woman has an image in order to render herself desirable. It is not important to know what the desire is for: desire itself suffices. In time the image will justify itself.

LAURENT, ALAIN. Féminin-masculin: le nouvel équilibre [Feminine-masculine: the new equilibrium]. Paris: Seuil, 1975, 189 pp.

    No more "repose for the warrior," for women no longer wish to remain in "their place." A group of men felt compelled to express their views in the increasingly strident French debates over feminism. Among the solutions they propose are: don't antagonize masculine neuroses; don't kill the "difference"; divide the care of children, even that of the newborn. These are French male views approved by some feminists, condemned by others.

LAUWICK, FRANCOISE. Quelle drole de veuve: chronique [What a strange widow: a chronicle]. Paris: Flammarion, 1979, 180 pp.

    This essay considers the difficulties widows encounter in adjusting to their situation. If widows are no longer subject to denunciation for immorality with possible loss of their inheritance, as they were in eighteenth-century France, society still appears uncomfortable with women who are no longer married, some of whom are financially independent.

    Widows are victims of society's rejection. They need strong character and health to confront family battles, problems over their children's education, the jealousy of other women, and attacks from the "exterior." Widows cannot understand why they should be the victims of such treatment. Why do they appear to lose their interest to others, their role in society, when they lose their husbands? Is their life in society wholly dependent upon having a man? In this troubled, troubling twentieth century others, including the happy young couple of the moment, should consider this current problem.

Widows find an apparent reversal of values. Devotion to a dying husband is criticized by a society "allergic" to courageous acts: "She was too good"; "Why did she become her husband's nurse?," etc. French widows appear to be more discreet. They do not partake of group psychotherapy as do an increasing number of American widows. Different situations and stories are recounted. The subject is also treated in Marthe Massenet's Madame veuve (1977).

LeBRUN, ANNIE. Lâchez-tout [Let everything go]. Paris: Sagittaire, 1977, 180 pp.

Here, as in earlier articles, Annie LeBrun attacks what she calls "femellitude": female terrorism, or "Stalinism in skirts," the author's terms for militant feminism. She refuses to be enrolled in the army of feminine militants solely because of a biological hazard and professes a deeply felt individualism. The French feminist movement and its shock militants--Xavière Gauthier, Hélène Cixous, Benoîte Groult, Annie Leclerc--are criticized.

The extreme weakness of de Beauvoir's propositions, her false academic perspective, and her error in envisioning the feminist question in light of Sartre's theses are all attacked. LeBrun castigates "Saint" Luce Irigaray and all those who obscure women's discourse by their experiments in women's writing. They invite caricature.

The book offers insights into a French woman's views from a different school.

Le GARREC, EVELYNE. Un lit à soi: itinéraires des femmes [A bed of one's own: women's itineraries]. Paris: Seuil, 1979, 253 pp.

Communal dwellings with shared labor have long been features of utopian communities, such as Fourier's phalansteries. But privacy was generally not considered even though the concept of personal sanctity has been a frequently voiced feminist demand. Feminist journalist Evelyne Le Garrec follows the itineraries of women, women who have become single again through widowhood, divorce, or separation. Her study includes comments on the chapter of "the theory of the bed" from Balzac's La physiologie du mariage, ou méditation de philosophie éclectique sur le bonheur et le malheur conjugal (1828), a part-satirical, part-pseudo-sociological work.

LEMOINE-LUCCIONI, EUGÉNIE. Partage des femmes [Divided women]. Collection le champ Freudien, directed by Jacques Lacan. Paris: Seuil, 1976, 182 pp.

This work examines the problems entailed in being a woman. The author draws her conclusions in part from interviews with pregnant women. Pregnancy is held to be the time when women feel their womanhood most intensely. And yet, as both partakers of creation and objects of creation, they are divided. For some, this period is marked by narcissism. This is one possible reaction for women caught in the paradigms and systems of virile representations. The references in this feminist psychoanalytic exploration are Freud, Lacan, Lévi-Strauss, and literature, including Greek tragedies.

LEROY, SUZANNE. C'est dur la solitude [Solitude is difficult]. Collection Une Femme et son Métier. Paris: Robert Laffont, 1972, 235 pp.

Suzanne Leroy directs a matrimonial agency. When she set up her agency over twenty years ago, there were few such services in France. Now they are much more numerous, indicating changes in French mores.

Long experience has brought Leroy familiarity with the many problems of those who seek mates. Most have their personal "history," which they decide to share with her. She has thus learned of the needs, demands, and caprices of clients in this little-documented domain, which she now shares with the public.

Several initial chapters explain how marriages were organized or arranged in ancient China, Greece, Rome, and North Africa, as well as in France of former days.

LESPÉRANCE, EMMANUEL. L'ère de la femme moderne: essai sur le féminisme [The era of the modern woman: essay on feminism]. Brive: Nouvelle Maugein, 1970, 147 pp.

This essay in the style and tradition of Montaigne is based upon years of reflection on the problem of feminism. Personal considerations, historical events, anecdotes, and aphorisms intermingle with poetry and literary citations. Emmanuel Lespérance considers the "shocking" lack of rights for women in so many modern societies.

For the author, women are yet another group among those who suffer unjustly. Suffering is attributed to two causes: the corrupting influence of capital and the wars that are the consequence of this system of values.

MAILLARD, CLAUDE. Le présent des femmes [Women's present]. Paris: Robert Laffont, 1978, 212 pp.

Under the direction of Claude Maillard, a doctor and psychologist, a group of thirty women spent two years exploring the problems entailed in relationships between the sexes. This continuous, collective history is the result of their discussions. Its aim is to make French men more aware of what women are like.

They do not know women well, not even their girl friends and wives. An effort must be made to listen to and understand women.

A number of areas were considered. The child: is having one a trap? or a passionate experience? Boy or girl: why a preference? Nourishment: is food a source of feminine alienation? For or against a dining room? Would a salaire ménager (housewive's salary) tend to restrict women to that activity? Time: how do women relate to it? Is this possibly another form of death? The women touched upon many topics that most affect their lives: life, love, and children. For some it was the first time they had been able to confront these questions.

Until now, men presumed to be the only ones with knowledge (savoir). They must learn that women also have a knowledge that is proper to them. Women's knowledge is more visceral, it has its own discourse. Thus far there has been little dialogue. French women must understand and utilize their strength. In this difficult undertaking of the present, their tenacity and persistence of the past will aid.

MASSIP, RENÉE. La femme et l'amitié [Woman and friendship]. Paris: Centurion; Grasset, 1970, 153 pp.

The novelist and essayist Renée Massip, author of L'entente du couple (1970), continues her analyses of women. To many people, the notion of friendship between men and women seems impossible. Part of the problem is terminology. Everyone has a particular idea of what friendship entails. The standard definition from the nineteenth-century Larousse dictionary states that "friendship requires strong, calm souls, above all independent souls" and goes on to add that "since subordination is the civil and economic condition of women, and since they bring passion to all their activities, and since they are in constant rivalry among themselves, and above all, because love and maternal love take such an intense place in their lives, women can scarcely know true friendship." Most women are but "faint" friends because most are mistresses and admirable mothers.

Massip discussed the question of friendship with family and friends. There are quotations on the topic from literary figures such as Diderot, George Sand, and Colette. True friendship, it would appear, cannot be satisfied with either camaraderie or false intimacy. Renée Massip concludes that it is more difficult for women to find the right tone for friendship because women tend to be more secretive and sometimes fearful, and therefore measured in their acceptance and offering of friendship. For the French the classic text on friendship is Montaigne's essay describing his feelings for La Boëtié, written thirteen years after his death. It was a friendship that surpassed all Montaigne's relationships with women.

French Feminisms

MENASSEYRE, CHRISTIANE. Les Françaises aujourd'hui [French women today]. Que sais-je? Paris: Hatier, 1978, 79 pp.

This concise, inexpensive work summarizes the general situation of women in contemporary France. The disparity between the image of French women and reality is examined. Their situation in regard to work, education, motherhood, and public life is outlined. The author concludes that French women wish "to be," that is, to live normally, without heroism, in their professional, civic, and private spheres. They want an existence determined solely by their choice.

MICHEL, ANDRÉE. Le féminisme [Feminism]. Paris: P.U.F., 1979, 125 pp.

A short, general outline of feminism is sketched by one of France's leading sociologists. Some of the material is drawn from Elise Boulding's The Underside of History: A New View of Women Through Time (1977). There are several sections on the French women's movement of the 1970s, which are integrated into a concise, well-documented global view.

_____. Femmes, sexisme, et société [Women, sexism, and society]. Paris: P.U.F., 1977, 208 pp.

Virtually all the articles in this volume Andrée Michel edited are based upon papers presented at the 1974 world congress of the International Association of Sociology held in Toronto by the International Committee of Research on the Roles of the Sexes. Consequently, a number of the articles are French translations of papers presented in English. The majority, however, were written by French scholars.

Marie-José Chombard de Laüwe considers the socialization of children; Marguerite Lorée, the images of publicity. There are contributions by Christine Delphy, Nicole-Claude Mathieu, and Helen Yvert-Jolée. The three sections deal with the social sciences and sexual stratification, production and reproduction of the roles of the sexes in different societies, and women's innovations in the system of sexual stratification and new perspectives. Economists substantiate the claim that the "free" services of women rendered in the context of the family represent almost a third of the gross national product, the PNB (produit national brut).

Since this is a Franco-American endeavor, a number of articles include comparisons between the two countries. Lorée, for example, analyzes women's image in French and North American publicity. The historical movement of "enclosing" women has been studied in both countries. Efforts to present rational, unprejudiced, scientific analyses of problems are seen as impeded by sexual prejudices. This volume proposes new ways of developing a sociology of the role of the sexes that will not be restricted to androcentrism.

MICHEL, CLAUDE. Toutes les mêmes? [All women alike?]. Paris: Syros, 1979, 170 pp.

On one level women constitute a group. Whatever their situation in society, the movie star and the militant worker have more in common than do the president and the mechanic. Until quite recently most women shared the same segregation and the same education. Yet to be a woman signifies different things to different women. This study analyzes the differing situations of women according to their socioprofessional status in France.

Claude Michel is a feminist militant with a degree in demography. The mother of six, she directs the Breton Family Planning Movement. Her volume summarizes studies of the problems of women: marriage, children, work, home. Contrary to widespread opinion, the choice of becoming a housewife, a woman who remains at home, is comparatively new. In the last century, this "profession" was open only to women of the bourgeoisie. Even today, the "free" choice between family and work is available to a small minority.

Michel calls for the suppression of all remaining restrictions on abortion. It should be free and available to all, including minors and immigrants. The humiliating steps to be undertaken--consultations with medical and social workers--should be removed. (Some of these restrictions have since been removed by the Socialist government; others are destined for elimination.) In the end, she concludes, it is women alone who must take their destiny in hand. The difficulty is that many women are still fearful, reticent, and resigned.

MONTRELAY, MICHÈLE. L'ombre et le nom: sur la féminité [The shadow and the name: on femininity]. Paris: Éditions de Minuit, 1977, 172 pp.

The author, a French psychoanalyst who follows the Freudian school, offers a collection of texts on the problem of femininity. Some have been previously published. The style is dense and hermetic; Freud and Lacan are the names most frequently cited. The fluctuating shades of the word "femininity" pose implicitly, it is held, the existence of the Shadow, the kingdom of nothingness. In this realm the real assumes a corporeal existence as the feminine "imaginary." Does psychoanalysis repress this Shadow, where the poet, like Rilke, or the mystic, like Michelet, are engulfed? Why are they the ones to invoke and speak of its power rather than Freud? These are some of Montrelay's concerns as she analyzes femininity, the dark continent.

NOËL, MICHÈLE. Le commerce des dames [The commerce of women]. Paris and Tournai: Casterman, 1974, 167 pp.

The "commerce" in question is an exchange of views with eight women who are questioned about their lives and their thoughts on feminism and women's situation today. Michèle Noël envisions her role as that of a narrator introducing each dialogue of this possible play and providing the epilogues.

French Feminisms

Perhaps the most interesting of the group is Solange, a prostitute. Her story is all too typical: orphan, on welfare, virtually doomed from birth. Yet she shows innate dignity and courage. Seduced, she refused to give up the child for adoption. It developed tuberculosis; hospital bills mounted. Solange did not want to disturb her sister's precarious domestic situation, so she took up prostitution, the only "profession" open to her. She strongly challenges the public's views on prostitutes. She has a heart: she is a mother whose child will not lack.

The actresses of this "drama" are unanimous in their feeling that their childhood was marked by sexual repression. The pill has dramatically changed women's lives. But at the same time, it has relieved men of responsibility.

NOKOVITCH, MILENA. Ce que femme veut [What woman wants]. Paris: Bonne, 1977, 154 pp.

Adjunct mayor and head of a firm, Milena Nokovitch examines what women can attain in a constantly changing society. What are the means available to the French woman to try and ameliorate the roles of mother, wife, and worker? The new legislation implemented since 1974 links women to their domestic and economic roles. These newly accorded rights are seen as at the heart of a new social ethic based upon individuals, not systems. The brief history of the efforts to obtain these rights is outlined. Relevant texts complete this general work.

Les nouvelles femmes [The new women]. Paris: Mazarine, 1979, 241 pp. (Preface by Benoîte Groult.)

This volume presents the results of a vast national survey, undertaken in April 1978, consisting of the responses of over twenty-thousand women who read the feminist magazine, F magazine. In addition to answering 104 questions concerning various aspects of their lives, many women added notes and letters with personal comments. Some of these personal observations have been included.

The "new" women are compared to the blacks of America in their struggle to obtain rights. If these women do not yet lead a "new" life, they hope, prepare, and dream of one nevertheless. Women in France have changed, are changing, will change. But their environment has changed little. Disparity between reality and aspiration is seen in all its ramifications. This volume presents a comprehensive view of a more enlightened and better informed segment of the French female population.

PARTURIER, FRANÇOISE. Lettre ouverte aux femmes [An open letter to women]. Paris: Albin Michel, 1974, 191 pp.

The "open letter" is but one of the missives in an ongoing epistolary polemic employing a favored French mode, the ironic dialogue. The subject here is male prejudice and women's lack of solidarity.

Initially, Françoise Parturier wrote a Lettre ouverte aux hommes (1968), to answer Francis Jeanson's Lettre ouverte aux femmes (1965). In this letter Parturier denounced masculine pretensions and phallocracy in general. Jean Larteguy then took up the challenge with Lettre ouverte aux bonnes femmes (1972), to which Parturier now responds. Jean Larteguy had criticized "female imperialism." By attempting to best men, women are not just reversing and repeating repression but they are also deceiving themselves. It is not a question of superiority or inferiority, but of difference and women's specificity. However, it was felt that his comments lacked objectivity.

Françoise Parturier takes up and then refutes all the idées reçues about women. She also points out that a third of France's married young men do not work. They study while their wives support them. It is not accurate to claim that all feminists are either homosexuals or sexually frustrated (mal baisées, névrosées, etc.). Such views distort the problem of women's freedom. It is the inequalities, not sexual differences, that must be remedied.

To help break the masculine cultural hegemony, Parturier became the first (unsuccessful) candidate to the French Academy. It was not a personal gesture, she maintains, but rather one to call attention to French women's lack of recognition. Women's efforts should involve sharing; community endeavors should take precedence over personalities, a reproach she makes against the young women of the MLF. The women who have "arrived" must remember those who have not, and this, even though the public and press want names, not anonymity.

She chides the women's press of that time for not helping women to change themselves for the best. It caters to the traditional view of women. The Gaullist women politicians are accused of giving in to the party's paternalistic politics. Her criticism extends to all women who sacrifice women's interests to those of the male power of the hour. Women must form new political groups, change the tone of the old political debates, and use clear, direct language. She feels that as feminism asserts itself more in France, its language tends to become more obscure. The author endeavors to counter this trend with frank, direct language, a familiar tone, and many contemporary references.

The volume includes some examples of male "hysteria," letters Parturier received after she took up the defense of women. This "letter" was answered by Michel Jobert's Lettre ouverte aux femmes politiques (1976). In it Jobert paid tribute to the contribution of women to the political scene.

PELLAUMAIL, MARCELLE MAUGIN. Le masochisme "dit" féminin [So-called feminine masochism]. Paris: Stanké, 1979, 214 pp.

Simone de Beauvoir describes this study as an important contribution to women's struggles. The problem analyzed is: Why do women appear not only to accept, but indeed to orchestrate and perpetuate the various forms of inferiority and inequality--unfavorable opinions, bad jobs, etc.--directed at them? Why this acceptance, this apparent fatalism?

The author believes that in spite of profound social changes during the past decade, women still retain most of their old attitudes. Close examination, she contends, shows that French society has not radically changed in regard to women. A critical survey of the development of the notion of feminine masochism is set forth. Psychoanalysis is faulted for having committed two major errors in its assessment of feminine problems. First, to have reduced the feminine problematic to purely psychological dimensions. Second, to have restricted itself to a pseudo-scientific point of view that blocks all possibility of evolution.

A new interpretation of so-called feminine masochism is required; one that will include both the psychological and the sociological-ontological aspects of the problem. This view must encompass a negation of women's unfavorable situation in society and an objective solution to the contradictions this condition engenders.

PERASSO, ELIANE. Ne pleure pas, hurle [Don't weep, scream]. Paris: Stock, 1973, 222 pp.

Eliane Perasso, a young lawyer and municipal counselor in Marseilles, urges women to let their anger and rage be heard--by neighbors, by society, by all. Only then can their sufferings and oppression be truly known. The problem is more than one of women's condition, civilization itself must be changed. Women have come of age. They must now participate actively in the revision of our civilization.

She describes her essay as a "simple" work, for it exposes the obvious; the fact that women are capable of assuming political responsibility. She is indignant that France has more bistros, even pharmacies per inhabitant than crèches, day-care centers. A true democracy should, above all, recognize in woman the special dignity that she possesses and assumes as mother, as manager of the family unit. She is invested by nature with the highest human responsibility, creating for the child a structure suited to his or her shelter and affective development. This expertise and this function are inalienable from the heart of society. They should be the basis for a comprehensive policy.

PERREIN, MICHÈLE. Entre chienne et louve [Between bitch and she-wolf]. Paris: Grasset, 1978, 250 pp.

Novelist and journalist Michèle Perrein feels that the only world that exists for women is a world of struggle. Women must be aware of this and not resign themselves. They must take an active part in events and partake of "active wisdom" (sagesse active). She speaks in sympathetic terms of the passions that separate men and women, passions that must be accommodated. It is better for women to refuse or invent their destiny rather than accept one that is imposed. Half-hearted participation is no longer possible; commitment is the order of the day.

Much in the essay is autobiographical. In evocations of her childhood, Perrein refers to her strict mother, to the women who marked her life. The films of Ingmar Bergmann were an influence: so too, were other films. Like many French women she finds that writing helps her to self-realization for it accommodates both her age and her sex.

QUÉRÉ, FRANCE. La femme avenir [Woman future]. Paris: Seuil, 1976, 156 pp.

In the future, women must accept la différence and all that that implies, the author holds. Women must not just imitate men. France Quéré castigates male psychologists who would presume to analyze women. She notes how biblical exegesis systematically accentuates Eve's guilt.

The study contains some interesting observations, including some on language, an area where French feminists have been active. Expressions of age tend to flatter men but to ridicule women: la force de l'âge (the strength of age) and buriné (engraved, hard-worked) vs. friser la quarantaine (on the verge of forty) and fripée (in rags). When women reach forty, la quarantaine, it is really that, a quarantine.

RIGHINI, MARIELLE. Écoute ma différence [Listen to my difference]. Collection le temps des femmes. Paris: Grasset, 1978, 192 pp.

Florentine Mariella Righini studied political science in Italy and France before turning to journalism and writing. She has written for the liberal Le Nouvel Observateur since its creation.

In this work she celebrates her difference--in spite of those who object to such an undertaking. And she does so in lyrical terms. This difference marks her to the very last cell. She categorically rejects the French tradition of misogyny. Woman is not the last thing that God created on a tired Saturday evening, as Dumas would have it. Righini issues a personal manifesto to other women. It is not sufficient to be born a woman, one must also become one. The major themes of contemporary French feminism are touched upon in this affirmation by a woman who accepts and rejoices in her specificity and will not accept the mute e.

SARTIN, PIERRETTE. Aujourd'hui la femme [Today woman]. Paris: Stock, 1974, 413 pp.

Pierette Sartin, a psychologist specializing in work, has written books on that subject and one on feminism, La femme libérée? (1968). Aujourd'hui la femme focuses on women in France. However, data from other countries is also included. America is the country most frequently cited.

There is an informative chapter on the legal situation of French women (at the time of publication), and texts of some of the earlier discriminatory sections of the Napoleonic Code are also cited. They indicate graphically all that French women have had to overcome. There is a chapter of almost a 100 pages on sexuality, one of the earlier of the recent feminist views on the topic. Other questions examined include: How is women's situation presented? What are the problems women encounter in professional training, crèches, divorce? What is the situation of the woman at home?

VALABRÈGUE, CATHERINE. Eux, les hommes [They, the men]. Paris: Stock, 1976, 267 pp.

Catherine Valabrègue is the author of a number of works including one of the first studies in the recent (and finally successful) effort in France to obtain reproductive rights, Contrôle de naissances) (1960). Editor also of La condition masculine (1968), she here surveys men's attitudes toward the developing feminist movement in France in the midseventies. To find out how men perceive women in that society, she undertook a number of interviews with men--predominantly younger ones--and some women in order to provide a counterpoint and to set forth women's problems in the world of men.

The men range from those who feel extremely threatened as traditional images of virility and the mother are called into question, to those who recognize that the images of masculinity are questionable. In general the men are confused and concerned with women's demands: they echo Freud in their question, But what do women want?

What becomes clear from their comments is that stereotypes persist. Profound changes in French society will be difficult to affect. Men's reactions to the "threat" of feminism and the growth of the MLF are expressed in a common vocabulary, that of terror. There are also the same references, whatever their background. Many of these men recognize the weight of tradition in France's view of woman and motherhood, views resulting from the heritage of Catholic France. Woman is a mystery, a myth. Her special sphere should be the family: she is not fit to command. Sexism is present in the ranks of the presumably sympathetic male liberals. Since man is misogynist by nature, the MLF hasn't really altered the situation. In spite of exterior changes, nothing fundamental has changed.

VINCENT, MADELEINE. Femmes: quelle libération? [Women: what liberation?]. Paris: Éditions Sociales, 1976, 166 pp.

Madeleine Vincent joined the Communist Party when she was a young working girl in Paris. During the war she was deported for her Resistance activities. Upon her return to France, she became general secretary of the Union des Jeunes Filles de France and later, a member of the steering committee of the French Communist Party in charge of women's issues. (One third of party members are women.) Her book covers the twenty-second party congress of 1976 and the party projects of the preceding year, the International Year of Woman.

The author decries the abstract quality of so many of the recent studies on French women. To remedy this situation, Madeleine

Vincent provides facts and figures that show women's actual status. She stresses their difficulties in finding housing and the problem of unemployment, which is higher among women. Her solution is the party's traditional one. Only the revolutionary current, as it gradually affirms itself, can provide viable solutions. All must see the fundamental reasons for inequalities and analyze the social structures and social givens. Men and women should not be opposed: they must join in attacking exploitation and oppression.

Vincent puts the emphasis on material goals. She refuses to accept women's demands as differing from those of her male comrades. The Communist party does not follow the patriarchal model in oppressing women, she insists (as some party women have claimed). All women cannot be subsumed under the rubric "female condition." This blurs class lines and hinders solving the real problem, that of class oppression.

Vivre au féminin [Living in the feminine]. Paris: Documentation Française, no. 171, May-August 1975, 64 pp. plus a forty-page supplement issued thus far.

A collective work, this issue covers the main details of the status of women in France to the date of publication. The subjects included are: the problems of work and age; the difficulty of reconciling professional and domestic obligations; the processes that differentiate social roles. While this is a general presentation, the information is pertinent, and relevant texts are included.

*DACO, PIERRE. Comprendre les femmes et leur psychologie profonde. [Understanding women and their profound psychology]. Verviers: Marabout-Gérard, 1974, 354 pp.

*_____. Les femmes [Women]. Verviers: Gérard, 1979, 353 pp.
Practicing psychologist Pierre Daco analyzes masculine fears of women and in so doing, presents an analysis of women as well.

CREATIVITY

AGULHON, MAURICE. Marianne au combat: l'imagerie et la symbolique républicaines de 1789 à 1880 [Marianne in combat: republican imagery and symbolism from 1789 to 1880]. Paris: Flammarion, 1979, 256 pp.

France represented in female form is the subject of rich inquiry. Marianne is the familiar name for the republican form of government. This identification increased as the nineteenth century progressed. First used to designate republican government, by extension she came to represent the French Republic. To define the word emblem the Larousse dictionary states that "the woman with the phrigian bonnet is the emblem of the French Republic."

Agulhon studies this iconography using sculpture and painting, theatrical presentations and the busts of town halls, cartoons, and even postage stamps. Prominence is given to sculpture, the most public and the most political of the plastic arts. The study covers history, politics, art history, and the history of mentalités.

The French Republic represents the result of three major conflicts: the new sovereign against the actual monarchs; a virtual religion against the established religion; and a popular force against the dominating social groups. Marianne was truly in combat. And, like the women of the nineteenth century, she was alternately exalted and vilified. In fact, the pronounced inequalities in women's situation, the disdain women were then subjected to, makes the association of the newly emerging republic with a female representation all the more intriguing. The author touches upon the implications of this aspect of republican affirmation. A fuller exploration is promised for the second volume, Marianne au pouvoir (from 1880 to the present).

There are rich insights into the topic and many pertinent citations. Perhaps the most famous recent personification of France as a woman is that expressed by de Gaulle in the opening of his Memoirs. All his life the General held a "certain idea of France." This idea appeared as a fairy tale princess or a frescoed madonna.

BOLSTER, RICHARD. Stendhal, Balzac, et le féminin romantique [Stendhal, Balzac, and the feminine romantic]. Paris: Lettres Modernes, 1970, 226 pp.

This study is devoted primarily to literary criticism, but it also covers the history of ideas during the period of French romanticism. Both Stendhal and Balzac exerted influence far beyond literary circles and both wrote on love. Stendhal's De l'amour (1822) is a detailed study of passion and the relations between the sexes. Balzac's La physiologie du mariage (1829) is a reply to Stendhal's study. While Balzac's work is ironic, it is tempered by social realities.

Richard Bolster argues that de Beauvoir "misread" Balzac and that the latter's work on marriage is more than an antifeminist manual. The novelist analyzed the theme of the strong woman and the femme-objet. His female public wrote and confided in him.

French Feminisms

CALO, JEANNE. <u>La création de la femme chez Michelet</u> [The creation of woman in Michelet]. Paris: Nizet, 525 pp.

    Here is a richly documented study of Jules Michelet (1798-1874), a man described as the "incarnation of history" (for the French). Those only superficially acquainted with this powerful personality--historian and poet--are struck by the disparity among his historical writings; his works on women, the family, love, and nature; and his private writings, especially the intimate <u>Journal</u> that he kept from 1828 on. Yet there is an underlying unity. Michelet noted of his work that while the form and appearance might vary, the substance (<u>fond</u>) remains the same.

    Calo examines the central, pervasive theme of woman in relation to Michelet's creative activity and his psychology. Woman as symbol, woman idealized, ideal woman, and the real woman all enter into this vision of women; heroines of past and present, figures of myth and dreams. The links between the romantic historian's writing and his life are analyzed in detail. In this manner the long evolution of Michelet's views on the mythical duality of woman is traced. Because this prolific writer has become the object of much recent study and because many of his writings on women are currently being reissued, such an overview is extremely helpful, as is the extensive bibliography.

CARDINAL, MARIE. <u>Autrement dit</u> [Differently said]. Paris: Grasset, 1977, 224 pp.

    This book was inspired by the correspondence Marie Cardinal, a philosophy teacher and writer, received after the publication of her very successful <u>Les mots pour le dire</u> (q.v.). Here Annie Leclerc, another philosopher asks questions focusing on the problems Cardinal shares with her women readers: love, death, women, writing, and politics. The exchange is frank and free.

_____. <u>Les mots pour le dire</u> [The words to express it]. Paris: Grasset, 1975, 343 pp.

    This is an extraordinary narrative--somewhere between fact and fiction--describing a young woman on the verge of breakdown who finally seeks help through analysis. In the course of her analysis the stages of her life unfold. Her past is revealed as she reveals herself. The words employed are words seldom employed, intimate words that help express and free women. The work shows the central role of blood in its various appearances--sexual maturity, sexual initiation, birth--in women's lives.

    Cardinal's autobiography, <u>Cet être-là</u> (1979), has recently been reissued.

CLÉMENT, CATHERINE, and HÉLÈNE CIXOUS. <u>La jeune née</u> [The newly born woman]. Collection féminine future. Paris: Union Générale d'Éditions, (10/18), 1975, 296 pp.

    Written in prophetic and poetic prose, this essay is one of a series devoted to analyzing the questions that arise in women's history. Teacher and writer Catherine Clément examines "La coupable" in the first section. Guilty women have been featured in myth and highlighted in history. Witches are an obvious example of this phenomenon. Culpability and seduction are discussed as well as sorceresses and the problem of hysteria. "Sorties," the second section, is by feminist writer Hélène Cixous. It includes "La venue d'une femme à l'écriture," a frequently cited text.

The third and final section of the volume brings the two women together to discuss women's issues, including writing and the problem of the <u>maîtresse femme</u>, <u>femme maîtresse</u>, or <u>maître femme</u> (the play on the words master, mastery, and mistress are typical of those found in this work which frequently employs neologisms).

DURAS, MARGUERITE, and XAVIÈRE GAUTHIER. <u>Les parleuses</u> [The women speakers]. Paris: Éditions de Minuit, 1974, 243 pp.

These dialogues are printed, just as they took place, with all the repetitions, digressions, pauses, etc. The two women decided that to put them in "good" logical order and in correct grammatical form would be to exercise a form of censure. These are women's words, as they are so often found, in the interstices of "correctly" expressed masculine discourse. Women's words might be compared to the weeds that grow between old stones--and finally crack the cement. Both the style and content of this work provide insights into the question of French women's writing and female creativity.

Xavière Gauthier (b. 1940) is a teacher, writer, and editor of the feminist review <u>Sorcières</u>. These interviews were part of a group she undertook to prepare an article on <u>l'écriture des femmes</u>. In this interview Marguerite Durand (b. 1914), the writer and filmmaker, talks about how she writes. Duras also discusses some of the problems creative women have to deal with in a masculine world. For example, no one advised her to take a percentage rather than a set amount for writing what was to become the very successful film, <u>Hiroshima mon amour</u>. Consequently she made very little. Problems in other areas are also discussed.

DURAS, MARGUERITE, and MICHELLE PORTE. <u>Les lieux de Marguerite Duras</u> [The places/locations of Marguerite Duras]. Paris: Éditions de Minuit, 1977, 103 pp.

In these conversations Marguerite Duras explains the "place" of isolated locations--such as her country property where she shot <u>Nathalie Granger</u>--in her writing and films. In similar fashion, the women protagonists of her books have also occupied her "place." Photographs show both the author and her places/locations.

French Feminisms

FAUCHERY, PIERRE. La destinée féminine dans le roman européen du XVIIIe siècle [Feminine destiny in the European novel of the eighteenth century]. Paris: Armand Colin, 1972, 611 pp.

    Much information on women's situation in eighteenth-century France and Europe may be found in this study described by the author as an essay in "gynécomythie romanesque."

La Femme au XIXe siècle: littérature et idéologie [Woman in the nineteenth century: literature and ideology]. Lyon: Presses Universitaires de Lyon, 1978, 201 pp.

    This is a scholarly collection of articles. The first group deals with subjects such as the literary status of women in the nineteenth century and their portrayal within the context of the ideology of Larousse's Grand dictionnaire universel. One scholarly article treats the legal status of women in the nineteenth century. The second part deals with the portrayal of women in the literature of that century.

DES FEMMES DE MUSIDORA. Paroles . . . elles tournent [Speak up . . . women are filming/ words . . . they (fem) are turning]. Paris: Éditions des femmes, 1976, 248 pp.

    Musidora was an association of feminist actresses, film directors, journalists, and script girls founded in 1973. They organized the first Festival of Women's Films in 1974. The group has since disbanded after achieving its principal objective, to call the attention of commercial distributors to their work. However, at the time the women joined together, the notion of women directors, women in films, was still considered somewhat incongruous. Musidora's initiative encouraged other women to embark upon creative endeavors.

    These women speak of seizing the camera the way others seize the pen. They want to explore new territory or enter a fictional universe. Since no text was refused in this collective work, many voices and many views are presented in what might be termed a chorus, rather than a common language. They have determined to do battle on a number of fronts: language, filming, distribution, information. Their struggles will engage all their contradictions. A number of the contributions center on women's language. There are reflections on the practical aspects of their work and observations on films as well as pieces by non-French cineastes. Other Musidora works include a dossier, "Le cinéma au féminisme" of fall 1979, and a number of the review Cinémaction.

FRANCIS, CLAUDE, and FERNANDE GONTIER. Les écrits de Simone de Beauvoir: la vie, l'écriture [The writings of Simone de Beauvoir: the life, the writing]. Paris: Gallimard, 1979, 609 pp.

    The biography, bibliography as well as texts--including some that have never before appeared in print or are difficult to consult--of the central figure in contemporary French feminism

are assembled in this substantial volume. The biography details
de Beauvoir's activities, writings, and thoughts on many topics.
It includes selections from various autobiographical works,
books, articles, and lectures along with comments about her by
Jean-Paul Sartre and other familiars. One can follow Simone de
Beauvoir's activities as she goes from private to public concerns--from theory to praxis. Her many activities, speeches,
and appearances of the past decades are noted, testifying to the
profound influence she has exercised on world feminism. The
repercussions of her writings and activities on behalf of women
the world over are documented.

Readers can both situate de Beauvoir in the French feminist
movement of the past decade and learn more of her activities in
other countries. These activities include the Women's Film
Festival of May 1975 in New York; an interview in English for
PBS; and a dialogue with Betty Friedan published as "Society and
the Female Dilemma" (Saturday Review, 14 June 1975).

The bibliography starts with selections from her earliest
attempts at writing in 1933. References to all her published
works are included, as are details of various translations.
There are also selections from her writings and prefaces from a
number of studies and works.

The volume is a comprehensive presentation of Simone de
Beauvoir's ideas as they are expressed in her writings, lectures,
and interviews. It exemplifies her claim that "The fact is that
I am a writer; a woman writer is not a private woman who writes,
but someone whose very existence is determined by the act of
writing." (The Force of Circumstance [1965]).

GAUTHIER, XAVIÈRE. Surréalisme et sexualité [Surrealism and
sexuality]. Paris: Gallimard, 1971, 381 pp. (Preface by J.B.
Portalès.)

The ambiguous and ambivalent view of sexuality found in the
literary and artistic work of the surrealists is analyzed in
detail. On the one hand, surrealism exults a cult of love that
leads to an idealization of women in an extreme, mythical view.
At the same time, it advocates sexuality without constraints.
This opposition along with the complimentary myth of the "eternal
feminine" are, in the author's terms, "male forgeries."

Gauthier inventories some of these opposing presentations of
women found in surrealism: woman as child or prostitute, star or
sorceress, source of salvation or damnation. In their desire
for scandal--an old French tradition of "provoking the bourgeoisie"--Breton, Aragon, and the other surrealists proclaimed
and celebrated the subversive force of Eros. This was a major
contribution to the society of the 1920s. But paradoxically,
the movement also strengthened the monogamist ideal.

The author finds surrealism's exploration of sexuality central
to the movement's attempts to reconcile the world of reality and
the world of dreams. While not all may agree with Gauthier's
interpretations of the paintings, prints, and sculpture of the

surrealists (reproduced for the most part), her reflections on
the role of sexuality in surrealism offer much to ponder.

Elsewhere in her writing, in <u>Rose saignée</u> (1974) and <u>Les parleuses</u> (1974) and in the feminist review <u>Sorcières</u> which she founded in 1974, Xavière Gauthier has commented upon the problem of women's writing. She believes that women write as if estranged, or as if writing from a foreign land in a foreign tongue.

GEFFRIAUD, JEANNETTE ROSSO. <u>Montesquieu et la féminité</u> [Montesquieu and femininity]. Pisa: Libreria Goliardica, 1977, 635 pp.

In her French doctoral dissertation, Rosso Geffriaud presents an analysis of femininity as it was seen through the eyes of one of the outstanding figures of the Enlightenment, Montesquieu (1689-1755), the political philosopher. The problems of women in eighteenth-century society are analyzed. The analysis is pursued on three levels, through the biographical materials, the presentation of women in Montesquieu's work, and the doctrinal arrangement of his thought regarding women.

The debate on femininity found in both the dictionaries and encyclopedic treatises of doctors, theologians, scholars, and pamphleteers, and in the works of the great figures of the century, extended throughout the entire eighteenth century. An extensive bibliography of over a thousand entries covers all the major works and provides the material needed to study the topic of feminism in the age of the Enlightenment.

GUY, ALICE. <u>Autobiographie d'une pionnière du cinéma (1873-1968)</u> [Autobiography of a woman pioneer in the cinema (1873-1968)]. Paris: Denoël/Gonthier, 1976, 229 pp. (Presented by the Association Musidora with Nicole-Lise Bernheim and Claire Clouzot. Filmography by Francis Lacassin.)

This is yet another tale of a young woman rising above adverse conditions. Constrained to find a job by a reversal in the family fortunes, the young bourgeoise Alice Guy became a secretary with the Comptoir Général de Photographie. Secretary, then assistant to Léon Gaumont, the young girl assisted at the birth of the French film industry. Upon seeing the first documentaries of the Lumière brothers, she decided to film a story. The editors maintain that her <u>La fée aux choux</u> (1896) was the first film of fiction. Prior to that time there had only been action films, street scenes, trains arriving, and similar action shots. For the next seventeen years Alice Guy was the only woman film director. Some of the many films she produced during that period are now being again "brought to light."

In the early 1900s Alice Guy accompanied her producer husband to America. While family responsibilities and professional rivalries restricted her activities, "Madame" Alice managed nonetheless to continue her film work and to help the new industry develop in America.

French Feminisms

This volume is itself a Franco-American production, a fitting testimony to a woman involved in the beginnings of cinema in both countries. The men who pioneered, Gaumont, Lumière, Meliès, and Feuillade, have all been recorded in the annals of film history. Alice Guy has had to wait for the current feminist movement to find her deserved place among those who developed the film industry. History is now being rewritten. The third edition of George Sadoul's Histoire générale du cinéma finally attributes to Alice Guy La Esmeralda (1905), a film whose techniques are found in all subsequent versions of The Hunchback of Notre Dame. Her experiments with various techniques are just one of the fascinating areas that Alice Guy writes about in her unusual life story.

HERMANN, CLAUDINE. Les voleuses de langue [The tongue snatchers]. Paris: Éditions des femmes, 1976, 176 pp.

Claudine Hermann analyzes women's culture and language to determine what guile and subterfuge they have resorted to in the past in order to transmit their experience. Women, she insists, have their own linguistic concepts and modes.

Examination of the writings of men and women (and Jan Morrison, who has been both) clearly demonstrates that the two sexes write differently and that there is an expression of different perceptions. Hermann anticipates that women's writing will initiate a new culture now that women have become aware of their new identity. No longer will they have to follow the male-dominated culture of the past. There remains so much to be discovered, so much to be learned. Everyone should be able to adjust his or her lenses without limiting others. There should be enriched and extended creativity.

HOFFMANN, PAUL. La femme dans la pensée des lumières [Woman in the thought of the Enlightenment]. Strasbourg: Association des Publications près les Universités de Strasbourg, 1977, 621 pp.

This work is a representative French doctoral dissertation, lengthy, exhaustive, and extensively researched and documented. The author examines the diverse theories of womanhood found in the writings of doctors, physiologists, and obstetricians, the treatises of jurists, and the major works of the great writers of the eighteenth century.

"Womanhood" was then subject to an ontological "curse." It bore the dual heritage of the Aristotelian tradition and that of the Christian dogma of the Fall. The very tenacity of the traditions indicates the radical quality of those moralists and philosophers who, following Descartes, exhorted women to free themselves from the notion of their "innate infirmity."

Hoffmann concludes that in the century of "progress" it would be a simplification to reduce the feminine condition to an opposition between progressive and antifeminist currents. More complex and nuanced theories were present. Some tended toward utopianism while others posited "femininity" as a value and freedom for women to claim. In addition to the writers and theories discussed, two long sections are devoted to physiological models and pathology, eighteenth-century materials not always readily available to contemporary scholars. These sections present views on topics such as the mechanics of reproduction, information on contemporary obstetrical practices, and various psychological views of women.

HORER, SUZANNE, and JEANNE SOCQUET. [La création étouffée Stifled/crushed creativity]. Paris: Pierre Horay, 1973, 236 pp.

Why has the French language no feminine form for author, composer, sculptor, painter, or writer? Because from childhood on, feminine creativity is stifled. The woman who tries to express her creative impulses is rebuffed and "frustrated."

The authors' views on the problem are reinforced by the testimony of creative women, author Marguerite Duras and the composer Betsy Jolas. Education is assigned the principal blame for this state of affairs. It eliminates--at times destroys--all spontaneity and curiosity in young girls. Since there are few heroines in school texts, these girls lack role models. They have been manipulated by the problem of "difference." Like others, the authors note the impact of photo-novels, with their romantic, escapist images, on young French women.

Two pertinent texts are included. One is an article from the generally serious review Réalités deploring the entry of women into the prestigious École Polytechnique. In reality a young woman ranked first in the class when women were admitted for the first time in 1972. The other article, from Elle magazine, comments on the problems posed "when she earns more than he does."

IRIGARAY, LUCE. Ce sexe qui n'en est pas un [This sex that is not one]. Paris: Éditions de Minuit, 1977, 217 pp.

Psychoanalyst and writer Luce Irigaray has a style that matches the topic: rich, dense, and difficult. This collection of articles--most previously published--offers a series of questions provoked by her earlier work, Speculum de l'autre femme (1974). The central question What is woman? has no possible answer. Woman is neither one nor two, hence has no "proper" name. Further, woman has another sexuality, one that has limitless possibilities.

Irigaray sees as the central concern of the women's liberation movement that each woman become aware that her personal experiences, feelings, and resentments are shared by all women. This awareness can lead to politicization. Women must escape from the patriarchal culture found in discourse, theory, science. French women have been passive. Consequently they have allowed men, their eternal pedagogues, to define their nature. This situation must be changed. Women must order their lives. Such are some of the concerns of this work, which has been described as a post-Lacanian effort to deconstruct Freud and Western philosophical discourse.

LASCAULT, GILBERT. Figurées, défigurées: petit vocabulaire de la féminité représentée [Figured, disfigured: short vocabulary of femininity portrayed]. Paris: Gallimard, (10/18), 1977, 224 pp. (Preface by Michel Dufrenne.)

This book is written by a "masculine individual" who does not treat femininity (or womanhood) directly. Rather, he investigates the visual presentation of women by Western man. How have women figured in painting and sculpture? These figurations--more frequently disfigurations--often serve to exacerbate the war between the sexes. This makes women unhappy. And men suffer the consequences indirectly.

The format is that of the conventional dictionary. An article on coupeuses de tête (women beheaders, Judith, Salomé, etc.) follows one on cornes (horns, i.e., jealousy) and precedes the one on culottes (breeches or pants, the symbol of masculine power). The entries of this pseudodictionary are "open." Every feminine reader is expected to add her own.

The title may mislead. In addition to being an amusing and disconcerting parody, this is a scholarly work. The references range from Vasari and the Robert dictionary to recent feminist demonstrations and advertising exploiting women's representation.

LAURENT, MICHELLE, ed. En portées. Paris: Syros, 1979, 134 pp. (The title is a play on portées, disposed or inclined to, and emportées, the feminine plural of carried away or prevailed over.)

This collection offers seventy-three women's songs celebrating the stages of women's lives. Music is included for some and there are also several drawings. A number might be viewed as poems.

Women sing of their struggles, their work, their solitude, and their feelings. Some of the women contributors are known to the French public; a number have made records.

LeBRUN, ANNIE. Lâchez-tout [Let everything go]. Paris: Sagittaire, 1977, 180 pp.

Here, as in articles she had published earlier, Annie LeBrun attacks what she calls femellitude, female terrorism or "Stalinism in skirts," the author's term for militant feminism. For her part, LeBrun refuses to be enrolled with fighting women simply because of a biological accident. Thus she rallies against feminists from Simone de Beauvoir and the "poujadiste" Benoîte Groult to Marguerite Duras.

She holds that the author of the Second Sex "erroneously envisioned the feminist question in the light of Sartre's doctrines." This has made her a pioneer, but a pioneer in the long march toward "sensitive mutilation." There are comments about the "extreme weakness" of de Beauvoir's propositions.

Speaking of current French experiments in women's writing, l'écriture féminine, LeBrun sees such efforts as mere mystification. They will prevent the feminist message from being heard.

For her, they verge on caricature. The book is ironic and provocative. It offers some idea of a French antifeminist woman's views.

LECLERC, ANNIE. Parole de femme [Woman's word]. Paris: Grasset, 1974, 196 pp.

Philosopher, teacher, and writer Annie Leclerc offers a personal statement about the problem of women's language. But she does not see it as a personal problem; instead women's language entails the larger problem of women in today's world.

Men wish to master; they revel in heroics; they want to conquer and possess. Annie Leclerc rejects all the presumed courage entailed in heroic struggles. Women have other values and another language to express those values. Women must elaborate and refine a language that is not oppressive, a language that does not leave one speechless but that loosens one's tongue instead.

In collaboration with Hélène Cixous and Madeleine Gagnon Leclerc has written on this same problem in La venue à l'écriture (1977).

QUIGUER, CLAUDE. Femmes et machines de 1900: lecture d'une obsession moderne style [Women and machines in 1900: reading of a modern style obsession]. Bibliothèque du XXe siècle. Paris: Klincksieck, 1979, 439 pp.

The modern style of the title is more commonly referred to as Art Nouveau. Following the work of Jean Starobinski, the author traces the theme of the "woman as object" in literature and the arts at the turn of the century. He finds networks of correspondences and similar mythologies in all artistic media during this period that saw the appearance of the automobile and other machines, the period that ushered in the modern age.

Although written in French, there are also English and German texts and examples. The works of Rilke, Wedekind, and Oscar Wilde are utilized. France is represented by Octave Mirabeau, among others. There are many suggestive observations. Ideologies and interpretations are described in a critical style that employs terms like "plastic pan-homogeneity." Whether from literature or the plastic arts, the many examples included reveal that woman is the central image in Art Nouveau. Creative works in this style show a fear and fascination of woman and her sexuality. This ambivalence is the result of the fear of real women, a fear that leads to the mystique of purity--but a troubling purity of sensual innocence.

YAGUELLO, MARINA. Les mots et les femmes [Words and women]. Paris: Payot, 1979, 202 pp.

Marina Yaguello examines the sociolinguistic condition of women and analyzes the sexual diversity of language as cultural, not "natural." How do women speak among themselves? How are they spoken to, spoken of? What image of women does the mirror of language reflect and reveal? In exploring these questions, the role of sexual metaphors is also studied. These metaphors appear to fix the symbolic representations and echo the stereotypes and prejudices which they both nourish and sustain.

The chapters in this work are conceived of as individual essays which may be read as such. The first two are more technical and require some familiarity with linguistics. American research is frequently cited. The later chapters are less "scientific" and offer a more "feminist" interpretation of language. The chapter on grammatical gender is of interest since English does not have that feature. The absence of certain words in French, such as sorority, may be consonant with the lack of French women's experiences in working with groups.

There is an interesting chapter on contempt, "The power of language and the language of power." Yaguello cites some of the numerous French terms used to refer to women not found in standard reference works such as Guiraud's Dictionnaire érotique. Although the majority of these terms refer to prostitutes, they are frequently used as synonyms for women.

JOURNALISM, THE FEMINIST PRESS, AND ADVERTISING

ADLER, LAURE. À l'aube du féminisme: les premières journalistes, 1830-1850 [At the dawn of feminism: the first women journalists, 1830-1850]. Paris: Payot, 1979, 231 pp.

The author, herself a journalist, discusses the French feminist press from its beginning at the time of the 1830 revolution to the uprising of 1848 and its sequel. Not coincidentally, this period corresponds to the early days of the feminist movement. The undertaking and commitment of these early women journalists was not to be duplicated until 1968, when a comparable feminist press--diverse, lively, and provocative--again appeared.

One is struck by the overwhelming enthusiasm and vision of the working-class writers. Their joint efforts in publishing reinforced feminist solidarity and underscored their demands. Much more than a history of short-lived journalistic endeavors, this book chronicles the history of feminist activities during the early days of the movement and offers portraits of some of the important feminists of that period such as Claire Bayard, Jeanne Deroin, Eugénie Niboyet, and Suzanne Voilquin, for whom journalism provided an invaluable apprenticeship to feminist activity.

CHABROL, CLAUDE. Le récit féminin [Feminine narration]. Paris and The Hague: Mouton, 1971, 142 pp. (Contribution a l'analyse sémiologique du courrier du coeur et des entrevues ou "enquêtes" sur la femme dans la presse féminine actuelle.)

While this is primarily a linguistic study, it does provide much information about the French feminist press. Of interest also is the analysis of the "courrier du coeur," the lonely hearts' columns. Claude Chabrol finds these sections to be consoling and repressive. The overall impression received from these columns is that women expect too much from life, thus they are inevitably deceived and disappointed.

On a more general level, the author maintains that in spite of the many changes that have taken place in society in the last century, including the new and extended roles women have assumed, the notion of "difference" persists.

DARDIGNA, ANNE-MARIE. Femmes-femmes sur papier glacé [Feminine women on glossy paper]. Paris: Maspero, 1975, 165 pp.

In this challenging and stimulating analysis of the popular press, particularly the women's magazines Elle, Marie-Claire, etc., Anne-Marie Dardigna employs the categories of Roland Barthes. She believes that the oppression of women today has reached a point of acute contradiction, a contradiction between general advancement in the level of education women receive and the continued daily routine of many women. This routine offers little, if any, intellectual stimulation or possibility for self-development.

Articles in the women's magazines present a negative picture of women: they are often trivialized. Odd jobs around the house are elevated to the status of "professions," ("mes petits métiers," my little trades), in an effort to make women believe that their lives in the background, on the sidelines, are important. Dardigna notes that the word amour has pronounced sexual overtones in today's press.

The newer magazines and the new sections and articles of the established periodicals have all profited from renewed interest in women. But they have done so without making a positive contribution to women. The popular weekly Elle proclaims that the relations between men and women are always conflictual: "that is the way it is" (no. 1372). Anne-Marie Dardigna's reflections and comments are based upon years of working with the press, an experience she has found to be a continual source of impatience and irritation.

_____. La presse féminine: fonction idéologique [The feminine press: ideological function]. Paris: Maspero, 1978, 245 pp.

Here Dardigna updates and expands her earlier study, Femmes-femmes sur papier glacé (q.v.). In the intervening years much has happened in the lives of French women. And several new women's magazines have appeared. This more recent feminist press has provided special opportunities to manipulate women in new ways, to make them even more "womanly" than before. It also serves vast financial interests. To substantiate this claim, a detailed examination of the publicity, articles, features, short stories, and photo-novels in this recent women's press is undertaken.

The author notes that the photo-novel is a genre limited almost exclusively to Latin countries where there is a predominant

Catholic influence. This she attributes to vestiges of the former role played by priests. It is now the photo-novels that offer a "repressive" morality to their readers, mainly young girls who devour these works during job breaks or traveling to and from work. The examples of photo-novels she cites readily lend themselves to ironic commentary and mordant humor. There is a chapter on "Giscard d'Estaing and Griselidis," described as a moral tale for the working class. (Griselidis, heard of as early as Boccaccio, became the symbol of the resigned woman, servant to the master and the state.)

Whether one agrees with the political interpretations of the material or not, this careful analysis offers much to consider: women's lives in the corridors of power, the wealth women spend as "pioneers" of consumption. American women are seen in a worse situation vis-à-vis men. This is held to partially explain the more violent character of their "rebellion."

LAVOISIER, BÉNÉDICTE. Mon corps, ton corps, leur corps: le corps de la femme dans la publicité [My body, your body, their body: woman's body in advertising]. Paris: Seghers, 1978, 256 pp.

The exploitation of women's bodies discussed a decade earlier in Rocard and Gutman's work continues, and this in spite of the growing attention feminists have brought to the problem. Bénédicte Lavoisier's study encompasses not only advertising, but also relations between the sexes in general. Her comments are based upon questionnaires, interviews, and documents, including many ads (some are reproduced). Sections are short. This is a sociological study, not a systematic theoretical analysis. Yet serious problems are touched upon: erotism, the frivolity of the consumer society, and the place of women in that society.

Lavoisier links the decreasing importance of motherhood to the increase in the use of svelte, sexually provocative women in ads. There is a mal de mère, fear of putting on weight and aging.

ROCARD, GENEVIÈVE, and COLLETTE GUTMAN. Sois belle et achète: la publicité et les femmes [Be beautiful and buy: advertising and women]. Collection femme. Paris: Denoël/Gonthier, 1968, 184 pp.

This study of France's consumer society cites Betty Friedan and Vance Packard among others. While still behind England and America in the amount spent on advertising, the French are endeavoring to catch up with their more "advanced" neighbors. Much of current advertising is aimed at women for they do eighty percent of the purchasing. And since they themselves do not earn the major portion of this money, women tend to feel reticient about making demands as consumers.

Successful advertising knows how to speak to women, how to promise them happiness and self-development through the acquisition of manufactured objects. Happiness for French women should consist in looking like one of the four prototypes the author identifies: the housewife, the bride, the mother, and the femme-femme, the feminine woman, sometimes the cover girl. These prototypes are not merely grotesque; they are dangerous, for they create images that penetrate and deform reality. The emphasis is not just on physical beauty but on youth as well.

Everywhere present, nearly always aggressive, advertising influences every facet of women's daily lives. A special, often esoteric, hyped, or pseudo-scientific vocabulary is employed in French advertising. Many terms are borrowed from English, resulting in what is known as franglais. (A chapter on a French Tupperware party is included.) Women must be vigilant in order to avoid being compromised and corrupted. They must reject the notion that "femininity" can be purchased. And they must make their claims as consumers heard.

Le sexisme ordinaire [Everyday sexism]. Paris: Seuil, 1979, 370 pp. (Preface by Simone de Beauvoir.)

A section entitled "Le sexisme ordinaire" was initiated by the review Les Temps modernes in 1974. A selection of these articles, published in succeeding years, is presented in this volume. Initially, flagrant examples of sexism were simply quoted. Gradually, however, there evolved analyses of sexism as it is found in books and films, essays and reviews--settings where sexism is often more subtly disseminated. The incisive, ironic, at times playful and humorous tone of these articles may surprise those who believe that women--particularly committed feminists-- lack those qualities. Here is ample demonstration that women too can display that Gallic wit known as l'esprit gaulois.

The collective looks forward to the day when there will be a law in France making sexist remarks illegal, just as there is now such a statute punishing racial remarks. (Such a law has just been passed.) The fact that the word sexism did not become officially "recognized," that is, make its way into the authoritative dictionaries until 1978, gives some idea of the problems encountered.

SULLEROT, ÉVELYNE. La presse féminine [The feminine press]. Paris: Armand Colin, 1963, 319 pp.

The "second press" is not a recent phenomenon: it has existed for more than two centuries in France. Until quite recently the topics covered had remained virtually the same. Évelyne Sullerot, the noted feminist historian, sociologist, and writer, saw this feminist press as a rich source for the study of society and its customs. It presented the domestic economy, social relations, attitudes, and moral viewpoints. To please, many women endeavor to correspond to the images portrayed in journals and reviews, a contention later studies have substantiated.

Sullerot divides the feminist press into two groups. There are publications that focus on duties: styles, modes, conventions, all characterized by "one should" or "one should not." The end result is that whether these women's journals speak of fashion or sentiment, they sound like catechism lessons. The other group puts the accent on rights: responsibilities, revolts, the long struggle French women have been engaged in to win what "rights" they have obtained.

This latter group of feminist journals proliferated during periods of revolution and revolt: 1789, 1830, 1848, and the beginning of the Third Republic after the insurrection of the Commune in 1871. The most important of these feminist journals was La Fronde, published from 1897 to 1903 and then from 1926 to 1928. It was the first major feminist daily written, edited, administered, composed, typeset, and distributed entirely by women.

Sullerot's study is often cited in more recent works: it provides a rich mine of pertinent information. All the principal French women's journals and magazines are summarized. Also included are publication dates, circulation, editorial orientation, format, publicity, and pedagogy along with a portrait of the typical reader. The materials and topics found in these journals are analyzed.

On the same topic see Évelyne Sullerot's subsequent Histoire de la presse féminine en France dès origines à 1848 (1966).

VICTOR, ÉLIANE. Une minute pour les femmes [A minute for women]. Paris: Fayard, 1975, 153 pp. (Written in collaboration with Martine Fell.)

This is an account of what was entailed in producing the television program of the same name, seen on TF 1. Addressed daily to "you who are millions," the program endeavored to inform French women of all that is taking place in this period of many transformations and to show how various events affect them as women. Material from diverse sources was presented in clear, concise language easily understood by all. Given the hermetic quality of some official documents, this is quite a task of "translation."

***

DZEH DJEN, LI. La presse féministe en France de 1869 à 1914 [The feminist press in France from 1869 to 1914]. Paris: Rodstein, 1934, 236 pp.

Although this work is considerably earlier than the decade covered in this volume, it merits inclusion for it has a comprehensive bibliography. The study is divided into periods: the initial section, from 1869 to 1891, discusses the pioneers, their journals, and their organizations; the second, covering 1891 to 1914, describes the work of those who continued the tradition. The work concludes with an assessment of the achievements of the early French feminist press, its intellectual and feminist conquests.

Sexual Politics

Central to French feminist activities of the past decade has been a concern with the body: women's efforts to control reproduction, to come to a fuller sexual self-understanding, to enjoy sexual relations. The emphasis placed upon sexual issues--whether they be sexuality, contraception, abortion, lesbianism, prostitution, or rape--is what distinguishes the current feminist movement from those of earlier periods.

SEXUALITY

Religious opposition reinforced by traditional views has made efforts to provide sexual education in France difficult. Until well into the 1970s, French women were not well informed on reproduction or contraception. The new Ministry of Women's Rights has launched an information campaign. Female sexuality is no longer restricted to the presumed expertise of specialists. It is openly discussed and written about by feminists, including innovative writers such as Monique Wittig, Catherine Clément, Xavière Gauthier, and novelist and journalist Benoîte Groult. The main theme has been that of <u>jouissance</u>, women's sexual pleasure. The insistence on women's specificity and on the difference between male and female has been more pronounced than in America.

The French Revolution abolished laws that made sexual activities illegal. This situation prevailed until the Vichy regime promulgated legislation aimed at male homosexuality. Marshall Pétain's law was reinforced after the Liberation. Homosexuality was made a social "scourge" like alcoholism and tuberculosis. For some time now, efforts have been under way to repeal the law. Women's homosexuality has never been openly prosecuted. Apart from the lack of specific legislation, France has a long tradition of comparative tolerance of those with alternative, "bohemian" life styles. (Virtually all the recent works by or on French lesbianism have been translated.)[1]

Sexual Politics

From the beginning, French lesbians have been active in the renascent women's movement. They participated in founding the Front Homosexuel d'Action Révolutionnaire (FHAR) in 1971. This past decade they have been living together somewhat more openly. Nevertheless strong social prejudice persists, not only in society, but among certain feminists as well. There have been conflicts over ideologies and tension between lesbians and heterosexual feminists and between lesbians and homosexuals. Simone de Beauvoir has suggested that they, through the radical exclusion of men in their lives, can play an important role in the cause of women.

Another area where French women have been breaking the traditional "conspiracy of silence" has been in denouncing female circumcision. It has been estimated that between thirty and fifty million women in the Middle East and certain regions of Africa have undergone some form of this operation, and with their migration to Europe, the practice has been brought to France. The problem is complex; there are cultural issues involved. It has been asked whether European women should not deal first with their problems rather than meddle with African customs. But it has also been maintained that torture cannot be tolerated and that the women of these countries have been so indoctrinated that they do not realize how they have been manipulated by their male oppressors.

This subject is treated in Benoîte Groult's Ainsi soit-elle and in several articles she did for F Magazine, as well as in Pierre Leulliette's Le viol des viols (1979) and Awa Thiam's La parole aux négresses (1978).

In the last year or so, this subject has received wide attention in France. Several infants were hospitalized, in some cases dying, after having been circumcised by relatives or fellow countrymen living in France. French authorities have started prosecution in these cases because the practice is not legal in France.

REPRODUCTIVE RIGHTS, FAMILY PLANNING, AND ABORTION

In 1900 the review Régénération first brought up the question of choice in having a child. In the following years, there were well-attended lectures on women's right to elective motherhood. (Male sterilization is a taboo subject in France because the penal code considers it a crime of voluntary mutilation [Articles 309 and 310].) However, the war halted this growing movement and the 1920 law on contraception and abortion effectively silenced it. During the interwar period there were a few who dared to speak out against this restrictive legislation: teacher Henriette Alquier, tried in 1927 for advocating sexual education; Bertie Albrecht, who published the review Le problème sexuel in 1932; and Dr. Jean Dalsace, who opened the first consultation center on family planning at Suresnes in 1935. Then yet another world war intervened. The movement for contraceptives for women resumed in the mid-1950s with the founding of Maternité Heureuse. It was not until the Neuwirth law of 1967 that contraceptives were first legalized in France. However, distribution, even information, was restricted.

Thus it was that in the early 1970s, French women were preoccupied with efforts to repeal the stringent law of 1920 on abortion and to make family planning information more widely available. Because of the prominent part this campaign for reproductive rights played in the current French feminist movement, details of the long, arduous, and acrimonious battle are outlined in the introductory essay. As late as the early 1970s, French doctors received no formal training in family planning. Each time the issue arose, the doctrine of privacy was invoked. Hence it is not surprising that French women have had to assume charge of their sexual lives and their reproductive rights. Their efforts to reform the laws--laws that only affected women, voted on only by men--have helped French women develop skills and expertise in promoting women's concerns. Women's issues were brought from the personal sphere into the public forum.

PROSTITUTION

The problem of prostitution finds its place in this debate on sexuality in society. Encouraged in part by feminist demands, French prostitutes organized sit-ins and demonstrations in the early 1970s. The dilemma persists. Are prostitutes victims of patriarchy or willing participants?

The Romantics opposed the harsh views and measures of the Revolution on prostitution. They favored comprehension and help rather than condemnation. Throughout the nineteenth century feminists were ambivalent and divided in their views on the institution. Marx, Engels, and their followers saw prostitution as the worst evil of capitalism. Anthropologists reject that view, contending that it existed in precapitalist societies and represented the total extension of male power. Most feminists today view prostitution as the most obvious and most degrading symbol of women's subjugation and exploitation by the male hegemony. Still, there are those like psychologist Judith Belladonna who recently researched the topic. She sees a potential revitalizing mission for prostitutes. Prostitution could become not a profession, but a way of living one's sexuality.

Reform efforts have been undertaken by Le Nid (the nest), founded by Father Talvas in 1936, an association that now exists in several countries. Le Nid has a number of foyers and training centers for adult female prostitutes. Support includes work experience and references, both of which are needed for employment. Salaried work enables women to figure on social security records and receive benefits. Since many prostitutes are single mothers, they would qualify for aid. Le Nid also supported the protest movement of the prostitutes in the early 1970s. On the other hand, the then head of the Secretariat of the Feminine Condition, Françoise Giroud, refused to deal with them. She argued that they were victims of repression and directed them instead to the Minister of the Interior. Their repression was the "direct result of the masculine condition, not the feminine."

French prostitutes are caught in the dilemma of being both legal and illegal. They are often compared to immigrant workers, their marginal male counterparts. Prostitutes cannot marry, for their husbands would automatically be subject to prosecution for "living with one who prostitutes." They are subject to income taxes (on figures arbitrarily arrived at) but receive no benefits. In their Manifesto to the People (Le Quotidien, June 1975), they charged the state with being the main procurer: it profits from their earnings. Additionally they asked for justice and for all the advantages and rights of women.

RAPE

Rape--total physical and moral violence done to women--was focused on by French feminists in the Trial of Aix in 1978. Defense witnesses included women deputies from the entire political spectrum ranging from the Parti communiste français (PCF) to the Union pour la démocratie française (UDF), and the Rassemblement pour la République (RPR). The transcript of the trial (as well as the Bobigny trial on abortion) was published by Gallimard for the association Choisir. These volumes provide material for study of both the problems of women in France today and the workings of the French judicial system. The Aix rape trial helped to lift the barrier of silence and bring about a revision in the penal code in favor of more stringent punishment for rape. Previously it had not been a serious charge. Often it was prosecuted as assault and battery, a comparatively light charge. And, all too often, the woman was made to feel guilty, to be suspected of provocation.

French women have brought up subjects that had heretofore been taboo: abortion, rape, conjugal abuse, and [female] circumcision. They have proclaimed their right to control their bodies and to enjoy pleasure and happiness. They have attacked sexism in all its manifestations. They have exposed repression and sexist representation of women, both held to be present to a greater degree in France. A growing number of French women have come to refuse to accept this degrading situation. The personal has become political. French women are engaged in sexual politics.

NOTES

1. Robert Aldrich, "Homosexuality in France," *Contemporary French Civilization* 7, no. 1:1-19.

Sexual Politics

SEXUALITY

Apprenons à faire l'amour [Let's learn to make love]. Paris: Maspero, 1973, 53 pp.

It is hard to imagine that this slight volume could have caused the scandal it did when it was published a few years ago. Then that is to forget that the French, particularly the bourgeoisie, are not yet as "emancipated" as are those who currently speak out and write on sexual education. The aim of this collectively written text is to speak about sexuality and to further discussion on that topic--not on the book, which is how events turned out. Factual materials are set forth with an open discussion of problems and other aspects of sexuality, such as homosexuality.

BÉNABOU, MAXIME. Être femme après 40 ans [To be a woman after forty]. Paris: Jean-Pierre Delarge, 1977, 139 pp.

The author maintains that menopause must be seen as a natural phenomenon by women who reach that age, by the doctors who would console them, and by society as a whole. With prevailing attitudes the prospects of reaching that age are depressing both for younger women and for those reaching what the French tactfully call women of middle age, femmes d'un certain âge.

CRESSANGES, JEANNE. La vraie vie des femmes commence à 40 ans [Women's real life begins at forty]. Paris: Fasquelle-Grasset, 1979, 279 pp.

Jeanne Cressanges's other works include Les chagrins d'amour (1976), a work in which she criticized Simone de Beauvoir for basing her comments and observations about menopause upon pathological cases. The "real" life promised by the title may be exaggerated. Nevertheless the study does explore the problems and possibilities of an age group often omitted in assessments of women's life today.

The virtually obligatory survey necessitated by such a study was further extended in this work by personal contacts with about a third of the women who responded. Thus the statistics are rounded out by portraits, case histories, and comments from these women, as well as by materials from a number of recent books dealing with the problems of older women.

Most women in this age group in France today had a traditional upbringing with a strict education. The prospects of a new future are at times difficult to deal with. These women feel that they reached their full potential in the affective, intellectual, and sexual aspects of their lives after they passed the age of forty. In a country which places much emphasis on physical appearance and where publicity is directed to the younger woman, the potential consumer, it is helpful to have some idea of how this older group of women feels and acts.

Maguelone Samat-Toussaint has written on this same topic in *La femme de 40 ans* (1973).

DALLAYRAC, DOMINIQUE. *L'important, c'est la femme* [What's important, is woman]. Paris: Tchou, 1977, 280 pp.

A journalist, Dallayrac has contributed to many foreign as well as French reviews. His publications include *Dossier prostitution* (1966) and *Dossier homosexualité* (1968). Here he offers new views on the relationships between the sexes. He credits women with the power to change the world. Their task is to instruct men in what are the fundamental values, values women have preserved from time immemorial. This ambitious study of sex includes cultural comparisons, interviews, views, and commentary.

The initial section deals with sexual venality. The demand that women enter marriage as virgins is viewed as the direct consequence of the institution of patriarchy and the values upon which it is established. The middle chapters treat the development of sex as a consumer product and include notes for a presentation of sex consumption. Theories of sociability, nomadism, property and the institution of patriarchy, and the repression of sexuality to affirm authority, are among the topics examined. The concluding section deals with the problems of "masculine, feminine, pleasure." What will be women's situation in the future as the war between the sexes gives way to the more "revolutionary" sexual mores of today? Are we proceeding to social androgyny and to a society based upon values different from those of the past are questions explored by the author.

The book raises a number of major issues, including that of sexual liberation and its potential for change. A sexual revolution may indeed be under way, but it has much further to go. How will it affect—possibly overthrow or destroy—male/female relations? Will it call into question the sociofamilial system? The author is working on the second part of this project, one he calls a "Liturgy for times to come," in a work focusing on violence, *Et les hommes vivront d'amour*.

GAUTHIER, XAVIÈRE. *Dire nos sexualités* [Speaking of our sexualities]. Collection coup pour coup. Paris: Galilée, 1976, 320 pp.

From 1973 to 1976 Xavière Gauthier recorded the comments of friends and casual acquaintances on their sexuality. She endeavored to be resolutely antijudgmental. Her introduction underscores the fact that all the authorities, from Krafft-Ebbing to Zwang, have denied desire. Here differing opinions are voiced. Each interviewee expresses his or her sexuality as it was and is experienced.

These personal views contrast with the many recent works on the topic, such as Dr. Zwang's *La fonction érotique* (1972). For all such studies the point of reference is science. These scientific works consider only white sexuality, consequently they are racist. Further, only the bourgeoisie is examined so they have a class bias. Only adults are included; there are no children, adolescents, or older people, a group made to feel "guilty" for having sexual desires. Since only the couple is considered, these works are based upon the traditional family model. Further, this recent expertise is masculine, producing a profoundly misogynist discourse.

Gauthier's long introduction contains many excerpts from this contemporary "scientific" work: these excerpts are followed by the author's acerbic and incisive comments. Our sexualities and the many varieties of love need free expression. The feminist author inveighs against authorities, whether medical, social, or religious. She also rejects psychologists who would presume to set down norms for something so individual as sexuality.

HANS, MARIE-FRANÇOISE, and GILLES LAPOUGE. Les femmes, la pornographie, l'érotisme [Women, pornography, erotism]. Collection libre à elles. Paris: Seuil, 1978, 400 pp.

Here assembled are varied--at times contradictory--views and responses by women (and a few men) on erotic art and pornography: books, pictures, and films. This topic is one women usually are reticent to discuss. Those interviewed fall into two groups: anonymous women of different social classes and the observers, psychoanalysts and feminist writers including Luce Irigaray, Vivianne Forrester (a specialist on Virginia Woolf), and Régine Deforgues, editor of numerous popular and serious erotic texts (including a book on Pauline Réage, author of the Story of O). Also involved is psychoanalyst Judith Belladonna, who worked as a stripteaser for a short time to research her book on prostitution, Folles femmes de leurs corps (q.v.).

The reactions of the two groups range from curiosity to arrogance, disgust, anger, fear, fascination, or indifference. A philosophy teacher who acted in a pornographic film sees teaching as but another form of seduction. Two words that reappear are those of "violence" and "power." The male presumptuously claims pornography in these terms. There is general agreement that women have a horror of violence and have difficulty in accepting what men believe they should appreciate.

HOURAY, PIERRE. Pour la libération de la femme [For the liberation of woman]. Paris: Buchet-Chastel, 1973, 310 pp.

The liberation in question is sexual liberation. Houray, author of a number of works on sexual problems and sexual education, takes as his starting point the MLF mainfesto of May 1971, Le Torchon brûle (The dishrag is burning, i.e., commotion in the kitchen). He hopes that the current women's revolutionary movement will be accompanied by a revolution which will eliminate all censorship and taboos. French society, dominated as it is by a bourgeois ideology that equates money with power, permits the reign of accountants and censors.

For the author, one of the most insidious and, at the same time, one of the most effective forms of sexual repression is the systematic "mystification" of women. Among the expressive myths examined in this scholarly essay are the notions of "castration," frigidity, the great love, etc., as they are revealed in case histories. Given the immense erotic possibilities of the female body, the long-deferred exploration and celebration of its resources should constitute one of the paths to the true liberation of women. The work concludes with a long bibliography.

MAURE, HUGUETTE. L'amour au féminin [Love in the feminine]. Paris: Calmann-Lévy, 1973, 264 pp.

Huguette Maure undertakes an inquiry into feminine psychology. Like her earlier Aventure au masculin, this work is written in an ironic and humorous vein: it is thought-provoking, perhaps upsetting to some. Rather than attempt yet another survey on the subject of women and love, she explores it in depth, drawing upon personal experience. She questions why women—at least those brought up in the past—have difficulty in engaging in casual adventures and why men say "my great loves," not "my great love."

*VERGEZ, SUZI. Pipi debout, quelle injustice [Pipi standing up, what an injustice]. Paris: Grasset, 1977, 193 pp.

Suzi Vergez discovered at an early age that she could not urinate standing up. This was but the first of many subsequent discoveries about the injustices women experience, the many things that serve to put women "in their place." Daily life is composed of those thousand and one little differences. (Verge is the anatomical term for penis.) Source: Des livres et des femmes.

REPRODUCTIVE RIGHTS, FAMILY PLANNING, AND ABORTION

L'alternative: libérer nos corps ou libérer l'avortement [The alternative: free our bodies or free abortion]. Paris: Éditions des femmes, 1973, 62 pp. (By women of the MLF.)

From its beginning, the MLF has been engaged in an offensive for legal abortion and, in a larger sense, for women's personal control of their bodies, their reproductive rights. This booklet presents a political position based upon a "collective work on sexuality and the body." It presents and summarizes one tendency of the MLF in France. These views, first set forth in issue number five of Le Torchon brûle, are views of militants of the Psychanalyse et Politique tendency. They have been expanded and developed for this publication.

ASSOCIATION CHOISIR. Avortement: une loi en procès, l'affaire Bobigny [Abortion: a law on trial, the Bobigny affair]. Paris: Gallimard, 1973, 254 pp.

This work summarizes the trial of a young girl, seduced and abandoned, who underwent an abortion, and her mother and those women who helped her, who were also indicted. The movement Choisir la Cause des Femmes grew out of this trial. In this case feminists decided to put the restrictive law of 1920 on abortion on trial. For the first time an open, national debate on the topic of abortion would be held.

It was estimated that in the early 1970s there were over a million clandestine, illegal abortions in France and that over five thousand women died from these illegal procedures. Those who suffered in one way or another from this operation were the least favored women in society. They could not pay for trips abroad to receive proper medical care. The testimony at the trial included that of Nobel Laureate Jacques Monod, who supported rescinding the law.

Simone de Beauvoir, cofounder with Gisèle Halimi and Jean Rostand of Choisir, writes that the law prohibiting abortion is one obvious way society oppresses women. The politics of natality keep women at home (the long-held ideal of la femme au foyer) and out of the work force. Momentum initiated by the Bobigny trial led to the legislation of 1975 permitting abortion (with some restrictions) for an initial five-year period. The law was made permanent in 1979. Since then it has been modified to permit IVG (interruption volontaire de grossesse, voluntary interruption of pregnancy, the legal term for abortion) to be covered by social security.

L'avortement: histoire d'un débat [Abortion: history of a debate]. Paris: Flammarion, 1975, 292 pp.

The several-thousand-page official dossier of the proposed bill over abortion is condensed in this volume. It offers selections from the debates held from the summer of 1973 to the end of 1974 in hearings, working committees, and the National Assembly and Senate. This is the basic source for information on the legislative process that implemented the law on the complex and controversial subject of abortion.

The task was difficult. Nevertheless, the approach to the new legislation was democratic. The entire spectrum of contemporary views on the topic was heard from the various groups who appeared before the working committees. The opposition was well represented by women, doctors, and conservatives such as Professor Pierre Chaunu, who founded an association of Professors of Letters and Human Sciences for the Respect of Life, a group composed of more than 600 professors of higher education. Chaunu maintained that "this group was more sensitive to the problem [of abortion] because it was composed of people who reflect upon [France's] heritage."

The final text of the law on abortion was short. But over 110 possible amendments were discussed. In the end, the bill, a bill which the majority of French citizens supported, was passed. Dr. Henry Berger, president of the Commission of Cultural,

Family, and Social Affairs of the National Assembly and sponsor of the legislation, offers a brief outline of the debate in his preface.

Avortement et libre choix de la maternité: textes et documents [Abortion and free choice of maternity: texts and documents]. Paris: Éditions Sociales, 1974, 128 pp. (Preface by Roland Leroy, editor of the Communist daily, L'Humanité.)

The French Communist party (CPF) has often been behind the times in its official positions. It was long critical of family planning and abortion, viewed as the vices of the rich. Family limitation was seen as a bourgeois plot to limit the proletariat. In the past years it has had to modify its views to accommodate the women of the party, as this work reveals.

For the party, this complex question must be considered in the context of its relation to all the forms of exploitation that workers and the population undergo. The question of abortion must be seen from the working-class viewpoint.

The statement is twice made that the French Communist party rejects theories that would make the right to abortion one of the essential means for the "liberation of women" or that would offer the "refusal" of motherhood as a solution to social questions. In contrast to its earlier, more conservative views, the CPF has now come to see the right to abortion as the recognition of individual liberties and responsibilities. Nevertheless, abortion is viewed as the ultimate recourse, one to be resorted to only when there is a "grave social problem" without possible solution for the mother or the family.

Speeches reprinted include those by Madeleine Vincent and Georges Marchais. The laws on this topic proposed by the Communist group of the National Assembly are reproduced.

COLLOQUES DU CENTRE CATHOLIQUE. Avortement et respect de la vie humaine [Abortion and respect for human life]. Paris: Seuil, 1972, 250 pp.

Here is the report of the 1972 colloquium sponsored by the Catholic Center. Doctors, theologians, and scientists gathered to discuss the theme "Abortion and the respect for human life." The debates recorded underscore the urgency and complexity of the issue. At that time abortion was a serious crime under French law. A critical assessment of the problem based upon a survey of 7500 doctors is included. There are no formal conclusions. However, these predominantly male voices tend to speak for themselves.

COMITÉ POUR LA LIBERTÉ DE L'AVORTEMENT ET DE LA CONTRACEPTION. Libérons l'avortement [Let us liberate abortion]. Paris: Maspero, 1973, 139 pp.

A team from Grenoble reports of 300 abortions undertaken using the Karman method. The advantages and problems of this method are reviewed. Use of a new form of paramedicine in undertaking these abortions is advocated. There are comments from women who have undergone abortions under varying conditions and under various medical procedures.

Contraception et avortement: dix ans de débat dans la presse (1965-1974) [Contraception and abortion: ten years of debate in the press (1965-1974)]. Actions thématiques programmées, ATP. Paris: Éditions du CNRS, 1979, 126 pp. (Research directed by François A. Isambert and Paul Ladrière.)

The larger question of the reciprocal interaction between the press and the evolution of social ideas and mores is examined in terms of the principal demands of French women--laws permitting contraception and abortion. The period covers the decade preceding the adoption of the initial law on abortion.

The press, extensive in France, presents both fact and opinion. This analysis, substantiated by graphs and tables, was limited to the six major Parisian dailies. It studies the role of these papers in the articulation of the problems of contraception and abortion. An examination of the feminist press complements the study. In this press one finds an ambivalent attitude, reflecting that of women themselves. Some feel that women must have complete freedom, including freedom over their bodies. Other women see abortion as violence done to women's bodies. This latter group insists that women should not have to undergo abortions, a form of oppression that parallels the oppression of women in society. The feminist press reveals that women share the view that abortion should be eliminated, not banalized. The comparatively recent, widespread introduction of contraception permits women greater freedom in taking charge of their bodies and their lives.

GUERRAND, ROGER-HENRI. La libre maternité (1869-1969) [Free (elective) maternity (1869-1969)]. Tournai: Casterman, 1971, 161 pp.

Though short, this historical survey of family planning in France is well documented. There is an eight-page bibliography. One finds it frequently cited in more recent works. There is good coverage of the late nineteenth and early twentieth centuries, periods which have received little study. It was in 1898 that Daniel Richie's Stérile, the first work of fiction based upon neo-Malthusian doctrines, appeared. Between 1900 and 1914 there were many popular works, plays, and novels on the subject. Their interest resides in showing how important the concern for family planning was at that time; they have but limited literary qualities.

Paul Robin and Eugène Humbert were pioneers in early twentieth-century efforts to introduce contraception in France. A counter-attack was led by the church and the medical corps. These early efforts were interrupted when France lost a million and a half men in the war. Natality became an overriding concern. The severe law of 1920 against birth control and abortion passed with the complicity of the highest medical authorities. There was little public awareness of what was taking place.

In 1956, Dr. Marie Andrée Lagroua Weill-Hallé helped found Maternité Heureuse (later Le Planning Familial) to provide family planning advice. The first clinic was opened at Grenoble in 1961, the same year she published La grand' peur d'aimer, about women who "feared making love," whom she encountered in her medical practice. Six years later the Neuwirth law modifying the 1920 legislation was passed. The Neuwirth law provided for the distribution of contraceptives only on doctors' orders; many did little to inform women of these rights. A more liberal law was passed in 1974. Texts of these laws are provided.

HALIMI, GISÈLE. La cause des femmes [The cause of women]. Paris: Grasset & Fasquelle, 1974, 206 pp. (Comments assembled by Marie Cardinal.)

The Tunisian-born, Paris-trained lawyer Gisèle Halimi became involved in political causes early in her career, serving as defense attorney for the Algerian and Basque Liberation Fronts. For the last decade she has dedicated her talents and energies to women's causes. With the eminent biologist Jean Rostand and Simone de Beauvoir she founded the movement Choisir. (De Beauvoir wrote the preface to her 1962 book defending the young Algerian revolutionary Djamila Boupacha.) Choisir wanted to protect the many women who had undergone abortions, including the signers of the Manifesto of the 343, and assure the defense in trials focusing on the crimes of abortion and rape, those of Bobigny and Grenoble, and later that of Aix.

Before outlining the trials of Bobigny and Aix, Halimi provides some autobiographical materials. To be born female in a colonial land and, as she was later to realize, Jewish at that, represented several misfortunes in a world made for men.

An unsuccessful clandestine abortion obliged her to go to a hospital for a curettage, undertaken generally at that time without anesthesia. Memories of that painful, punitive experience helped shape her views on the need to legalize abortion. She stresses that the pregnancies she wanted were experiences of immense joy.

In her detailed comments about the early days of the Choisir movement, Gisèle Halimi reveals the difficulties of those who had chosen "the cause of women."

LAGROUA WEILL-HALLÉ, MARIE A. L'avortement de Papa: essai critique pour une vraie réforme [Outmoded abortion: critical essay for a true reform]. Paris: Fayard, 1971, 122 pp.

The author was one of the principal founders of the Family Planning movement in France. The American example is credited with inspiring her. In this volume she considers the problems and confusion accompanying growing discussion of the issues of contraception and abortion in France. Jacques Derogy, the first journalist to take up the problem of contraception (in the review Libération, 1955), assists her in this analysis.

Unpublished documents indict the massive failure of contraception after it was first legally authorized in the late 1960s, albeit on a limited basis. Fewer than seven percent of French women were found to be using modern contraceptive methods. The cartoons included in this book are by the well-known artist Siné and are characterized by the rather broad humor known as l'esprit gaulois.

MAILLARD, CLAUDE. Avortement: les pièces du dossier [Abortion: the documents of the dossier]. Paris: Robert Laffont, 1974, 272 pp.

The events immediately preceding and during 1974, the year of the debate on abortion in France, are presented quarter by quarter. The materials cover over 4,000 clippings from Parisian and provincial newspapers. There are no analyses of comments, just a presentation of facts. They prove eloquent enough.

In April 1971, 343 women signed a manifesto declaring that they had undergone an abortion, thus risking prosecution. In June of that same year, 600 doctors signed a manifesto in favor of legal abortion. However, the doctors, unlike the women, did not publicly acknowledge that they had practiced abortions. To do so would have meant risking suspension, possibly revocation, of their medical licenses.

French women had come to realize that their determination to be in charge of their lives and their bodies led inevitably to political combat. The founding of the movement Choisir and the Bobigny trial ensued. Then followed the debate in the press here documented.

The preface is by Dr. Paul Milliez. He was publicly censured by the conservative Council of the Order of Physicians (comparable to the AMA) for having been a defense witness in the Bobigny trial.

MORIÈRE, HUGUETTE. Vivre avec la peur au ventre [Living with fear in one's womb]. Femmes en mouvement. Paris: Pierre Horay, 1979, 157 pp. (Preface by Benoîte Groult.)

The oldest of ten children--half of whom died before they turned four--Huguette Morière recounts her life in a very poor family. Early on she decided not to repeat her mother's experience. When, after four years of marriage, she found herself the mother of three, she decided to induce an abortion each time she found herself pregnant. And this Morière did, with primitive homemade means, ten times.

The sinister folklore of abortion described here recalls Zola. Yet such was the situation in France until the Neuwirth law of 1967 was passed.

Prior to that time women could not even be told about contraception without risk of prosecution for those involved. The only woman to be executed in France in this century was Mme Giraud, a washerwoman guillotined in 1943 for having performed abortions: a 1941 decree of the Vichy government counts abortion among "crimes against the security of the state."

PEYRET, CLAUDE, with CLAIRE BRISSET. Avortement: pour une loi humaine [Abortion: for a humane law]. Paris: Calmann-Lévy, 1974, 254 pp.

Dr. Peyret, a practicing Catholic and Gaullist, found all his previous views called into question when a young woman died in his office after a self-induced abortion. He decided to try and inform others about the previously little-discussed topic of abortion. He was asked by the Council of the Order of Physicians to look into revising existing legislation on therapeutic abortion. There was need for reform. The laws were broken daily, often by some of the best-known doctors.

Dr. Peyret prepared material for the debate preceding passage of the law on contraception in 1967. There were difficult days and appearances on television. He received much correspondence, some of it abusive. But the results were positive: the silence on abortion had ended. The political and ethical, as well as medical, aspects of the problem are well articulated.

TOULAT, JEAN. L'avortement: crime ou libération? [Abortion: crime or liberation?]. Paris: Fayard, 1973, 155 pp.

Jean Toulat, the author of a number of works on religious subjects, including Paul VI on Holy Ground, summarizes the French Catholic position on abortion. Any attempt to legalize abortion Toulat views as a step on the road to Auschwitz. The protection of life he links to recent ecological concerns over the protection of nature.

*BOSMANS, FERNAND. L'avortement: clandestine! . . . légal? [Abortion: clandestine! . . . legal?]. Paris: Fernand Nathan, 1973, 173 pp.

*DOURLEN-ROLLIER, ANNE-MARIE. Tout savoir sur l'avortement [Everything about abortion]. Paris: Filippachi, 1972, 160 pp.

*DOURLEN-ROLLIER, ANNE-MARIE, with JEAN DALSACE. L'avortement [Abortion]. Paris: Casterman, 1970, 156 pp.

*FLANDRIN, JEAN-LOUIS. L'église et le contrôle des naissances [The church and control of births]. Paris: Flammarion, 1970, 255 pp.

*GERAUD, ROGER. Avortement et eugénique [Abortion and eugenics]. Vervier: Gérard, 1974, 318 pp.

*GUY, FRANÇOIS, and MICHÈLE GUY. L'avortement: documents pour une information sur un problème d'actualité [Abortion: documents for information on a contemporary problem]. Paris: Édition du Cerf, 1971, 240 pp.

*LEJEUNE, JÉRÔME. Laissez-les vivre: non au génocide [Let them live: no to genocide]. Paris: Lethielleux, 1975, 351 pp.
"Laissez les vivre" is the name of the anti-abortion movement in France.

*VALENSIN, GEORGES. Je suis un avorteur [I am an abortionist]. Paris: Filippachi, 1974, 240 pp.

*VELLAY, PIERRE. Le vécu de l'avortement [The actuality of abortion]. Paris: Édition Universitaire, 1972, 176 pp.

PROSTITUTION

BELLADONNA, JUDITH. Folles femmes de leurs corps: les prostituées [Women wild in their flesh: the prostitutes]. Paris and Fontenay-sous-Bois: Recherches, 1977, 242 pp.

The title of this essay on prostitution is drawn from a 1254 ordinance stating the punishment for folles femmes de leurs corps was "to be expelled from their dwellings, chased from the towns, burgs, and villages, with their goods duly seized once they had beeen stripped of their garments."

Judith Belladonna's work is not another sociological inquiry. It is one woman's attempt to understand women and prostitution. Further, she insists, it is not written from the traditional feminist viewpoint. Feminists, she feels, do not really want to try to understand prostitution. They condemn it unequivocally as an exploitation of women in the worst sense. There would seem to be an ambivalence in reactions to prostitution: fascination and terror, secret seduction and repression.

Study of and contact with prostitutes led Belladonna to conclude that the vast majority want to continue to exercise their profession--but under better conditions. For many it offers the opportunity to give, to offer themselves. They may contribute to the newly evolving sexuality. Even though they use a vocabulary of suffering, most do not want to leave their situation or find another profession.

It would appear that the institution of prostitution is but another product of capitalist society with sex capitalized. Both prostitute and client are consumers. The author's provocative views are completed by comments from several other writers and testimony from the prostitutes themselves. The volume includes a brief history of prostitution in France with useful citations and documentation.

CONINCK, CHRISTINE, and BARBARA. La partagée [The divided woman]. Paris: Éditions de Minuit, 1977, 190 pp.

This is the story of a divided woman, a woman with two names. There is Barbara, the prostitute, the public woman, and Mireille, the private woman. Barbara/Mireille was brought to the home of Christine de Coninck when the prostitutes of Lyon were expelled from the Church of Saint-Nizier. They had occupied the church--with the aid of the pastor and the association NID--to protest the brutal torture-murders of several of their number in the past few years. They also protested increasing harassment by the local police (embittered perhaps by a reputation compromised when several top police officials were found to have profited from regional prostitution). And they decried the treatment of prostitutes in general.

Barbara/Mireille details the 1975 revolt of the Lyon prostitutes, a movement that soon encompassed prostitutes in other major cities. She credits the current feminist movement with aiding these women to protest in public. This was the first time they had met and worked together. Demands set forth included the right to prostitute themselves and the right to leave prostitution without bearing a stigma for live.

To Christine, Barbara/Mireille recounts her life. The ward of public assistance, she was brought up by an unloving couple and raped by her stepfather at nine. There were stays in a psychiatric clinic for aggressive behavior, in a sordid home for the "protection of minors," and four years in prison for attacking her seducer. Like many prostitutes, she took up the trade when she found herself a single mother with children to support and educate. Since the events of 1975, which she helped lead, Mireille has left for other work. Reinsertion is a difficult undertaking.

CORBIN, ALAIN. Les filles de noce: misère sexuelle et prostitution (19e et 20e siècles) [Good-time girls for a fling: sexual misery and prostitution (nineteenth and twentieth centuries)]. Paris: Aubier-Montaigne, 1978, 571 pp. (Noce also means wedding.)

Historian Alain Corbin studies prostitution in France during the nineteenth and twentieth centuries in what has come to be recognized as the definitive work on the subject. The author contends that prostitution has heretofore been less well understood in France than in America. His extensive documentation includes a lengthy bibliography and citations of primary sources such as manuscripts, official documents, printed inquiries, and newspaper articles. French emphasis on record keeping has meant that exhaustive records, for example, forty-eight very complete dossiers for lieux de débauche in Marseilles covering a few short years, exist.

Corbin traces the changes in forms and styles of prostitution, changes that parallel changes in French society. As the clientele becomes more bourgeois, the bordellos of the working class give way to "houses": venal relations are patterned more on the conjugal model. Increased prosperity in the second half of the nineteenth century brought increased demand and the rise of more elaborate sexual practices.

The "French system" of regulated prostitution was set up after the Revolution. Registered prostitutes and designated locations would provide the sanitary control central to the system. This way vice and disease would be concentrated and controlled. But it did not work that way. To begin with, there were many part-timers and "free-lancers." Registered prostitutes were required to undergo weekly medical examinations, but often these were superficial. Those infected tried to hide their condition for, if detected, they would be sent to the prison hospital of Saint-Lazare or similar establishments in the provinces. Little effort was made to help these women. Treatment was both harsh and punitive.

The failure of supposed sanitary control became the best argument for those who wished to abolish houses of prostitution. The fear of venereal disease became a major concern at the turn of the century, a concern voiced in a number of novels and plays. The principal difficulty in dealing with prostitution in France has been the inability to distinguish between concerns for morality and health. The prostitutes themselves--often victims of both class and gender discrimination--have seldom been considered; only their patrons were.

Corbin's study reveals the underlying dilemma of a society trying to come to terms with sexual mores. The emerging, triumphant bourgeoisie idealized woman and stressed her purity. At the same time, concern for proper "establishment" deferred marriages. Prostitution was the inevitable outcome. In the 1830s Dr. Alexandre Parent-Duchatelet set up the hierarchies and classifications of prostitutes in a work of social medical anthropology that informed literature on prostitution for half a century. He was the first to point out, in his De la prostitution dans la ville de Paris (1836), that prostitutes play an important role in society. French men have sensual desires. Were it not for the prostitutes, men would pervert daughters or servants (which they appear to have done anyhow). Prostitutes are a necessary "evil."

JAGET, CLAUDE. Une vie de putain [A whore's life]. Paris: Les Presses d'Aujourd'hui, 1975, 212 pp.

In 1975, the International Year of the Woman, women prostitutes occupied the house of the Lord, (that is, the church of Saint-Nizier in Lyons). Thus went the headline of one of a series of articles Claude Jaget wrote for the review Libération, virtually the only publication to call attention to their cause, as it had earlier championed birth control and was later to condemn rape. His aim was to call public attention to the problems of the prostitutes themselves.

Jaget details the events that led to the occupation. The abbot of the Church of Saint-Nizier, which harbored the women, spent time with the prostitutes and supported their protest. For this he was vilified. Efforts were made to prove that he was a procurer. Such was (is) the mentality on the matter of prostitution.

In the volume, six women prostitutes tell their life stories. One describes prostitution as an "assassination," but a temporary one. Factory work, on the other hand, she sees as "continual assassination." The appendix sets forth French legislation on prostitution.

A number of recent French works by prostitutes have appeared in English. Other titles on the topic are:

*MAILLARD, CLAUDE. Les prostituées [The prostitutes]. Paris: Robert Laffont, 1975.
   "What they recount when they talk with a[nother] woman."

*ORAISON, MARC. La prostitution . . . et alors? [Prostitution . . . and so?]. Paris: Seuil, 1979, 149 pp.
   A Catholic doctor and psychologist considers the moral and religious aspects of the problem of prostitution. His study is placed under the biblical injunction "The prostitute will precede you into the kingdom of Heaven."

*SACOTTE, MARCEL. La prostitution, que peut-on faire? [Prostitution, what can one do?]. Paris: Buchet-Chastel, 1971, 315 pp.

*TEXIER, CATHERINE, and MARIE-ODILE VEZINA. Profession prostituée [Profession prostitute]. Paris: Éditions Libre Expression, 1978, 354 pp.

RAPE

ASSOCIATION CHOISIR. Viol: le procès d'Aix, avec un texte inédit de Gisèle Halimi [Rape: the trial of Aix, with an unpublished text by Gisèle Halimi]. Paris: Gallimard, 1978, 416 pp.
   This is both a fascinating and frightening document. It details the efforts of the Choisir movement to make France and the world aware of this all too common crime of violence against women. The trial transcript provides insights into the workings of French justice, which differs from Anglo-Saxon law. Choisir undertook the legal defense of two young women who brought suit for rape against three young men in the south of France, a region where Mediterranean machismo is deeply embedded. It was decided that, as in the trial at Bobigny over abortion (which Halimi also defended), this would be the trial of rape itself. "Rape is total physical and moral violence done to women."

Sexual Politics

The punishment for rape in France was then less severe than that for bank robbery, although rape robs a woman of her body and her dignity. Women deputies from the entire political spectrum-- from Conservatives to Communists--came to testify. All involved were determined that the barrier of silence be lifted. The successful prosecution of the case, in spite of some harassment, brought favorable changes in the penal code. They included prosecution of sexual aggression against minors and more stringent punishment for rape. Provisions already implemented and those under consideration are outlined in the documents which complete this dossier: depositions, (statements by those unable to attend the trial), closing arguments, press reviews, and the text of a law proposed by Choisir that would make conjugal rape a crime.

FARGIER, MARIE-ODILE. Le viol [Rape]. Collection le temps des femmes. Paris: Grasset, 1976, 224 pp.

Marie-Odile Fargier, a journalist with the Quotidien de Paris, conducted an inquiry on rape among lawyers, police, doctors, sociologists, psychoanalysts, victims, and aggressors. There is no consensus on the reasons for this crime against women, the only crime in which the burden of proof is born by the victim. Some allege that it is biological "fatality," others speak of a social or cultural phenomenon. There are men who attempt to explain and justify, in some instances even deny, the very existence of rape.

The author indicts French justice for refusing to call rape by its proper name, instead, charges are brought for "bodily harm," "physical aggression," etc. The chapter headings are eloquent: "The law of silence" (the fear of women, particularly the young, in reporting rape); "Open season year round for hunting women"; "Rape does not exist . . ."; "Because there are no rapists"; lastly, "Rape is not destiny."

A portrait of the typical French rapist based upon 1974 trial records belies the stereotypes. He is generally French, often a younger married man, someone the victim knows. At the time the book was written, justice was on the side of the men. Various trial excerpts show how the woman victim is frequently presented as having provoked or consented to the act. The situation has changed somewhat. Three women's groups have done much to affect this change: Choisir, the Ligue pour le Droit des Femmes, and the Union pour la Dignité de la Personne Humaine.

Women in French Society

THE FAMILY AND CHILDREN

The family in France, as in most Western countries, is in constant interaction with all other institutions. At the same time, it underlies the structures of those other groups. Philippe Ariès and others have pointed out that the pre-Revolutionary French family differed considerably from the modern family. One important divergence was in function. These earlier families were generally units of production and consumption concerned with the common practice of a trade and, for those possessed of patrimony, its transmission. There were matrimonial systems during the <u>ancien régime</u> that offered women various possibilities for keeping their property and name. However, this latitude was gradually lost and ultimately, when Napoleon drew up the Civil Code in 1804, abolished. The legal incapacity of married women was institutionalized by the code's depiction of them as unfit. According to Patrick Kay Bidelman, the code also "established the legal and 'spiritual' premises for a series of judicial and administrative decisions that further lowered the status of women in the course of the nineteenth century."[1]

Families of the sixteenth, seventeenth, and eighteenth centuries were patriarchal. Cissie Fairchilds's recent analysis of marriage patterns and other relationships, <u>Domestic Enemies: Servants and Their Masters in Old Regime France</u>, shows how the concept of patriarchy pervaded French society then as the concept of "service" had pervaded the society of the Middle Ages. "The authority of the father of the family was the model for all authority: a king was the father of his people, God was the Father of all mankind."[2]

A child was not always joyously accepted in these earlier centuries. For women, it meant justifiable apprehension given the medical conditions of the times. As a Gascon proverb puts it, "A pregnant woman has a foot in the grave" ("<u>Femme grosse a un pied dans la fosse</u>"). The state made some effort to train midwives, but most had little formal instruction. Doctors were seldom called in. Although privacy was invoked the real reasons were more often prejudice and expense. The acceptance of a child in the family was further influenced by its sex. When asked about his progeny, a mid-nineteenth-century Breton farmer replied that he didn't have any children; he had only daughters.[3]

Nevertheless, during the sixteenth and seventeenth centuries, attitudes were changing. As the modern concept of childhood was developing, a growing concern for the child slowly evolved despite the fact that parents did not become too attached to their young children, only half of whom lived to be ten. Rousseau's Émile (1672) was widely read, if not widely followed. Rousseau opposed the then common practice of swaddling infants and advocated that women nurse their own children. City children of that time were generally sent out to wet nurses (nourrices), a practice that resulted in a high mortality rate.

Wet-nursing was a particularly French institution, one with a long history.[4] In 1350 King Jean set forth an ordinance regulating wet-nursing. By the eighteenth century, not only the aristocracy but also the bourgeoisie and the artisanate were hiring wet nurses. Many children died while en nourrice. The trip alone took a heavy toll. While at their nourrice, some succumbed because of ignorance or neglect. By the beginning of the nineteenth century, almost one in every five French children did not survive beyond the first year. Only toward the end of the century did this figure start to decline. The Roussel law of 1874 endeavored to reinforce and improve measures regulating the practice of wet-nursing that had been passed through the nineteenth century.[5] This law, progress in hygiene (particularly pasteurization), France's growing concern with "depopulation," a concern Karen Offen has shown was intrinsically linked to the debate on women's rights in fin-de-siècle France, and a debate conducted in sociobiological, medical, and demographic terms[6] helped reduce the number of infant fatalities and encouraged women to nurse their own children. By the outbreak of the First World War, nourrices were mostly memories in France's past.

Toward the end of the eighteenth century, the mistress of the household--la femme au foyer--made her appearance. She was a woman of the upper classes who devoted herself almost exclusively to home and children. Both conservatives and liberals enthusiastically promoted this model throughout the nineteenth century; the former wished to reinforce traditional Christian values while the latter wanted to establish secular republican values. This essentially bourgeois concept of the femme au foyer--and its accompanying cult of domesticity--is now on the wane in France although its influence persists among working-class men who are just now able to indulge in the "luxury" of a wife who can devote herself exclusively to home and family. In the past, women of the people could not afford to be totally absorbed by their families, to be "homemakers."

Women in French Society

In recent years there have been fewer marriages in France in spite of the arrival at marriageable age of the "baby boom" generation. A 1984 report on matrimony and its legal, fiscal, and social consequences presented by Evelyne Sullerot found that from 1973 to 1983 there were over 100,000 fewer marriages than would normally have been anticipated.[7] The report concluded that there had been changes in family patterns that had no precedent in peacetime France. These "missing marriages" will probably not take place, at least not in legal form. Further, if figures remain at the 1981 level, within one generation thirty-seven percent of the men and thirty-five percent of the women in France will never marry. These figures are in marked contrast to those of from eight to twelve percent of just a few years ago.[8]

This decrease in the marriage rate has been accompanied by a marked increase in the number of unmarried young couples living together. Although precise figures are understandably difficult to obtain, the Sullerot report estimates that about half of today's younger couples cohabit, as compared with fewer than a fifth in 1969. A generation ago such living arrangements would not have been acceptable to most families. If liaisons existed, they were not openly acknowledged or accepted. The current women's movement and a freer moral code have helped bring about a profound change in French mores. In 1976 the state extended its considerable social services to support children born out of wedlock. The concern is to provide for the children, not dole out moral censure.

Historically France has been preoccupied with preserving the family unit. Since the Popular Front was voted in in 1936, extensive legislation has been enacted to help parents raise their children. Current measures to aid families include permanent supplementary income such as family allowances and special financial aid for births, maternity, illness, disability, and housing. All families with two or more dependent children are eligible to receive family allowances, regardless of their marital or occupational status. Both parents have the right to take time off when a child is born. The working mother is entitled to sixteen weeks' maternity leave. Social security pays ninety percent of her normal salary during this period. A recently passed law provides for an elective parental leave (congé parental d'éducation). One parent may take up to two years' leave to raise a new baby or an adopted child under three years of age. (Only workers in firms employing 200 or more are now eligible; efforts are under way to extend this option to all workers.) Under the terms of the law, the returning worker must be given the same position or a comparable one, without loss of seniority.

Among many younger French women there has been another silent revolution whose impact has not yet been fully discerned. These young women refuse patriarchal society and any living arrangements that place women in a disadvantaged position. They want personal autonomy and professional possibilities. For some this has meant the deliberate choice of becoming a single parent. The 1984 matrimonial statute report reveals that current well intentioned fiscal and social policies permit—and, paradoxically, even appear to favor—such decisions.

If a marriage proves unsatisfactory, it is now possible to divorce under less onerous and less expensive conditions, thanks to recent modifications in divorce legislation. The French divorce rate has doubled since 1950. Now one marriage in five ends in divorce, a figure still well below the American rate of one in two.

A number of studies on the French family and on children—notably the works of Claude Lévi-Strauss, Philippe Ariès, and more recently, Elizabeth Badinter (who argues that no such thing as a maternal "instinct" has existed everywhere at all times) have appeared in English.[9] The annotated entries reveal that although some basic women's demands obtain for France and the United States, the social goals that inform them are not necessarily the same.

EDUCATION AND SEX ROLES

Readers unfamiliar with French society will perhaps be surprised to find so few titles in this important section. This may be explained in large part by the fact that France has a highly centralized national educational system with little place for outside—that is, nonprofessional—participation in the educational process. A good general survey of this subject is Antoine Prost's Histoire de l'enseignement en France, 1800-1967 (Paris: A. Colin, 1968).[10]

With the development of a concern for children and the concept of childhood noted above, educational institutions were given a more extensive role in their formation and education. This role has been the subject of a number of studies; however, until quite recently female education was studied in the context of the history of French education in general. Little scholarly attention was paid to the nontraditional ways in which girls were frequently educated. Few studies were devoted to professional and technical education of the type organized by Elisa Lemonnier (1805-65) in 1862 to provide young women with solid, general professional training. Now a number of well-documented French master's theses and doctoral dissertations have been devoted to this neglected aspect of women's history.[11] Another important factor for female education in the past was the mother-teacher (mère-éducatrice). One of the many tracts published in the first part of the nineteenth century was Martin Aimé's widely read L'éducation des mères de famille, ou la civilisation de la race humaine par les femmes (1837). Training manuals and guides for girls, such as Dr. Chenu's Manuel de la dame de charité (1876), intended for nurses, are most revealing. In the past, many girls were

Women in French Society

educated in their families, through the family professions and through social work. Accounts of formal education do not fully detail the instruction of girls in the France of years past. A more comprehensive account of French women's efforts to obtain education is presented in the Introduction.

Education is now compulsory in France from ages six to sixteen. It is free of charge in public schools and universities. In 1981 there were over eleven million children attending primary and secondary schools and almost a million attending university. This enrollment gives France one of the highest school enrollment rates in the world. All textbooks through the second year of secondary school (5ème) are provided free of charge by the state. The Ministry of Education establishes a uniform curriculum for the entire country and grants all diplomas. Most private schools follow the state system of education and prepare their students for the regular state-sanctioned diplomas since they cannot by law grant their own. The question of the state's financial contribution to the private schools--which are mainly Catholic--and whether or not their teachers should become state functionaries has evolved as the focus of a nationwide debate in France.

One area that French feminists of the 1970s have addressed, one where their concerns may have some impact on the education process, is that of the image of women and girls in school textbooks. In spite of the accomplishments of French women--both past and present--they are still largely presented in situations of weakness and dependence, conditions often symbolized by poverty or illness. This image bears witness to a cultural model found throughout French literature. From the timid, fragile young girl to the devoted, ever-present married mother (no single or working mothers are included) and the poor worthy widow, women figure in school texts. But they are seldom portrayed as responsible, independent citizens. The presence of these stereotypes is abundantly documented. The implications of these outdated and depreciating views of women are being analyzed.

Initial research into this problem was undertaken in the 1960s by women connected with the national scientific research council, the CNRS. They included Suzanne Mollo, Marie-José Chombart de Laüwe. Liliane Kandel, and Andrée Michel. In 1974, the Ligue Française pour le Droit des Femmes undertook a campaign to publicize the problem. The following year Françoise Giroud made a survey of the image of women in French school books one of the first projects of her newly organized ministry of the feminine condition. The Union des Femmes Françaises has also mobilized its considerable strength to address this problem. In 1978 the Center for Feminine Information in Paris organized an exhibition on "The Image of Young Girls in Children's Books" at the popular Georges Pompidou Center, known as the Beaubourg Museum. Then, in 1979, Catherine Valabrègue and

Agnès Fichot founded an Association for a Nonsexist School. The campaign against distorted and sexist representations of women continues into the 1980s.

RELIGION

France is frequently referred to as the oldest daughter of the Catholic church. While it is true that there has been a special relationship between that country and Catholicism, it is also true that, as in many relations, there have often been quarrels and disputes. Catholicism is the traditional religion in France, as it is in other Latin countries. Formal religious rites mark the main events in life: birth, maturity, marriage, and death. Yet in a country where almost eighty-five percent of the population is Catholic barely fifteen percent of that number attend weekly mass-- a practice nominally required of observant Catholics.

Throughout the nineteenth century the church waged a long, energetic campaign to prevent women from enrolling in state schools. For sociologists Andrée Michel and Geneviève Texier, this is but part of a larger campaign. They maintain that from the right to education to that of contraception, women have had to contend with systematic obstruction by the Catholic hierarchy, one of the most powerful pressure groups in France.[12] Historically the church had always provided education for French women. It believed that it was better equipped to undertake this "mission." Women were felt to need special protection, protection the church could best provide. When republican politicians first endeavored to provide state secondary education for women, the church's principal spokesman, Félix Antoine-Philibert Dupanloup (1802-78), bishop of Orléans, asked if young girls brought up "on the knees of the church" were to be abandoned to base, materialist humanity?[13] Some contemporary Catholic feminists question the church's intransigeant position against contraception and abortion. They argue that an exclusively male group should not presume sole jurisdiction over and disposition of women's bodies. These women express the fear that if the church hierarchy does not come to terms with this central problem, it will lose women just as it lost the workers in the nineteenth century. And more women than men have been practicing Catholics. In the past, French women assured the continuity of religion through their instruction of their children.

A colloquium of French church figures in 1982 raised the question of whether one can be both Catholic and feminist. Some progress was reported at the gathering, the theme of which was "Women are also part of the church." Nevertheless much remains to be done. As one participant expressed it, "women must demand reparation for the enormous injustice done to them for centuries. This is not a personal demand, but a denunciation of the immense and absurd waste of spiritual forces."[14] The very fact that a number of recent books challenge the centuries-old views of the place of women in Catholicism suggests that changes are under way. Even among Catholic women, the authority of the Fathers is no longer accepted without question.

NOTES

1. Patrick Kay Bidelman, Pariahs Stand Up! The Founding of the Liberal Feminist Movement in France, 1858-1889 (Westport, Conn. and London: Greenwood Press, 1984), 5. Article 1124 of the code declared that "unfit" persons included minors, ex-convicts, and married women. Full details of the development of the laws governing marriage and the family in France from the final decades of the ancien régime to the promulgation of the code are set forth in James F. Traer's Marriage and the Family in Eighteenth-Century France (Ithaca and London: Cornell University Press, 1980).
2. Cissie Fairchilds, Domestic Enemies: Servants and Their Masters in Old Regime France (Baltimore and London: Johns Hopkins University Press, 1984), 138. Elsewhere (p. 6) she notes that the "metaphors of caring father and submissive child shaped all relationships between superior and inferior, not only those of master and servant but also those of king and subject, magistrate and citizen." See also Gordon S. Schochet, Patriarchalism in Political Thought (New York: Basic Books, 1975).
3. Charles Laurent, Les droits de la femme: droits politiques (Paris, 1888). Cited in Bidelman, Pariahs Stand Up!, 23.
4. See George D. Sussman, Selling Mother's Milk: The Wet-Nursing Business in France, 1715-1914 (Urbana: University of Illinois Press, 1982).
5. See Anne Martin-Fugier, "La fin des nourrices," Le Mouvement social 105 (October-December 1978):11-32. On this and other efforts by nineteenth-century legislators to control family life and women's activities see Jacques Donzelot, La police des familles (Paris, 1977), translated into English as The Policing of Families (New York: Pantheon, 1979).
6. Karen Offen, "Depopulation, Nationalism, and Feminism in Fin-de-Siècle France," American Historical Review, June 1984, pp. 648-76. In this important article Offen shows how the women question had risen to the forefront of French political discourse by the late nineteenth century. She contends that this centrality of the woman question--"la question des femmes" or "Frauenfrage" was a convenient term used by many nineteenth-century European writers to refer to the complex issues raised by women's subordinate status and the challenges they posed to existing social and political institutions by demands for change--compels a rethinking of French, and even European, history as it has traditionally been written and taught (p. 649).

7. Evelyne Sullerot, rapporteur, Le statut matrimonial: ses conséquences juridiques, fiscales, et sociales (Paris: Conseil Économique et Social, 1984). This study--the first of its kind in France--reveals the disparity between the intention of French matrimonial legislation and its application.

8. Ibid., 161. In 1982 there were 312,000 marriages while in 1972 there were 417,000, a decrease of almost one-fourth.

9. Elisabeth Badinter, Mother Love: Myth and Reality (New York: Macmillan, 1981). Additional works in French include: Jacques Gelis, ed., Entrer dans la vie: naissances et enfances dans la France traditionnelle (Paris: Luget, 1978); Yvonne Knibiehler and Catherine Fouquet, L'histoire des mères du moyen âge à nos jours (Paris: Montalba, 1980); Alain Lottin et al., eds., La désunion du couple sous l'ancien régime: l'exemple du nord (Lille: P.U.L., 1975); and Louis Roussel, Le mariage dans la société française contemporaine (Paris: P.U.F., 1975). Translations and recent studies in English include: Georges Duby, Medieval Marriage: Two Models from Twelfth-Century France (Baltimore: Johns Hopkins University Press, 1976); David Hunt, Parents and Children in History: The Psychology of Family Life in Early Modern France (New York: Harper & Row, 1970); Roderick Phillips, Family Breakdown in Late Eighteenth Century France: Divorces in Rouen, 1792-1893 (Oxford: Oxford University Press, 1980); Edward Shorter, The Making of the Modern Family (New York: Basic Books, 1975); Bonnie L. Smith, Ladies of the Leisure Class: The Bourgeoises of Northern France in the Nineteenth Century (Princeton: Princeton University Press, 1981); and Robert Wheaton and Tamara K. Hareven, eds., Family and Sexuality in French History (Philadelphia: University of Pennsylvania Press, 1980). Earlier but still useful is Wesley D. Camp, Marriage and the Family in France Since the Revolution: An Essay in the History of Population (New York: Bookman, 1961). Most of these works, as well as those cited, contain extensive bibliographies. Cissie Fairchilds's Domestic Enemies: Servants and Their Masters in Old Regime France lists treatises and medical works on child raising, for example, and moral tracts and etiquette books.

10. For additional information and other references see the section on education, "L'école des femmes," in the Introduction.

11. See the Spring 1980 issue of Pénélope--a French journal devoted to the history of women--on the theme "Éducation des filles: enseignement des femmes."

12. Andrée Michel and Geneviève Texier, La condition de la Française d'aujourd'hui, vol. 2 (Paris: Denoël/Gonthier, 1984), 11.

13. See the introductory section on education and the entries for Françoise Mayeur for additional details on the role of Monseigneur Dupanloup in the controversy over secular versus religious education for women that broke out during the 1860s.

Women in French Society

THE FAMILY AND CHILDREN

CARLIER-MACKIEWICZ, NICOLE. <u>Les veuves et leurs familles dans la société d'aujourd'hui: étude sociologique</u> [Widows and their families in today's society: a sociological study]. Paris: Caisse Nationale des Allocations Familiales, 1970, 284 pp. (Preface by M. Harzfeld; designs and graphics by the CNAF graphic team.)

Few studies have been devoted to widows who head families. The legislation pertaining to them in France is comprehensive but it is also often contradictory. Widows need to be well informed about their rights; most, however, are not. The widows interviewed for this study were termed very responsive, positive, and helpful. At last some concern was being shown about their situation.

Some of the problems widows encounter examined in this work include the tensions inherent in trying to assume all parental responsibilities and the difficulties found in the closed family. The social reinsertion of both the widow and her children is generally difficult. Often there is a strong feeling of exclusion. The death of the husband and father is a social as well as personal tragedy.

Much of the data of this study lends itself to psychological interpretation. The author, however, has restricted her inquiry to sociological considerations. There has been some improvement in both the legal and financial situation of French widows since this book was written.

CAYRON, CLAIRE. <u>Divorce en France</u> [Divorce in France]. Paris: Denoël/Gonthier, 1974, 222 pp. (Preface by Simone de Beauvoir.)

The year after this book was published the laws pertaining to divorce in France were changed. This book documents the difficulties entailed in obtaining a divorce in France until just recently. It dramatically portrays the many obstacles one young woman encountered in ending her marriage.

The dossier for the "Affaire C/C" included incriminating documents of the husband's debauchery, medical certificates attesting to the traumatic effects of his behavior on the older daughter, then not yet two, and the knife he used to terrorize his wife. However, it was only her abject physical appearance that gave Claire C. the legal document necessary to leave the "conjugal domicile" with her two young daughters. Had she left without this authorization, she would have been guilty of "deserting the home" and a divorce might not have been possible.

The remainder of this long, sordid account tells of the years of effort and expense entailed in trying to collect the pension the court initially awarded her. Her husband, son of a banker, had ample means. Yet he persisted in trying to evade his obligations; he even tried to bribe her lawyers. Fortunately for the harassed young woman, there were heroes as well as villains among the legal figures she dealt with.

French logic determined that divorce by mutual consent was not possible. If the couple could "agree," that negated the need for divorce. Such was the thinking that prevailed until just a few years ago. According to the law that originated in 1804 or earlier, was abolished in 1816 only to be reinstated in 1884, a husband could only be charged with adultery if he installed the mistress in the conjugal domicile, something few men would undertake. But Claire's husband did, and this fact--rather than any of the more damaging charges, such as physical abuse--finally enabled her to obtain a divorce after years of prolonged effort.

Simone de Beauvoir notes in the preface that this husband was more tyrannical, sadistic, and neurotic than most. Nevertheless, the case, however extreme, is salutory. It demonstrates the fallaciousness of views such as "a bad father is better than none," and it shows the shortcomings and contradictions of the laws that governed divorce in France for some 100 years.

CHABAUTY, MARIE-LUCE. Les enfants de la maternelle [Nursery school children]. Paris: Centurion, 1979, 277 pp.

Nursery schools, les écoles maternelles, are a generally acknowledged French success story. In 1770 Pastor Oberlin set up "knitting schools" for the care of the children of the poor. These schools prospered. In 1837 they were formally recognized by the national Ministry of Public Education. By that time they had become charitable establishments where children of both sexes were given some initial schooling. In 1881 these schools were officially integrated into France's national primary education system by Jules Ferry.

All children between the ages of two and a half and primary school entry age, generally five, are accepted in écoles maternelles. There are no fees, and the personnel have the same training and salary scale as do teachers in elementary schools. By age four, virtually all French children are enrolled in these noncompulsory schools.

Marie-Luce Chabauty is an educator who has been a pedagogical counselor in Catholic Education for eighteen years. Her work is a practical guide designed to help teachers in the maternelles and to apprise parents of the qualities required of these teachers: imagination, conviction, and competence. The aim is to awaken the potential adult (le petit d'homme) in each child.

DANA, JACQUELINE. . . . et nous aurions beaucoup d'enfants [. . . and we would have many children]. Paris: Seuil, 1979, 240 pp.

Here Jacqueline Dana, a journalist and writer who has written a number of studies on children and families, addresses those men who decry France's low birthrate and reproach women for not having enough children (on average, 1.8 instead of the 2.1 deemed necessary). These men need to become more preoccupied with the society their potential descendants will occupy. They must also pay more attention to women's varying responses to motherhood, here represented in interviews with nonmothers as well as mothers. Motherhood provokes many responses: women may feel exalted or devoured, sublime or guilty. If men were more involved in French women's concerns then perhaps indeed they "would have many children."

La famille [The family]. Collection vivre demain. Paris: Hachette, 1975, 300 pp.

This sociological study explores the implications of the facts and figures available at the beginning of the 1970s. The French were marrying at a comparatively steady rate in spite of a changing society, and doing so at an earlier age. (The 1984 government report on the matrimonial status presented by Evelyne Sullerot indicates that the situation has changed dramatically, with fewer and fewer marriages.) The possibility of an increased aspiration toward "family happiness" is examined and the problem of reconciling this aspiration with the more and more "liberated" woman is raised. Graphs and statistics in this study were drawn up at the request of the French Planning Commission.

FLANDRIN, JEAN-LOUIS. Familles: parenté, maison, sexualité dans l'ancienne société [Families: kinship, houshold, sexuality in pre-Revolutionary society]. Paris: Hachette, 1976, 283 pp.

Historians long restricted their research to the public sphere. Today they are examining the private sphere as well. The respective rights and duties of husband and wife, their authority over their children, and the possibility of divorce and contraception or abortion have all become family affairs.

Jean-Louis Flandrin examines these issues in pre-Revolutionary French society, when the French king was viewed as the father of his subjects. The relation of parent and child often served as a model for political and social relations in liberal societies. Under the ancien régime, leading families such as those composed of relatives of Richelieu and Colbert played a major role in French political life. But what of the family as we understand the term today?

Flandrin considers the historical ambiguity of the term itself. A family may mean vertical descendants or horizontal extension, people linked by kinship or marriage. In France, lineage was more important among the privileged classes. For the rest of society, the family was a domestic group depending upon the father (père de famille).

In the seventeenth century, entire families, parents and children alike, frequently shared a common bed. The church became concerned about the morality of this situation. Flandrin also raises the question of why birth control spread in France a century earlier than it did in England. The author assumes that the higher rate of infant mortality in France--due in large measure to the custom of sending children out to wet nurses—made parents finally accept the responsibility implied by being a parent.

GROS, BRIGITTE. Les Paradisiennes [The women of/in Paradise]. Paris: Robert Laffont, 1973. 248 pp.

The initial section of this study of the lives of contemporary women living in large, modern apartment complexes (called cités in France) describes the building of one such complex in Meulan, a town twenth-five miles from Paris. The complex was named The Paradise, for it seemed to Brigitte Gros the realization of a dream for better housing for many. Gros undertook the project of building this paradise when she was elected mayor of Meulan in 1965 on the Union Républicaine d'Action slate.

Transposing dream to reality entailed many time-consuming steps through France's highly hierarchized administration. First the land had to be acquired. Endless delays and difficulties ensued. To get minimal telephone service meant going to higher authorities in Paris. Once the material problems had been more or less worked out and the families moved in, other, unforeseen problems arose. These problems form the major subject of the book.

French housewives in such housing complexes are cut off by distance from places of possible employment. Thus deprived of outside activities, they tend to consecrate all their time to minute, time-consuming domestic tasks. The author argues that this situation is detrimental to society as a whole, for these women's time could be more creatively and more usefully occupied. There is a further consequence of their situation: young women "condemned" to remain at home show an increased tendency to alcoholism, nervous breakdown, even suicide.

LARRIVE, HÉLÈNE. Les crèches: des enfants à la consigne? [Day-care centers: children in the checkroom?]. Paris: Seuil, 1978, 217 pp.

Crèches are state or private day-care centers for infants from six months to two and a half years. Hélène Larrive expresses her views on the problems still facing these centers. These views are based upon the author's three years' experience in using them for her own child.

Reality, Larrive points out, is not reflected by statistics. Statistics cannot measure the parental guilt that is aroused by leaving a very young child for eight hours a day or more. Yet the women who place their infants in crèches do not generally have any other alternative. Only working mothers are currently eligible for the state-funded centers; preference is given to those who are least-favored financially. This means, among other things, that only a limited socioeconomic group is served.

The personnel in these establishments is almost totally female and often poorly equipped and underpaid. This contrasts with the nursery schools, the écoles maternelles, which are part of the

national education system. More crèches must be built so that
women from all levels of society can have the option of using
day-care centers.

Several pages reproduce the official laws governing their
operation. Crèches are defined by law as places which "keep
during the day while their mothers work, healthy children under
three years of age." Thus the needs of the mother and her work
constitute the key factors for admission. Sick children who must
be kept home become a real and unpredictable problem for the
working mother.

LAUWICK, FRANÇOISE. Quelle drôle de veuve: chronique [What a
strange widow: a chronicle]. Paris: Flammarion, 1979, 175 pp.

Widows are victims of society's rejection. They need strong
character and health to confront the situation in which they find
themselves, be it in family battles, education of the children,
jealousy of other women, or attacks from the "exterior."

Widows cannot understand why they should be victims of such
treatment or why they should lose their interest when they lose
their husband. Is their life in society wholly dependent upon
having a man?; Can the absence of a man in their lives be responsible for so many problems? In this troubled and troubling
twentieth century others, including the young couple happy at the
moment, should consider the dimensions of the current problem in
France.

Françoise Lauwick speaks from personal experience. Psychologists contend that the loss of a spouse is the greatest loss in
life. That death reminds the survivors of their mortality,
further reinforcing the loss. Widows observe an apparent reversal of social values. Devotion to a dying husband is criticized by a society "allergic" to courageous acts. She was too
good: why did she become her husband's nurse, etc. French
widows tend to be discreet. They do not partake of group psychotherapy, as an increasing number of American widows do. The author recounts different situations and stories involving French
widows.

LEBRUN, FRANÇOIS. La vie conjugale sous l'ancien régime [Conjugal
life under the ancien régime]. Paris: Armand Colin, 1975,
179 pp.

A good general introduction to the recent scholarship on the
family in pre-Revolutionary France, this study draws upon many
sources including folklore. Marriage ceremonies are described.
In some areas of France, the bride was dressed by her attendants
in garments such as a long tablier, or apron, symbol of household occupations. Wedding songs spell out the uncertainty of
the newly married girl who is "linked" until death. "Who says
my husband,/often says my master."

Scrutiny of the records of civil trials for separation offers
precise evidence of what conjugal difficulties were in pre-Revolutionary France: the husband's brutality (often linked to

alcoholism), financial complaints, and so forth. The legal formula defined a married woman as "so and so, wife and under the authority of so and so." The husband imposed his name, dwelling, and social and financial condition, in addition to his authority over the children, the finances, and related matters. Legally women passed from the tutelage of their father to that of their husband. However, as this study shows, reality was somewhat more nuanced.

The Catholic church attempted to regulate sexual behavior. But records of illegitimate births noted in parish records show that the church tenets were not always observed. In certain parishes in Brittany the entry was made upside down, as a sign of reprobation. Illegitimate births were often the result of broken promises of marriage or of the seduction of servants by their masters. There was total social, legal, and cultural subordination of the "guilty" woman, but not of her partner. Rather than view these statistics for illegitimate births as a sign of the growing "dechristianization" of French society, as some have suggested, Lebrun sees them as graphic illustrations of the inferior condition of women.

The absence of the most elementary precautions for infants (for example, taking them to church for baptism, whatever the distance or weather) appears in retrospect to have been a more or less implicit form of birth control. Growing numbers of abandoned children--Rousseau's five are the best-known example-- were seen among the favored as well as the poor. Lebrun argues that just at the time that there was a tendency to focus on the nuclear family, economic, constraints made smaller families necessary. A growing interest in raising the child, noted from about 1760 on, accompanied the trend toward fewer children.

MÉTRAL, MARIE-ODILE. <u>Le mariage: les hésitations de l'Occident</u> [Marriage: the hesitations of the West]. Paris: Aubier-Montaigne, 1977, 320 pp. (Introduction by Philippe Ariès.)

In this study of the institution of marriage, Marie-Odile Métral uses the scriptures, the writings of the church fathers, and literature. Her approach incorporates structural and deconstructivist presentations and references to feminists theoreticians.

Study of the early church confirms what today's Catholics do not always realize, that from its very beginning the church has maintained a critical attitude toward sexuality. Christianity was the first religion to consider virginity desirable, to make it divine, following Christ's example. This preference for virginity led to placing marriage in tutelage. Phillipe Ariès tempers the author's views by pointing out that in early days the church's influence did not in fact extend to many rural communities. Roman law still prevailed. Popular Christian customs did not necessarily coincide with the views of the clerical elite.

Ariès approves of Métral's description of l'amour courtois, the passionate love lauded by the troubadours. By nature adulterous, the woman chose and conducted the relationship in courtly love. The woman "merited" love and her pleasure was central. This courtoisie contrasted with chivalry, which excluded love. Courtly love is seen as doubly compensatory, compensating the woman qua woman and the man, generally of a socially inferior rank.

According to Métral, a "Thomistic tour de force" takes place with St. Thomas. Pleasure is restricted and love neutralized in marriage. Until the end of the ancien régime, reserve characterized marriage. Lack of privacy was probably a factor, as was the growing concern with birth control. The nineteenth century is credited with introducing passionate love into marriage iself. The family has come to provide social and productive cohesion. How will this be reconciled with an apparent decrease in true sociability? Recent surveys, such as that of L. Roussel for INED, show that the links between French parents and their married children are still strong. The author contends that the institution of marriage is undergoing many changes. The hidden and paradoxical nature of the recent alliance of marriage with the couple must be understood to comprehend these changes.

MICHEL, ANDRÉE. Activité professionnelle de la femme et vie conjugale [Women's professional activity and conjugal life]. Paris: Éditions de la CNRS, 1974, 190 pp.

One of France's leading sociologists, Andrée Michel, who has written extensively on women and the family for the past twenty-five years, here presents the results of a 1966 survey of families from Paris and Bordeaux.

French women, she maintains, work outside the home more than do their American counterparts. This is due to sheer economic necessity. The survey found that the vast majority of French women choose marriage for spiritual considerations: love, companionship, and understanding. The nineteenth-century marriage of family interests found in the novels of Balzac is very much on the decline. Today's French family no longer represents the alliance of two patrimonies.

Among the areas analyzed by Michel in this report are: decision making and its relation to a woman's professional status; the effects of career on marital satisfaction; and the life-style of a family in which the woman works. The findings are then compared to studies made in several other countries.

PILLORGET, RENÉ. La tige et le rameau: familles anglaise et française, 16e-18e siècles [The trunk and the branch: English and French families in the sixteenth-eighteenth centuries]. Paris: Calmann-Lévy, 1979, 324 pp.

This comparative history traces the development of the family in France and England during three centuries. The author maintains that these two nations shared many common features in earlier times and only began to differ substantially in the mid-eighteenth century. Demographic evidence from both nations is utilized by Pillorget to show how two peoples with a common range of problems and values made their respective families both the recipients and laboratories of their virtues and vices and how in adopting particular solutions, they developed national characteristics.

In France, as in England, the modern family prolonged the hopes of the Middle Ages by transforming them. The family became the core of society, a unity of production, consumption, procreation, and education. The family transmitted the patrimony from generation to generation, endeavoring to both maintain the lineage and enrich it. Family clans evolved throughout this period, developing into households. Conjugal love manifested itself. In the second half of the eighteenth century there was a veritable crisis in society, reflected in families.

PITROU, AGNÈS. La famille dans la vie de tous les jours [The family in everyday life]. Toulouse: Privat, 1972, 220 pp.

Between 1968 and 1970, over seven hundred people were questioned about their daily family lives. The results of this survey offer some idea of the manner in which women's work--in and out of the home--is viewed.

RIBEAUD, MARIE-CATHÉRINE. Les enfants des exclus [The children of the excluded]. Paris: Stock, 1976, 255 pp. (Written with the teams of Science and Service.)

Marie-Cathérine Ribeaud, a psychologist concerned with the marginals in French society, here examines the children from the poorest milieus--the "under" proletariat, many of whom come from non-French backgrounds. Thorough research, she says, must be undertaken to understand the motivations of these women. In the past, campaigns to implement conventional family planning methods have failed, presumably because they were based upon French assumptions and traditions. She insists that family planning efforts in these groups, if they are to succeed, must be targeted at the subculture. The early and repeated pregnancies in these groups, accompanied by childhood spent under difficult conditions, accentuate this need.

_____. La maternité en milieu sous-prolétariat [Motherhood at the lowest socioeconomic levels]. Paris: Stock, 1979, 278 pp.

As the title indicates, this work--part of the author's efforts to study French poverty--describes the situation and views of the economically least favored women who are mothers. Many of these women are mères de familles nombreuses, that is, mothers of large families. This can be attributed to some extent to the economic benefits parents receive for additional children as part of France's longstanding natalist policy. This study helps explain why many poor women are virtually permanently confined, in the several meanings of the term.

The approach is psychological, not statistical. A representative group of twenty-three women ranging from twenty-four to fifty years old was interviewed. The main social unit in this group is that of mother and child. The majority of these women came from large families themselves, hence as they grew up their role model was a mother with many children. Most had to assume heavy familial responsibilities while still young and most had little information in sexual matters. They had been plunged into the world of adult sexuality while still young. The author observes that the interviewees tend to be passive and fatalistic, with a fatalism that equates the future of girls with marriage and children.

SEBBAR, LEÏLA. On tue les petites filles [Little girls are being killed]. Paris: Stock, 1978, 357 pp.
   Until the women's movement there were few studies of the violence inflicted upon young girls. Since the 1976 Trial of Crimes Against Women held in Brussels, however, attention has been focused on the problem. This book is a catalogue of the mistreatment, abuse, and violence suffered by young girls under the age of fifteen in the decade 1967-77. This is difficult but necessary reading. The violence many women underwent as young girls has profoundly affected their lives and their understanding of sexuality. According to Sebbar, children have more to fear from those they know--family, especially stepfathers, relatives, and friends--than they do from the typical child molester depicted in the early twentieth century by Krafft-Ebing. Some of Leïla Sebbar's extensive documentation comes from police and social services reports, but most comes from the voluminous correspondence addressed to Menie Grégoire through her national talk show.

_____. Le pédophile et la maman: l'amour des enfants [The paedophile and the mother: the love of children]. Collection voix des femmes. Paris: Stock, 1980, 301 pp.
   Mother, teacher, journalist, and feminist involved with two feminist publications, Sorcières and Histoires d'elles, Leïla Sebbar was prompted to write this book because of the silence of the French women's movement on this central subject, children. Discussion focuses on the problems of birth control, abortion, and child care. She argues that virtually nothing was being published on women's feelings toward children, an extremely important subject that should be examined. Areas explored in this volume include childhood, its representation, and the love of and desire to have children.

VILLAIN, PIERRE. 130,000 familles prennent la parole [130,000 families speak out]. Paris: Cerf, 1973, 210 pp.
   Selected responses from the extensive survey undertaken by the weekly La Vie catholique are used to investigate new aspects of family life in France. In Catholic milieus the parent-child link

is still very important, yet today some of the young are attracted to the idea of communities. This is a new phenomenon among French Catholics. Current difficulties in today's family include reconciling individual liberty and familial authority. One woman summed it up by pointing out that in the old days one said "I am marrying my daughter." Today one says "my daughter is getting married."

These recent findings also indicate changing mores in the realm of sexuality. Even in Catholic circles premarital relations are viewed as virtually inevitable. Abortion remains a painful and controversial topic. (The survey took place when the law on abortion was being discussed.) On balance, it would appear that Catholic attitudes do not differ so significantly from those of non-Christians or nonbelievers.

This survey is compared with one of several thousand adults and youth done by the Institut Français d'Opinion Politique (IFOP), a survey focusing on family relations, authority and liberty, and marriage and sexuality. Data from both surveys complete the volume.

*COHEN, SUZY. Les crèches [Day-care centers]. Paris: Éditions Sociales, 1979, 226 pp.

*GUITTON, JEAN. La famille, l'amour, et le démon du midi [The family, love, and the demon of the heyday of life]. Collection foi vivante. Paris: Aubier-Montaigne, 1971, 125 pp.

The prolific Catholic author Jean Guitton, a member of the French Academy, touches upon divine and worldly love. The principal focus is on parent and child, but aspects of love among other members of the family are also covered.

*HASSOUN, JACQUES. Entre la mort et la famille, l'espace crèche [Between death and the family, the day-care center]. Paris: Maspero, 1973, 111 pp.

The author, a psychiatrist attached to the Bureau of Maternal and Infant Protection (PMI), subtitles his work "History of the tribulations of a psychoanalyst in a departmental crèche and of what he viewed of the misery of the salaried worker and that of the child caught in a system of necessity."

*SALTIEL, MICHÈLE, and ÉVELYNE SULLEROT. Les crèches et les équipements d'accueil de la petite enfance [Day-care centers and the equipment needed for young children]. Paris: Hachette, 1974, 250 pp.

Women in French Society

EDUCATION AND SEX ROLES

BASTIDE, HUGUETTE. Insitutrice de village [Village school teacher]. Paris: Mercure de France, 1969. Reprint. Collection femme. Paris: Denoël/Gonthier, 1973, 184 pp.

This is an account of the difficulties faced by a young woman of modest background in southwest France when her husband was called up for military service. (Conscription is required of all French males, although marriage and dependents sometimes permit deferment of service.) Unlike many working-class parents, Huguette Bastide's family had encouraged her to pursue an education. After the birth of her first child, she undertook the demanding baccalauréat, a degree necessary for virtually any professional occupation in France. Subsequently she prepared the certificates needed to serve as a substitute teacher so that with her husband's departure, she could provide for herself and her child. To Bastide, paid work represented more than just financial necessity; she needed it for intellectual and emotional development.

The rest of Huguette Bastide's story is an indictment of the treatment of teachers who are sent into isolated areas to take charge of one-room schools, sometimes under the most primitive conditions. She criticizes the closed nature of an educational system that teaches routine rather than methods and history books which focus mainly on wars and colonization. Nothing is said of the portrayal of women in these texts: this only became a concern of French feminists in the 1970s.

In addition to exposing the shortcomings of the French national education system, this book documents the life of a young French woman trying to balance her roles of housewife and civil servant in the years preceding the events of 1968. The conditions of village school teachers Bastide describes have recently been modified by the rural population's accelerated exodus to the cities. This has meant the end of many hamlets such as the one in which Bastide taught.

BÉDRINE, NICOLE, RÉGINE LILENSTEIN, and CLAUDE-ROSE TOUATI. Idées reçues sur les femmes [Preconceived notions about women]. Anthologie de l'humour involontaire. Paris: Hier et Demain, 1978, 189 pp.

From Saint Thomas, Diderot, and Balzac to contemporaries such as politician Jacques Chirac, current mayor of Paris, and singer Jacques Brel, men have uttered ridiculous statements about women. This anthology of their remarks is in the tradition of the medieval sottisier, that is, a collection of stupid sayings. A number of pertinent advertisements are reproduced.

CHOMBART de LAÜWE, MARIE-JOSÉ, and CLAUDE BELLAN. Enfants de l'image [Children of the image]. Paris: Payot, 1979, 295 pp.

Although this book is not restricted to the image of women transmitted to young girls, it nevertheless contains much on that topic. Images in children's literature, especially in illustrated books, in comic strips such as Tin-Tin, and in cinema and television are studied. The authors employ an interdisciplinary approach in their psychosociological study of childhood. The book also contains a good bibliography on the topic.

Media plays an important part in children's socialization, hence the importance of the image. The authors note that portrayals of the activities of young girls today more closely resemble those of boys. In this process of equalization, the role of sex has become profoundly ambiguous--perhaps at the risk of loss of identity. One visible result of the trend towards equality has been that fewer and fewer girls' publications are produced. French girls now prefer reading boys' periodicals. Questionnaires reveal the role of appearance in choice of heroes. Girls favor richer descriptions with emphasis on the physical appearance of the character.

COLLANGE, CHRISTIANE. Madame et le bonheur [Madame and happiness]. Paris: Robert Laffont, 1972, 227 pp.

From her journalism and daily, hour-long radio program, "Women's Actuality," Christiane Collange discovered the silent majority. They are the sixty percent of French women who see themselves as happy (according to a 1970 survey of Elle magazine) and who have difficulty in accepting this state.

Collange points out that happy women feel they are not "normal." While the notion that most women are happy is not one that many feminists would readily accept, Collange believes that the positive must be recognized.

She argues for a rehabilitation of féminitude. To bring this about, education is central. The French still bring up boys according to Jesuit precepts of the eighteenth century. They are instilled with a sense of competition, a respect for logic, and a love of order and discipline. This being the case, parents must take a greater part in their children's education than does the state. Boys must be taught to assume more domestic tasks at home, just as young girls are now entering into occupations once reserved for males.

DECROUX-MASSON, ANNIE. Papa lit, maman coud [Papa reads, mama sews]. Paris: Denoël/Gonthier, 1979, 160 pp.

The distorted image of women in school texts has been the subject of a number of recent studies. Here, school texts from twenty primary schools arbitrarily chosen from different regions, rural as well as urban, were examined. The major finding is predictable: woman equals mother and housewife.

Gender, so basic to French grammar, is one of the first lessons children receive. In school books the masculine is symbolized by a young boy, a cock, or a book, indicative of intellectual endeavors. The feminine is represented by a young girl, a chicken, sometimes a pot or kitchen implement; domestic duties are designated. And so forth. (The authors indicate that virtually all the publishing firms contacted refused to allow reproduction of illustrations that would have graphically underlined the points made.)

These school texts have been reprinted year after year, generation after generation, without changes. Single-parent families are never presented, nor are working mothers or fathers helping at home. As the title indicates, stereotypes prevail. Mother is never accorded an extrafamilial life. When the possessive form is studied, women are given physical attributes, men, strength and intellectual prowess.

FALCONNET, GEORGES, and NADINE LEFAUCHEUR. La fabrication des mâles: du sexisme ordinaire aux pièges de la libération sexuelle [The fabrication of males: from ordinary sexism to the traps of sexual liberation]. Paris: Seuil, 1975, 205 pp.

In this essay Georges Falconnet and his collaborators point out how women are taught to be passive, patient, quiet, and resigned. French society seeks, hence teaches, different roles and values for the two sexes. How men view themselves and how they formed their ideas about women are but two of the questions posed.

The book has three major divisions: Power and possession; private life; and the formation and reproduction of the masculine ideology. Traditional men are found to be threatened by women's sexual, economic, and legal emancipation. This holds for such legislation as the recent reforms on responsibilities of parents. They are attached to their masculine "nature," to masculine rights. Many of these French males are concerned about losing their "superiority." Women are a masculine accessory--according to the various ads included. Many men approve of abortion but not contraception. This paradox may be explained by the fact that the latter permits greater sexual liberty for women.

In L'enfant et la vie familiale sous l'ancien régime (1960), Phillipe Ariès underscored the emphasis on the mastery of self in boys' education. From the seventeenth century on, this is seen as distinguishing men from women. Masculine education is completed by military service, an experience women do not share.

FLAMANT-PAPARATTI, DANIELLE, and EMMANUELLE. Emmanuelle ou l'enfance au féminin [Emmanuelle or childhood in the feminine]. Paris: Denoël/Gonthier, 1979, 187 pp. (Preface by Elena Gianini Belotti.)

Danielle Flamant-Paparatti recounts one French woman's efforts to give her daughter a nonsexist education. This project was complicated by the fact that the father is Italian and the child's first years were spent in Sicily, in an environment more provincial and peasant than that of France.

The mother is determined that her daughter's education not repeat the traditional one she received. Emmanuelle is encouraged to reflect, rebel, question everything. The child's comments and observations are interpolated into her mother's diary. Efforts at encouraging the young girl to question and, if need be, to reject traditional values are reinforced by the militant political stance of the family.

LAÏK, MADELEINE. Fille ou garçon [Girl or boy]. Paris: Denoël/Gonthier, 1976, 319 pp. (By a team of analysts and researchers, with the collaboration of Annette Roïc.)

In most cases children seek the answers to questions about their identity from adults. Here the process has been reversed. The aim was to find out what young children knew about their origins and the differences in the sexes, and to examine how sexual discrimination takes root in childhood. It attempts to define the boundaries in children's concepts of masculine and feminine.

The study contrasts the perceptions of a group of children aged five to eight--how they talk about themselves and how they view themselves--with the views of the researchers themselves. a young team of sociologists and psychologists. The team determined that traditional research methods were unsatisfactory. They further found that analysis of children's perception of sexual identity brought into question their own sexual repressions and condition. While the work offers many suggestions and ideas, there are no formal conclusions and no theories are promulgated. The volume consists primarily of excerpts from interviews with children and the researchers' observations on children.

MAYEUR, FRANÇOISE. L'éducation des filles en France au XIXe siècle [The education of girls in nineteenth-century France]. Paris: Hachette, 1979, 208 pp.

Here, the historical scope of Françoise Mayeur's earlier study (q.v.) is extended. She outlines the development of women's education in the century that saw the most changes in that domain. In the early nineteenth century the view prevailed that education for women was a private matter and one of little consequence. Toward the end of the century, the subject became the center of a national battle between the liberals and anticlericals on the one hand, and the church, aligned with a basically conservative establishment, on the other. The church feared the entry of women into public life and wished to continue its long-held control over the instruction of girls. Women became the pawns in one phase of the struggle between the forces of the republic and those of the ancien régime.

In the early nineteenth century, two types of primary education were offered to young girls: that of religious institutions and that done with mothers' assistance. The many titles on this topic, such as Mme Tastu's Éducation maternelle, simples leçons d'une mère à ses enfants (1836; 7th ed. 1869), attest to this less-known "mother's instruction." Most education, however, was offered by religious orders; many were formed expressly for that purpose. In 1820 the Bourbon restoration dispensed the religious sisters from taking the exams required of school mistresses. Their vow of obedience to the convent was thought sufficient. Eventually the lack of qualifications of many of these religious teachers became one of the chief targets of those who advocated lay control of girls' education. The latter argued that religious institutions stressed piety and rote learning to the detriment of competence, and that they did not encourage intellectual inquiry.

When state elementary schools were set up, the school mistresses led a heroic life not unlike those of missionaries. With teaching certificates their salaries were still half those of cooks or domestic servants.

In the second half of the century, the principal spokesman for the church on the matter of female instruction was Monseigneur Dupanloup, Bishop of Orléans. He wanted girls to continue to be educated "on the knees of the church." They were not to be "thrown into the arms of humanity at a base price." He insisted that women be better educated so that they could refute freethinkers and inculcate moral and religious values into their children, and, indirectly, into their husbands as well. Any proposal for lay education was perceived as an attempt to destroy the faith. When Victory Duruy attempted to introduce lay secondary education for girls in the late 1960s, he was vilified. Dupanloup opposed his efforts. Pastoral letters, economic boycotts, and various pressures were utilized to discourage parents from enrolling daughters in Duruy's first lay secondary courses.

Jules Ferry delineated the issues in a famed speech of 1870. "Women must belong to knowledge (science) or to the church. Who holds women, holds all. First through the child, then through the husband, the older one who is fatigued or deceived by life." Neither group was concerned with women's education principally for its intrinsic merits or for its potential to advance women.

_____. L'enseignement secondaire des jeunes filles sous la Troisième République [Girls' secondary education under the Third Republic]. Paris: Presses de la Fondation Nationale des Sciences Politiques, 1977, 489 pp., and an extensive bibliography.

This dissertation is now the authoritative study of girls' secondary schooling in France. The work is designed around an institutional history of the École Normale Supérieure de Sèvres, founded in 1881 to train secondary level women teachers. Mayeur details the legislation initiating this state education.

Setting up this system was one of the main achievements of the Third Republic, known as the Republic of Professors. In 1880 the Camille Sée law established state secondary schools for girls in France. To implement the Sée law, lycées were built, beginning with the Lycée Fénélon of 1883, to provide state secondary education for women. Curriculum centered on the humanities;

there was little science and no Latin. This was consistent with
the long-held French view that education should be in harmony
with social position and the life one would lead. Education was
not seen as a means of advancement and rising above one's parents was not favored. It was assumed that young ladies of the
upper levels of society would never work.

What happened was that the "new classes," the petite and
moyenne bourgeoisie, took fullest advantage of this educational
opportunity. They saw it as a chance to provide their daughters
with a livelihood in place of a dowry. Often there were no dowries; many did not marry at all. This new clientele was helped
by the free tuition granted children of fonctionnaires (civil
servants) and the scholarships some municipalities offered worthy
but needy candidates.

At first, growth was slow in the state secondary schools for
girls. Then there was a brisk acceleration in enrollment at the
turn of the century. On the eve of the First World War about
38,000 girls were enrolled. More and more found themselves
obliged to earn a living. They sought to enter not only the
liberal professions but also fields heretofore closed to them,
an aim aided by the shortage of men. Girls were eventually permitted to take the baccalauréat required for higher education.
Their separate program, however, did not provide the curricula
necessary to pass that exam. Reorganized in 1924, the programs
of the lycées for boys and girls became identical in 1937.

This study helps put women's achievements in France in context
by detailing the many difficulties they faced in order to obtain
an education. Further, it shows that for a long time girls'
education was more secondary than superior, terms used interchangeably during that period. Girls' education was "secondary"
to that of boys. Girls' needs and aspirations were secondary to
political, religious, and ideological concerns. The book also
makes a valuable contribution to understanding change in French
society by showing to what extent education is the product of
ideology. Françoise Mayeur contends that state secondary education did not play an important part in liberating women in France
for those working to found these schools had conservative aims.

PELLETIER, MADELEINE. L'éducation féministe des filles [The feminist
education of girls]. Paris: Syros, 1978, 175 pp. (Followed by
Le droit à l'avortement, La femme en lutte pour ses droits, la
tactique féminine, and Le droit au travail pour la femme. Preface, notes, and introductory materials by Claude Maignien.)

One of the most original of French feminist figures, Madeleine
Pelletier (1874-1939) came from very modest origins. At twelve
she left school but continued to pursue her studies, completing
those needed to obtain a medical degree. She was the first woman
doctor admitted to the concours des médecins des asiles, which
permitted work in mental wards. From participation in Freemasonry she went on to investigate anarchism and Russian nihilism. After the Russian revolution, she undertook a trip there on
her own.

Madeleine Pelletier's life was characterized by an abiding concern with social injustices, particularly those experienced by women. She was responsible for having the Socialist party adopt the principle of rights for women in 1905, though the party subsequently did little to support her efforts to acquire such rights. In 1939 she was charged with the crime of abortion, and interned in an asylum where she died a few months later. Throughout her life she wrote pamphlets and brochures. They are often undated and difficult to find. Fortunately the Bibliothèque Marguerite Durand holds many of her works. This volume reissues several of these works.

ROCHEBLAVE-SPENLÉ, ANNE-MARIE. Les rôles masculins et féminins [Masculine and feminine roles]. 2d ed. Paris: Éditions Universitaires, 1970, 535 pp. (First published in 1964.)
 The conclusions of this study are based upon findings about families of engineers living in France, England, and Germany. Viewed by both men and women, the French male is seen as having a taste for theoretical ideas, an aptitude for mathematics, and the gift of leadership. He is sure of himself, combative, creative, and domineering. The French woman appears as capricious, coquettish, possessing a gift for arranging her appearance and her outfits and being intuitive and frivolous. These findings are in striking contrast to the ideal characteristics French women want for themselves: affirmation of self, affectivity, and intellectual qualities.

*CHABAUD, JACQUELINE. Education et promotion de la femme [Education and advancement of women]. Paris: UNESCO, 1970, 157 pp.

*L'image de la femme dans les manuels scolaires [The image of women in school texts]. Paris: Institut National de la Recherche et de la Documentation Pédagogique, 1975.

RELIGION

AUBERT, JEAN-MARIE. La femme: anti-féminisme et christianisme [Woman: antifeminism and Christianity]. Paris: Cerf-Desclée, 1975, 224 pp.
 Theologian Jean-Marie Aubert offers a Catholic (male's) view of the relations between Christianity and women. He recognizes that the church remains one of the last bastions of masculine hegemony and that women are not full-fledged members of the church. Accordingly, he urges understanding and appreciation of the forces of tradition, customs, and the Gospels. The principal ideological justifications for antifeminism and women's putative inferiority are reviewed. These views are real even though the

resulting discrimination is frequently held to be unconscious. The "true" causes of this traditional antifeminism--demographic, sociocultural, and psychological--are discussed. The hope is that some day Christian antifeminism will be a thing of the past.

Aubert does not see the advent of the woman-priest. This is due in part to historical forces and the traditional image of women that evolved in Western civilization. In its early days of stuggle, the church had to prohibit female participation in the celebration of services because there were priestesses in the pagan cults the church was trying to eradicate. A possible end to this historical discrimination against women may come about when all take up the injunction to "become one with Christ" (Gal., 3:28).

BAKER, CATHÉRINE. Les contemplatives, des femmes entre elles [The contemplatives, women living apart]. Paris: Stock, 1979, 460 pp.

A lengthy inquiry into the lives of a small group of religious women, those who have chosen the contemplative life and renounced the world, may not seem relevant to today's feminist concerns. And yet these women are active in a very real sense. Independent and rebellious, they share with the militants of today a desire to change the world as it now exists. In the course of her converations with 130 women in seventy different convents--convents with differing rules, rituals, and activities--the young atheist author found that she was deeply moved by these encounters. Still, she cannot forgive the Catholic church for having been so profoundly misogynist.

To those concerned with women's efforts to find a language proper to women, the modes of expression of women who live in a world without men are of particular interest. Cathérine Baker judges the impact of the women's movement in France by the fact that these women in isolation are aware of its existence: they discuss the implications both for themselves and for society. She notes that there are fewer differences today between the contemplative orders. All seem to share a joy in contemporary efforts to return to the monastic simplicity of former times and a renewed and intensified study of Holy Scripture.

BOUYER, LOUIS. Mystères et ministères de la femme [Mysteries and ministries of woman]. Paris: Aubier-Montaigne, 1976, 108 pp.

Catholic apologist Louis Bouyer adds his observations to the growing controversy over whether or not women should be priests. For the author, the views expressed in this debate frequently reveal a profound uneasiness with the Judeo-Christian heritage. He examines the Jewish heritage, one not all that familiar to French Catholics.

Bouyer maintains that the equality of women in religion would lead to their "masculinization." This would entail a loss of what is "feminine." The mystery of God implies the mystery of woman. Man needs woman to meet God. Further, God appears as the Father, therefore He has masculine attributes. People see God as the Spouse. There are precedents for a female diaconate (though not female priests), with women who had brought up their children in Christian fashion admitted to it. The educative mission of women should be considered an apprenticeship, a form of ministry.

FRUCHET, HÉLÈNE. La femme dans la vie et dans l'Église [Woman in life and in the church]. Paris: Éditions du Senèvre, 1972, 92 pp.

A historical survey starting with the Middle Ages is followed by summaries of women and work (mainly drawn from Sullerot). There are observations on the role of the church in women's lives. Women are the more numerous sex among the faithful. The author points to the "admirable" feminism that flourished in praise of the Virgin Mary during the High Middle Ages. Other holy women are described in an effort to refute the claim of de Beauvoir and others that the church has been a "source of oppression for women."

Fruchet admits that many French women resent the Catholic church's exclusively masculine priesthood and its highly hierarchical organization. Nevertheless women must continue their important contribution to resolving the many moral dilemmas one faces today. Reflecting traditional Catholic values, the book concludes with a chapter on the most highly esteemed women, the religious, "authentic" women who are, the author argues, the most feminine in the fullest sense of that word. They have given themselves wholly to God. Further information may be found in:

> MOLETTE, CHARLES [Abbé], ed. Guide des sources de l'histoire des congrégations féminines françaises de vie active [Guide to sources for the history of French female congregations in the "active life"]. Paris: Éditions de Paris, 1974.

LECLERQ, JACQUES. La femme: aujourd'hui et demain [Woman: today and tomorrow]. Paris and Tournai: Casterman, 1968, 134 pp.

With Imprimatur approval, Jacques Leclerq, author of many religious books, sets forth the orthodox Catholic position of the late sixties. At that time, changes in the situation of women were becoming increasingly visible. Jean XXIII's Encyclical Pacem in Terris is taken as the starting point. There are those who claim that the world is in difficulty today because it is ruled exclusively by men. God's wish, however, is for all to serve Him. He does not want women to serve men. The problem of women-priests is not viewed as a question of doctrine. The Holy Spirit will show the way.

Politics, Law, and Crime

The fact that France was one of the last Western nations to award women the vote is not well known. It was the result of a long, arduous battle that did not culminate until 1944. Women first voted the following year. Among the many arguments brought forth in opposition to women's suffrage at various times, some presented the idea that women were but pawns of the church; that they were not politically "sophisticated"; and that the vote would compromise their "mission in life," that is, home life. French society has been historically structured around the family, and the family has been centered around the father.

The long, laborious efforts required by French women to obtain the right to vote exemplifies the struggle to obtain civil and political legal reforms. Details on these efforts are set forth in the introductory essay.

What do French women want now? The platform of the movement Choisir la Cause des Femmes for the March 1978 elections—which appropriates many of the measures first sought by the Secretariat of the Feminine Condition under Françoise Giroud—and the more recent report of the Ministry of the Rights of Women under Yvette Roudy, <u>Les femmes en France dans une société d'inégalités</u>, both indicate that French women have not acquired full equality.

The preamble to the Constitution of 1946, reinforced by the Constitution of the Fifth Republic of 1958, maintains that women are guaranteed rights equal to men in all domains. That is the theory; practice is another matter. The Civil Code still retains inequalities. They are linked, almost exclusively, to women's domestic situation as wife and mother. The misogyny of the old Civil Code was epitomized by the notorious Article 1124 which deprived minors, married women, and the insane of their legal rights. This law was in effect until the end of 1942. Two years earlier the Vichy regime had passed an even more restrictive law excluding married women from working in the public sector. The Civil Code has made it extremely difficult for women to participate fully in their society. Until quite recently married women could not even open a bank account without their husband's written consent. In most marriages of the past, the property was the husband's to dispose of as he saw fit—even if some of it was purchased with his wife's income.

Given the lack of autonomy the laws afforded them, it is not surprising that when women did finally receive the vote, their vote was more conservative. Until just recently married women--with the exception of professional couples, where political differences might be tolerated--tended to vote as did their husbands. The 1981 elections saw a dramatic change. Women had been moving more to the left in the last few years. It was in large measure the women's vote that brought about the election of a Socialist president and, subsequently, a Socialist parliament. Reforms have already been undertaken under the aggressive leadership of Yvette Roudy, who as minister has undertaken to inform women of their legal rights. Historically women have not been well apprised of laws that pertain to them. Dissemination of information is now helping make women equal with men. At the same time, while women are making their vote count, their presence in the actual political process is limited. Political power remains concentrated in male hands.

When women were first eligible to hold office in Parliament in 1946, forty women were elected among the 630 deputies. This proportion was higher than that in England or the U.S., countries where women for several decades had been eligible to vote and hold office. By 1962 there were only eight women deputies among 482, in 1978, nineteen. France now has a lower rate of female participation in Parliament than do its European neighbors. To change that record, quotas have been set up for the next elections.

There is an obvious disparity between the number of women active in political life and those in professional life. In this latter category, French women are well represented. Yet the two are inextricably linked. When women do become active in politics, they do so with intensity and spontaneity, as French history amply documents. Men tend to distrust these qualities.

Among the factors hindering women's fuller participation in political life are problems of available time and a lack of determination to become involved in politics. In the acquisition of and access to power, the masculine mode prevails. More fundamental and more profound are the attitudes of the sexes. Some women do not feel that the patriarchal political system permits them to express their views. Women are present in the major political parties as female party workers, not as feminists.

French women have been exercising political power in their own way through pressure groups. The most recent example is the campaign for contraception and abortion. These women's issues were largely ignored by the major parties. By publicly proclaiming that they had broken the law by undergoing abortions, by taking over trials to try <u>their</u> issues, women have brought their concerns about laws pertaining to them into the public forum.

Perhaps one of the remaining problems is the ambiguity of the term "political." For some it equals struggles for power. Women for the most part have had little interest in politics as it has been defined and practiced by men. Their notion is closer to that of Aristotle: government in order to pursue the common good of all citizens. To this end, women want to eradicate, not appropriate, power.

The major unresolved legal reform women seek is to change the concept of "head of the family," a situation that adversely affects married women. In 1970, following a long evolution, paternal authority gave way to parental authority, that is, joint authority, in theory. Yet the fiscal and social laws continue to retain the concept of "head of the family." Discussions to ameliorate the problem have been met with claims that the excessive work entailed in changing these provisions and the delays that would ensue would impede France's economic growth. It might severely "prejudice" the national economy. A top former government figure recently stated that it would be "dangerous" to brutally change legislation and do away with habits acquired over the centuries.

With the persistence of such attitudes, it is not surprising that French women continue their assault on discrimination. Their general goal is to bring about a nonsexist society in which men and women may live in dignity, fully exercising <u>all</u> their rights. As this book goes to press, the struggle continues.

Politics, Law, and Crime

POLITICS AND LAW

ASSOCIATION CHOISIR LA CAUSE DES FEMMES. Le programme commun des femmes [The joint program for women]. Paris: Grasset, 1978, 206 pp. (Presented by Gisèle Halimi with Andrée Michel and Geneviève Castre.)

Because politics is "something too serious to be left to men alone," Choisir organized a joint program drawn up by women from all social, educational, and professional backgrounds. The occasion was the 1978 legislative elections. Women needed to be informed about the parties that had endorsed Choisir's proposals. Among concrete, immediately applicable proposals were measures such as the establishment of a national fund to guarantee food pensions, equality of the sexes on juries, penal punishment for sexist discrimination, proportional representation in all elections, and a quota of women for leadership positions in all the political parties. The program offers a general view of French women's demands in the late 1970s.

BLANQUART, LOUISETTE. Femmes: l'âge politique [Women: the political age]. Paris: Éditions Sociales, 1974, 183 pp.

Early in her writing career Louisette Blanquart was a journalist for the Jeunesse Ouvrière Chrétienne. But, after spending some time working in a salaried position, she became active instead in the CGT (Confédération Générale du Travail), the Communist-oriented labor union. Subsequently she became editor-in-chief of Antoinette, the party's feminist publication. (The format of the magazine is similar to popular glossy women's magazines such as Elle and Marie-Claire, so too is much of the content, which has been a subject of criticism.) Since 1970 she has been the editor for domestic politics of L'Humanité, the Communist daily.

This experience in party publications and organizations provided Louisette Blanquart with the background to critique former president Giscard d'Estaing's establishment of a Secretariat of the Feminine Condition, as well as to answer the repeated charges that the Communists are antifeminist. Blanquart denounces a feminism that advocates women opposed to men, whom she considers women's companions and coworkers in the struggle against exploitation.

Consistent with the publications of the party publishing firm, Éditions Sociales, this book provides many statistics, along with personal testimony and documentation.

BRIMO, ALBERT. Les femmes françaises face au pouvoir politique [French women confront political power]. Paris: Montchretien, 1975, 123 pp.

Here is a concise summary of the topic up to the 1975 date of publication. Albert Brimo divides French feminists into three groups: 1) the Socialist-Feminists, who believe, following the tenets of Bebel, that women can be liberated only when the capitalist-patriarchal society changes into a Communist society. According to this group, the nuclear family reproduces the mechanics of social exploitation. To attain true freedom for women, society must collectively organize social services and child care and eliminate the existing patriarchal family. 2) The Liberationist-Feminists, who are linked to the Americans. They have been influenced by the works of Friedan, Millett, and Ware, as well as by Marcuse and Reich. 3) The Modernist-Reformist-Feminists who are, in the author's view, the most restrained and the most effective. Françoise Giroud is seen as their best representative. For this group there is no "women's problem," just the problem of society in general. Changes must come from within society through the modification of the relations of men and women on the economic, social, political, and sexual level.

Brimo does not wish to offer yet another history of French feminism, but seeks to examine the question of women's participation in French society. He believes the female electorate represents the key element in France's current political life (as since proved by the 1981 election of the Socialists, where the women's vote was a deciding factor). In a democracy, Brimo argues, power, like liberty, is open to all; women must have the courage and strength to exercise it. Democracy permits women to express themselves and to act in the public sphere. Like all revolutionary movements, the women's revolution is born of a current of ideas that cannot be stopped nor silenced.

CAUVIN, CLAIRE, and DOMINIQUE PONCET. Les femmes de Giscard [Giscard's women/wives]. Paris: Tēma, 1975, 149 pp.

The double entendre of the title reflects the tone of this work, an ironic and humorous presentation of the former French president's female appointments and political allies. The authors travelled to some of the candidates' fiefs to gather fellow townspeople's opinions. In other instances, they use comments from the media. Anecdotes and sarcastic observations abound. While some of this material can only be compared to the gossip columns of popular magazines, there are also basic outlines of these women associates' careers. The authors contend that, in spite of the additional numbers brought into political office, French women's political participation has not been as extensive as Giscard claimed.

CHARZAT, GISÈLE. Femmes, violence, pouvoir [Women, violence, power]. Paris: Jean-Claude Simoën, 1979, 271 pp.

Described as an essay in political anthropology, Charzat's study covers women of other times and other lands, as well as France. Several initial chapters are devoted to historical consideration of men's political oppression of women. The second part focuses on more recent times.

The French workers' movement, she argues, has remained fundamentally conservative throughout the twentieth century, for it is influenced by bourgeois ideology. Women of the upper bourgeoisie patronate receive an education that assures the continuity of their class values. Few pursue higher education: most devote themselves to charitable activities. Women in this class serve the French power structure, where homogamy is widely practiced. A 1967 survey of major company presidents showed that almost 60% married the daughters of patrons. Yet thus far, not a single woman of the upper-level group of executives has held a management position herself. There is a brief analysis of the political discourses of the major French political parties.

Charzat concludes that the only concept that responds to the profound aspiration of women--an exploited group--is that of instituting a society without masters. This is a new, revolutionary vision of a free and egalitarian society. Only a society without masters is capable of the revolutionary resolution required to accommodate the contradictions of capitalistic society. Family, work, the conditions of life, and politics will have to change together or they will not change at all, for they are inextricably linked.

_____. Les Françaises sont-elles des citoyennes? [Are French women citizens?]. Paris: Denoël/Gonthier, 1972, 202 pp.

This is a compact, useful, and inexpensive book that briefly traces the history of French women's political participation and their exercise of political power. Paradoxically, now that the long, difficult struggle to gain voting rights has been won, French women still remain "minors" in the sense that, though of age, their status recalls that of a minority group. The situation has changed somewhat since this was written. However, many women still do not participate actively in politics. Although dated, the graphs and statistics are concise and useful: the situation of French women at the beginning of the resurgent feminist movement of the 1970s is well documented.

Les communistes et la condition de la femme [The Communists and woman's condition]. Éditions Sociales, 1970, 172 pp. (A study by the French Communist party's Central Working Commission on Women, edited by Yvonne Dumont; this is a revised edition of La femme et les communistes [1950].

The pronouncements of Engels, Bebel, and Lenin on women are presented in a collection of texts that includes Maurice Thorez's speech of April 11, 1945 stating that "women want words to become acts." Other texts concern women and work, the Communists and the family, and women and socialism. These texts provide a selective historical overview of the party's position on these topics. The only woman included is Clara Zetkin, who offers her recollections of Lenin.

Politics, Law, and Crime

DARMON, PIERRE. Tribunal de l'impuissance: virilité et défaillances conjugales dans l'ancienne France [Tribunal of impotence: virility and conjugal nonperformance in pre-Revolutionary France]. Paris: Seuil, 1979, 315 pp.

Pierre Darmon traces the strange and little-known drama of those men brought before a judge in the name of the ancestral myth of virility. For centuries, nonconsummation of marriage was one of the few ways of evading the rule of its absolute indissolubility. Under Pope Gregory (1227-41), the church had formulated the doctrine that the sacrament of marriage required physical consummation. Until the sixteenth century, trials for impotence were decided on the basis of the proof of septima manus (the testimony of seven relatives, friends, or neighbors). This was found to be inadequate. Consequently, what had been a sober and serious undertaking took on a scabrous character as the trials became public. A wide public was attracted and a carnival air prevailed at times. These reactions provoked criticism. Nevertheless the proponents justified the trials on the grounds that since marriage is contracted in public, with great ceremony, the dissolution should also be public.

The most famous description of these trials is to be found in Saint-Simon's Memoirs. He details the 1713 trial, of the poor Marquis de Gesvres. The proceedings of these trials were published: songs and limericks ridiculing the unfortunates circulated. Both medical and religious experts participated in the investigations. Some "specialists" would seem to have had an obsession on the matter.

The public nature of these trials would appear to substantiate Michel Foucault's claim that sex was "brought into discourse" at the end of the sixteenth century (La volonté de savoir [1976]).

DHAVERNAS, ODILE. Droits des femmes, pouvoirs des hommes [Women's rights, men's powers]. Collection libre à elles. Paris: Seuil, 1978, 389 pp.

This feminist lawyer's critique is based in part upon her experience working with the legal group of the MLF, the Mouvement d'Action Judiciaire, a group dedicated to educating women about their rights and how to use them. Initial collaboration between militants and legal professionals proved impossible, so the women jurists concentrated on helping women in difficulty.

The first two sections of the book summarize French law on "family government" and "the duties of motherhood." Another section outlines fiscal discrimination against women and the problems of women in public activities. School, work, politics, and civic participation are also discussed.

Since formal equality does not constitute real equality, the author finds women are still disadvantaged. There is still discrimination, not only in the texts, but especially in their application. An official distinction in roles still exists, and considerable distance remains between the rights women have obtained and those their actual situation permits them to exercise.

Dhavernas considers the law permitting abortion to be the most important single legal achievement for French women in recent years.

Les femmes à la mairie: nous, conseillères municipales [Women at the town hall: we, the city councilwomen]. Paris: Éditions du Cerf, 1976, 126 pp.

French women could not vote until 1945, yet ways were found before that time to utilize their resources and talent. Beginning in 1935, a number of municipalities named women municipal councilwomen using a law which permitted the naming of adjunct counselors for their expertise. Villeurbanne was the first town to take this initiative. It was soon followed by Dax, Périgueux, Aix-en-Provence, Marseilles, Chambéry, and others. And, as the record of their achievements shows, these women counselors accepted significant duties and responsibilities as well as titles.

GIROUD, FRANÇOISE. Cent mesures pour les femmes [A hundred proposals for women]. Paris: Documentation Française, 1976, 196 pp.

Writer and journalist Françoise Giroud (b. 1916) is well known to Americans for her association with the news magazine Express. Several of her works, If I Lie, What I Believe, etc., have been translated into English. In 1974 Giscard d'Estaing appointed her to be the first secretary of state for the newly organized Secretariat of the Feminine Condition.

Here, Françoise Giroud sets forth the program for her secretariat. The first measure actually implemented was the creation of a commission to examine, revise, and control the materials used in teaching. To no one's surprise, their report showed a definite bias in the image of women in French school texts. Another measure theoretically made sex education obligatory. However, until recently there have been only timid and inadequate applications of this directive.

The 100 proposals follow the stages of a woman's life, her needs during youth, maturity, and old age. Analysis of those measures implemented shows that there have been substantial gains in some areas, such as work and legal status, but few in others. More day-care centers and better housing are required. Specific suggestions are included for the future construction of additional units of state-subsidized, low-cost housing (the HLM), such as minimum kitchen dimensions, etc.

MACCIOCCHI, MARIA A., ed. Les femmes et leur maîtres [Women and their masters]. Paris: Christian Bourgeois, 1978, 440 pp. (Texts from seminars held at Paris VIII Vincennes, assembled by Jacqueline Aubenas-Bastié.)

Two seminars on women's studies were held at Vincennes: "Fascism, subordination, and the struggle for women" in 1975-76 and "Marxism and feminism" in 1977-78. These were the first such offerings in this discipline. (The term "seminar" is somewhat misleading since there were from 100 to 300 attending.)

Emphatic political positions are buttressed by many citations from Marx, Lenin, and Stalin; the scope of the discussions is international.

As the preface indicates, the aim was to analyze how fascism has mystified women, utilizing their tacit consent and complicity. Under fascism, women are glorified in their family role, with the family the microcosm of the patriarchal state. Now women must make the difficult but necessary choice and liberate themselves from the one "subjugation" that endures, dogmatic Marxism. The feminist struggle in Europe has been absorbed in the past: first into the French, then Russian revolutions, more recently by fascism and capitalism.

Maria Macciocchi, a former Communist deputy from Naples now residing in France, maintains that women must go beyond auto-exaltation and aspire to an intellectual and moral feminist revolution.

MAUDUIT, JEAN, ed. Ce que les femmes réclament [What women want]. Paris: Fayard, 1971, 460 pp.

This volume contains the main documents drawn up for the assemblies of the Estates General of Women described below, and the remarks of principal discussants.

MAUDUIT, JEAN, and ANNE-MARIE RAIMOND. La révolte des femmes [The women's revolt]. Paris: Fayard, 1971, 460 pp. (Organized by Elle: Les États Généraux des Femmes, with the assistance of Marie-Françoise Leclerc and others.)

The secretary general sums up the results of the Estates General of Women organized by Elle magazine in November 1970 and April 1971. (In pre-Revolutionary France, Estates General were assemblies of representatives from the three estates summoned from time to time by the king. Women generally could not participate, although there were some exceptions.) The 1970 and 1971 Estates General of Women explored many themes, such as: Will women revolt tomorrow? Has a revolt already begun? Where will it end? These theoretical questions led to some conjecture but also brought out a good deal of fact. In preparation for the assemblies, national surveys were conducted. One finding was that few French women were aware of their rights under the law.

The main areas considered in these gatherings were sexuality, politics, and work, as well as urbanism and education. Mauduit also looks into the "masculine condition." The volume offers a general idea of French women's views on themselves and their problems as the decade of the 1970s opened.

RENARD, MARIE-THÉRÈSE. La participation des femmes à la vie civique [Women's participation in civic life]. Paris: Éditions Ouvrières, 1965, 175 pp.

Published several years before the decade of the 1970s, this volume contains useful summaries and statistics from that earlier period as well as statements and conclusions from a questionnaire soliciting women's attitudes toward civic participation. Several hundred women from various cities and towns responded to this survey.

ROUDY, YVETTE. La femme en marge [Woman on the periphery]. Paris: Flammarion, 1975, 240 pp.

Yvette Roudy has had a longstanding preoccupation with women's issues. In 1964 she translated Betty Friedan's The Feminine Mystique, a work which served as a catalyst for the emerging French women's movement of the late sixties. At present Mme Roudy is Minister Delegate to the Prime Minister for Women's Rights.

She argues that now that women are no longer confined to their "feminine condition," emphasis can be placed on rights. She calls for "positive" discrimination for women.

President François Mitterrand notes in the preface that it is women who are affected first and foremost by whatever crises arise in society, whether it is the right to work, the length and conditions of work, the difficulties of youth and old age, or the rise in prices.

Roudy maintains that women are still en marge, that is marginal, like children, the handicapped, the elderly. They play supporting rather than leading roles. Women are virtually absent from parliament, where their future is decided. She is currently working to change the situation she severely indicts here. Her case is built upon an impressive collection of facts and figures. This book had been republished with the accession of the Socialists to power.

SEMAINE DE LA PENSÉE MARXISTE. Les femmes aujourd'hui, demain [Women today, tomorrow]. Paris: Éditions Sociales, 1975, 388 pp.

These are the transcripts of some of the proceedings, speeches, and discussions of the week of Marxist Thought (January 29 through February 4, 1975). The theme of the debates, "Women today, tomorrow," was linked to the International Year of Woman. The topics discussed were the feminine condition; images and reality; professional work and work at home; woman and sexuality; woman, child, and the family; and democracy, socialism, and the promotion of women. In addition to French Communist party members, there were outside speakers including educators, journalists, and feminists. Françoise Parturier, Catherine Clément, Luce Irigaray, and Menie Grégoire were among those who spoke.

Political polemics frequently intrude into these lengthy discussions. But then a congress of over 11,000 does not really permit debate as the term is generally understood. The work offers the French Communist view of women's malaise today.

Information pertaining to recent French legislation affecting women is set forth in:

CHAMPION, JEAN. Les problèmes juridiques des femmes seules [Legal problems of single women]. Paris: Delmas, 1969, 296 pp.

DELAIS, JEANNE. Le guide blanc de divorce [The white guide on divorce]. Paris: Fayard, 1971, 256 pp.

DURCA-JOURNET, ISABELLE, and PAULETTE ISTIN-AULITE. La femme et ses nouveaux droits [Woman and her new rights]. Paris: Albin Michel, 1975, 320 pp.

GIROUD, FRANÇOISE, et al., and LA LIGUE POUR LE DROIT DES FEMMES. Les femmes et le droit social [Women and social law]. Paris: Éditions Techniques et Économiques, 1976, 123 pp.

Guide juridique et social de la femme seule: célibataire, séparée, divorcée, veuve [Legal and social guide for the single woman: unmarried, separated, divorced, widowed]. Paris: Néret, 1969, 129 pp.

GUIDICI, MAURICE. Le guide juridique et pratique de la femme [Woman's legal and practical guide]. Paris: N.O.F., 1971, 154 pp.

CRIME

Cahiers sur la femme et la criminalité [Papers on woman and criminality]. Paris: Éditions du CNRS, 1979, 192 pp.
 These articles are based upon a collective investigation undertaken by the Departments of Psychology, Sociology, and Political and Legal Sciences of the CNRS (National Center for Scientific Research). The aim of the project was to better understand the psychosocial function of women and their roles as authors, accomplices, instigators, contributors to and victims of crimes.
 In France, as elsewhere, there are far fewer female than male criminals; there are only a few thousand in prison. Young girls and women prisoners questioned were compared to control groups in society. One paper examines the relation of a group of young women to their mothers and then to their own children. Another paper focuses on the language women convicts use. Structural analysis of some of their linguistic enumerations reveals how women criminals both perceive and define themselves.

ERHEL, CATHÉRINE, and CATHÉRINE LEGUAY. Prisonnières [Women prisoners]. Collection voix des femmes. Paris: Stock, 1977, 280 pp.

Thus far few works have been devoted to studying and determining the concerns of women prisoners. Little was known of their "lives" in prison. The feminist movement, coupled with prison uprisings in 1974, finally brought some attention to this group. This volume offers the testimony of women serving time in various French prisons. Their experience is expressed in their argot or prison slang. The daily "domestic" routine is described. Supposed widespread homosexuality is found to be exaggerated. Prison activities are found to reinforce typical "feminine" behavior.

The study also includes an analysis of women's crimes: infanticides, child neglect, and crimes of passion. The perspective of the work is both leftist and feminist.

The literary expression of women prisoners is found in Albertine Sarrazin's Journal de prison (1972) and in her partially autobiographical novels that have appeared in English, The Runaway (1967) and Astragal (1967).

Women and Work

With the exception of a small and highly privileged group, women in France have always worked. There are descriptions of feminine professions in the <u>Livre des métiers</u> of the late Middle Ages. In the past women were responsible for nearly all textile production, for the making of clothes and various products, for supplying water, for heating and washing, and for the care and education of young children. All this was undertaken in addition to commercial activities.

Except for the shopkeepers and artisans, this work done by women was generally unseen: it was not thought of as "work" in the traditional sense. However, that situation changed when, with the advent of the industrial revolution, women started to work more outside the home. Initially women were employed in textile manufacturing[1]--such as the Lyonnais silk industry--and then, increasingly, as unskilled laborers in factories.

Women's new visibility at places of work provoked protests and concern. For Jules Michelet, the very word <u>ouvrière</u> (woman worker) was impious. Fears were expressed that children would suffer from their mother's prolonged absences; that women in the workplaces would be easy prey to sexual harassment; and, as <u>voleuses d'emploi</u>, that they would deprive men of the jobs they needed to support their families.[2] The same objections were heard some decades later when women attempted to enter the professions.

In the 1840s timid initial efforts were undertaken to regulate female and child labor. Yet at the same time, women's demands that their traditional employments be protected from male intrusion were ignored. Single, widowed, and divorced women were particularly affected by this double standard.[3]

Not only the bourgeoisie felt that women belonged at home. French working-class men and their powerful unions were long hostile to women workers. Until well into the twentieth century these men saw women as competitors, workers who would accept a lower salary and take away their jobs. They also objected to the deplorable conditions of a number of workshops and factories. So they too took up the call for the <u>femme au foyer</u>. The International Workers Conference held in Paris in 1867 declared: "in the name of the freedom of conscience, in the name of individual initiative, in the name of freedom of the mother, let us snatch her from the workshop that demoralizes and kills her. That woman you dream of freeing . . . her essential goal is to be a mother. A woman should remain at home: work must be forbidden to her."[4] In his classic study of the working women, <u>L'ouvrière</u> (1861), Jules Simon held that women should not be permitted to work in the manufacturing sector. Instead, they should produce at home. Government measures were to be enacted to help improve their lot.

Women were poorly represented, sometimes completely absent from the many union and labor congresses that took place in France in the last decades of the nineteenth, and into the twentieth centuries. But they were active. They participated in and at times led strikes. During the 1970s, women initiated many strikes, such as the one at Lip, detailed in the entries for <u>Lip au féminin</u> and Monique Piton's <u>C'est possible</u>. Strikes often seemed to be the only way women could obtain their demands. French unions have finally had to drop their paternalistic stance and make efforts to accommodate women union members and their grievances. Margaret Maruani's <u>Les syndicats à épreuve du féminisme</u> outlines the long, difficult relationship between trade-unionism and feminism. Another study on this topic is Marie-Hélène Zylberberg-Hocquard's <u>Féminisme et syndicalisme en France</u>.

It is not possible in a few paragraphs to outline adequately French women's long, arduous campaign of the nineteenth and early twentieth centuries to obtain work in the same positions, under the same conditions, and for the same remuneration as their male counterparts. In general, their struggles parallel those of women in the other western European countries and in the United States. The history of French women's efforts to enter the industrial workplaces and the professions are set forth in a number of the entries in this section, particularly in the studies of Evelyne Sullerot.

Today every occupation in France has been accorded an economic value; every one, that is, except the one women engage in in their homes. This contribution (or "volunteer" labor) has yet to be taken into account in the national economy. Lack of economic recognition of household labor is held to account in large measure for the negative view women often have of themselves.

The conditions under which women work, the occupations they hold--traditional and nontraditional--their rank and remuneration have all been scrutinized in the studies included in this section. Various solutions have been proposed. Some hold that paid work procures women's autonomy and assures them an independent existence.

Women and Work

Employment is the determining factor in true equality, provided the working conditions and salary are satisfactory. Others maintain that the problem is more complex. They hold that French society should make it possible for women with children in low-income families to have the option of staying at home with their children. In this view, women should not be forced to assume the double burden of mother-homemaker and worker.

Women now represent over forty percent of France's work force. Nevertheless, prejudice still persists in the hiring of women, in spite of laws that would prohibit it. Over half the unemployed in France are currently women, although they represent two-fifths of the work force. Programs implemented in the past few years to improve women's position in the labor force include the Third National Pact for Employment (1979). More recently, the Ministry of Women's Rights has undertaken an aggressive campaign to reorient girls in their career choices, away from the "traditional" female occupations of teacher, secretary, and nurse, where opportunities are increasingly limited, and to direct them toward a wider range of career options. Increased access for women to stages (professional training internships) is being urged. Making work hours more flexible, giving Wednesday (a nonschool day) off to women with children, offering longer but fewer work days, and designing shared appointments are among the measures that have been proposed. With only seven percent of the work force in part-time positions, France is not in the same situation as the United States where the figure is closer to twenty percent.

Under a law passed in 1972 women have the right to bring cases of sex discrimination to trial, but few have done so. Only recently have women in any sizeable number been employed in higher level positions. They have been hindered by a lack of seniority, a particularly telling factor in the highly hierarchical French public sector where women constitute half the work force, yet are concentrated in the lowest categories. The pyramid effect prevails in the private sector as well. Women work fewer evenings and do less overtime (in some cases because of "protective" legislation that is now being reassessed). They often lack qualifications, hence the importance of stages. Some categories of female workers—artisans, those in agriculture and commerce—have been long overlooked. Attempts are being made to give them recognition as "co-exploiters" in family enterprises, permitting them to co-hold mortgages, and, in particular, making them eligible for the considerable benefits to the national social security system.

In assessing the professional accomplishments of French women, it must be remembered that only since 1965 have married women been able to work without the express authorization of their husbands. The current aggressive campaign to open more professions and higher-level positions to women should provide role models for younger girls. A survey published in F Magazine (24 February 1980) confirms that French women prefer to work even when it is not financially necessary. The women surveyed consider work necessary to their self-realization and self-esteem. That women's careers are now the subject of national concern indicates to what extent women have come "of age" in France.

NOTES

1. See Laura Strumingher, Women and the Making of the Working Class: Lyon, 1830-1870 (St. Albans, Vt.: Eden Press, 1979 and Louise A. Tilly and Joan W. Scott, Women, Work and Family (New York: Praeger, 1978).
2. See Susan Groag Bell and Karen M. Offen, eds., Women, the Family, and Freedom: The Debate in Documents, 1750-1950, vol. 1, 1750-1880 (Stanford: Stanford University Press, 1983).
3. Ibid., 140.
4. Madeleine Colin, Ce n'est pas d'aujourd'hui . . ., (Paris: Éditions Sociales, 1975), 25-26.

Women and Work

WOMEN AND WORK

ALLAUZEN, MARIE. La paysanne française aujourd'hui [The French peasant woman today]. Paris: Denoël/Gonthier, 1967, 204 pp.

Rural France is an interesting area to study at the end of the twentieth century, for its evolution has been slower than that of the country's other socioprofessional milieus. There has been a difficult transition from the nineteenth to the twentieth century. Women, rather than men, have borne most of the weight of actual changes. Therefore it is not surprising that twice as many young women as men are leaving the land in what has been termed the end of the peasants in French society. (Thirty percent of the active population in 1945, peasants now represent only eight percent.)

Whatever part of France they inhabit, it is the peasant women who suffer from the double duties of worker and wife and mother working in solitude and isolation. While they do share a close professional collaboration with their husbands, this contribution has yet to be fully appreciated and recognized. Their work continues throughout the year with no time off and no vacations in a country where other workers now enjoy five weeks of paid vacation.

This study describes a number of agricultural jobs for women created in the past few years. The aim is to slow the departure of women from rural areas. The jobs offer structure and some predetermined professional qualifications. These positions include counselors, teachers in home economics and related subjects and social workers and rural assistants. Perhaps the most innovative is this last-named group. Rural assistants help families in their own geographical area, but do so on the basis of clearly defined hours and salary. This is to assure the professional status of the work and, at the same time, to underline the value of the peasant/housewife's contribution.

ARONDO, MARIA. Moi, la bonne [Me, the maid]. Collection témoigner. Paris: Stock, 1975, 207 pp.

If conditions for French employés de maison, i.e. household help, are difficult, they are even worse for foreign domestics. Many do not have proper papers and hence are not eligible for social security benefits. They are particularly vulnerable to exploitation.

Maria's tale is typical. The oldest of eight children in a very poor Spanish family, she came to France to find work and, she thought, a better future. Deception quickly set in. Her first mistress--a former maid herself--was very hard on her. The events of 1968 brought hope for improvement. She was one of many women in France who were marked by the uprising that served as a catalyst to the recent feminist movement. Slowly but surely, working conditions are improving for this group.

In addition to Maria's story, this book includes comments from maids of varying ages in different regions. Their backgrounds and situations also differ.

BASILE, COLETTE. Enfin, c'est la vie [Well, that's life]. Collection femme. Paris: Denoël/Gonthier, 1975, 142 pp.

The life in question is that of Berthe, who works in the production line of a candy factory. Several days in her life are described in detail. This journal summarizes not only her daily cares but also those of her co-workers. These are women with problems: children young and old, husbands and lovers, bosses and supervisors, health and fatigue, material anxieties and unwanted pregnancies.

This is a realistic, not romanticized, view of working-class women written in a colloquial style that evokes the solidarity as well as the competition of the women. Its slow, relentless pace parallels the mechanical movements imposed upon those like Colette Basile who spend their days endlessly repeating mechanical gestures.

_____. Ma vie comme je peux [My life, as best I can]. Paris: Denoël/Gonthier, 1977, 138 pp.

The speculation--and eventual discovery--by co-workers that Basile was the author of the exposé of factory life, Enfin, c'est la vie, caused her to leave that job and move back for a time with her parents. This return to the parental foyer provoked memories of Basile's childhood and adolescence, here recounted.

There were the displacements caused by the German occupation (for the young Parisian, an enforced stay in the country seemed like a marvelous vacation); there was an early introduction to work in a hat shop; a period spent as a waitress in a provincial café; an extended convalescence for a back problem; and then the birth of a daughter in a home for unwed mothers. To support her child, Basile went to work in a factory, the work described in her first book. The story of her life--such as it is--is thus filled in.

*BÉCANE, GENEVIÈVE. Le travail à temps partiel dans la fonction publique, solution ou palliatif aux difficultés de la femme fonctionnaire [Part-time work in the public sector, a solution or palliative to the difficulties of women civil servants]. 2 vols. Paris: Université de Droit, Économie Politique, et Science Sociales (Paris II), 1974.

This doctoral dissertation examines the general problems of part-time work for women and in particular, women working in the public sector. The state is the largest employer of women in France, with one-fifth of all working women on its payroll. It has been ahead of private industry in attempting to introduce part-time positions for women.

Women and Work

BIDAULT, SUZANNE. Par une porte entrebâillée: ou comment les Françaises entrent dans la Carrière [By a half-open door: or how French women enter into the Career]. Paris: Table Ronde, 1972, 226 pp.

The title notwithstanding, this is not a book on the problems French women have encountered in entering the French diplomatic service (the career as far as the author is concerned). Rather, it is the account of how one woman made her way up the hierarchy of the Quai d'Orsay, the headquarters of the French diplomatic service.

There were many international adventures in the course of Suzanne Bidault's career, including work in the Resistance. She credits men with having helped her become France's first woman plenipotentiary minister. (Her husband was also a minister.) In the long, difficult struggle, men were her allies. "No feminist group aided me, not a single woman held out her hand." The last sentence of the book states "I prefer working with men."

BOURG, CLAUDE. Femme et chef d'entreprise [Woman and company head]. Paris: Robert Laffont, 1975, 288 pp.

This is the "rags to riches" account of an attractive young woman (featured on TV and in the press) whose father was killed in the Resistance when she was nine. At twenty she sold papers in the streets of Paris. Investing her modest savings, she set up her own firm, a part-time employment agency now operating worldwide. The problems of contemporary French women are discussed, including how to reconcile professional aspirations and family obligations.

Claude Bourg's views reflect her atypical career and experiences. The book was brought out in a collection entitled "A Man and his Profession"!

CALLET, CHRISTINE, and CLAUDE de RENTY GRANRUT. Place aux femmes [Make way for women]. Paris: Stock, 1973, 280 pp. (Preface by Edgar Faure.)

Women's continued entry into the work force and the problems inherent in this entry are elaborated. Interviews were conducted throughout France in factories, stores, offices, canteens, train stations, schools, and day-care centers. The authors spoke to managers, union leaders, top-level civil servants, and workers. They underscore the point that work constitutes the necessary entry point into social life.

The main resistance to women's work is still found among French working-class men. The men's own experience does not dispose them to see work as "liberating." Their ideal is to permit their wives to remain at home, something economic realities do not always allow. To help women find positions, flexible hours were introduced in France in 1970. Where they have been tried, such schedules have worked well in public and private (such as Peugeot) enterprises. But the number of firms permitting this practice is limited.

Studies reveal that women are in better emotional and physical health than men. The authors point out that fewer are to be found in mental institutions. Nevertheless French society still maintains a "certain idea of woman" and of her role. They assert that this idea is responsible for the oppression of women. From generation to generation a traditional image is perpetuated. The sociocultural model of woman must be changed. They conclude that while French women still have little voice and weight in politics and government, they are quietly but surely changing France's future.

C[ONFÉDÉRATION] G[ÉNÉRALE DU] T[RAVAIL]/Nord/Pas-de-Calais. <u>Les causes de l'absentéisme féminin</u> [The causes of feminine absenteeism]. Paris: Éditions Sociales, 1976, 126 pp.

The Communist dominated union, the CGT, was compiling statistics on the problem of women and work in France's highly industrialized north region when the Ministry of Work published a survey showing the North/Pas-de-Calais region to have the highest female absenteeism rate in the nation. To put the government report in perspective, the CGT published their own findings and accounts from women workers in that region. They viewed the government report as part of a campaign to downgrade social security benefits, which are far more extensive in France than in the United States.

The CGT maintains that better working conditions, not changes in social security allocations, are called for. The textile industries of the north have a higher percentage of women workers than do firms elsewhere. More of these women are young, in the fifteen- to nineteen-year age group. Consequently they have less schooling and less professional training. Many women textile workers are paid poorly for performing physically arduous tasks. One result is that this region also has the highest infant mortality rate in France, after Corsica. The real cause for women's absenteeism, they maintain, is the difficult conditions under which they work.

_____. <u>Les femmes salariées</u> [Salaried women]. Paris: Éditions Sociales, 1973, 247 pp. (Preface by Georges Séguy.)

Assembled here are some of the working papers, debates, proposals, and demands set forth at the CGT's Fifth Conference on Salaried Women hald in May of 1973. The conference brought together several thousand participants from Socialist groups and from the Communist party. The problems set forth are all too familiar, discrimination exists in every area of work. Given the fact that most women have interruptions in their careers, more time must be allotted to them so that their pensions will equal those of men.

The "events" of May 1968 played a decisive part in the growing militancy of salaried women, a militancy reflected in their

increasing participation in union activities. There remains a
fundamental contradiction between the effective role of women in
society and recognition of that role by institutions. It is a
problem easier to discuss than correct. Statements by many women
from varied backgrounds and different occupations throughout
France combine to present the official CGT view and buttress the
claims made.

CHARLES-ROUX, E., G. ZIEGLER, M. CERATI, J. BRUHAT, M. GUILBERT, and
C. GILLES. Les femmes et le travail du Moyen-Âge à nos jours
[Woman and work from the Middle Ages to the present]. Paris:
Éditions de la Courtille, 1975, 220 pp.

This illustrated collection of essays provides a historical
overview of French women and work. The chapters on the earlier
periods are the most useful, for this period is not as well
known. The extensive documentation available for the past two
centuries is lacking for the preindustrial period. However,
through the Livre des métiers of 1268, one learns of many women's
occupations of that time. This enumeration contradicts those
who think that women's work is a recent phenomenon. And this
history also proves that women's work has been anything but
marginal.

COLIN, MADELEINE. Ce n'est pas d'aujourd'hui: femmes, syndicats,
luttes de classe [It didn't just begin today: women, trade
unions, class struggle]. Paris: Éditions Sociales, 1975,
246 pp. (Preface by Henri Krasucki, secretary of the CGT.)

This study is devoted to women's early efforts and eventual
success in entering French labor unions. It then analyzes what
women have accomplished once admitted to the rank and file.
Women's dilemma remains central: how to reconcile family and
work.

The majority of French workers have had to struggle to obtain
better working conditions and better pay. Women, as the
"proletariat of the proletariat," have found themselves doubly
exploited, brought into industries because they were cheaper and
more expendable labor. As the Journal des Postes, Télégraphes,
et Téléphones put it in 1892, "the Administration does not want
any more men in its offices, only women. No more muscles,
nothing but nerves . . . since it seems that 'that' (ça,
perjorative) eats less, that costs less." Sometimes women
participated in--at times led--strikes, such as those of the
metal workers and mindinettes in 1917; the sardine packers in
1925; the textile workers of the north in 1927-28; and the massive strikes and occupations of factories, offices, and stores
in 1936.

The commendable, sometimes heroic contribution of the "alibi
women," the bourgeoises and the intellectuals, is recognized.
However, Madeleine Colin feels these women know little about the
vast majority of working women for whom work is anything but
"liberating." A labor leader who was the confederal secretary

of the CGT from 1955 to 1969, she presents the French Communist party's viewpoint. A summary outlines the CGT's efforts to improve women's working conditions and permit women's progressive entry into their union. Currently they represent about one-third of the CGT membership.

COLLECTIF. <u>18 millions de bonnes à tout faire</u> [Eighteen million maids of all work]. Collection points chauds. Paris: Syros, 1978, 198 pp.

This "black book" on women's work in France serves as a useful introduction to the subject. The opening chapter outlines a history of the various occupations French women have held since the Middle Ages. The situation today is detailed with facts, figures, and statistics. The ensuing chapters assess the problems women workers encounter, such as higher unemployment and lower wages than men, despite legislation that makes them legally equal. The authors are pessimistic about bills passed recently to improve women's working conditions. These are seen as superficial and, in some instances, impediments to real progress.

The problems are presented in general terms and are then followed by comments, interviews, and reports from women in various industries throughout France. One learns that in the textile industries of the north, the hierarchy is evident even in the color of the smocks worn; that there is exploitation and deception practiced by those who offer piecework to women at home; that there are both conflicts and solidarity among women working in a doll factory in the southwest, a situation also found elsewhere.

Sexism is seen in many forms. The constant interplay of personal and professional constraints prevails in women's work. For true progress to be achieved, it is held, the economic system must see women's work as more than just a supplemental source of profit. Further, the day-to-day relations of men and women must be changed. Surprisingly, there is no material on France's nearly one million female domestics, the real <u>bonnes à tout faire</u>.

ELY, MARIE, and ANNE ZEGEL. <u>Tous les métiers pour les femmes</u> [All the professions for women]. Paris: Solar, 1977, 540 pp.

Conceived as a directory for over 300 jobs open to women, this compendium indicates the qualifications required; the advantages and disadvantages of the professions; the schooling required; career prospects; and the names and addresses of establishments that provide such training. While designed for women considering careers in France, it indirectly provides much useful information on the status of the professions in general.

Women and Work

Femmes et immigrées: l'insertion des femmes immigrées en France [Women and immigrants: the integration of women immigrants in France]. Edited by Isabel Taboado Leonetti, Florence Lévy, and the CNRS team of research on international migrations. Migrations et sociétés no. 4. Paris: Documentation Française, 1978, 286 pp.

Foreign women were estimated to represent over six percent of the female population of France in 1980. Censuses taken in 1968 and 1975 show that in the intervening years, women immigrants in France entered the work force at a higher rate than did French women. And this entry has been twice that of male immigrants for the same period.

This volume considers women of two main cultural groups now residing in France: 1) the Iberians (the Spanish, who entered earlier, and the Portuguese, who came more recently); 2) Moslem women from Algeria, Morocco, and Tunisia, countries with strong ties to France. These women are now entering the labor force; for many the first job is as domestic help. Building and public works serve as the initial occupations of their male counterparts.

Statistics are analyzed in an attempt to better understand these women, to determine the conditions of their daily life in France. Many are found to be caught between two countries, two cultures, and at times, two societies in an ongoing state of ambivalence. The judicial and social status of women in their countries of origin are indicated. The Koran and Islamic law have marked one group; the Catholic church and the Napoleonic Code the other. Comments from these women immigrants are also included.

FRAISSE, GENEVIÈVE. Femmes toutes mains: essai sur le service domestique [Women in general service: essay on domestic service]. Collection libre à elles. Paris: Seuil, 1979, 248 pp. (Research, discussions, documentations, and interviews in collaboration with Martine Guillin.)

This feminist essay raises provocative questions about the relationship of mistress to maid, two women leading parallel but unequal lives, a situation more common in France than in the United States. The work is enhanced by scholarship: documentation such as journals and reviews; the proceedings of feminist congresses; and manuals for the "woman of the house" explaining how to treat domestics and run the household (such as those of Augusta Moll-Weiss, a pioneer in the field of home economics and author of Le livre du foyer [1912]). Regrettably, the book has neither bibliography nor index.

Efforts have been made to change the name of maid. Bonne, maid, is also the feminine adjective for good, i.e. good for all work or all-purpose. Where moral considerations are involved, the term "aid" is favored; where social considerations predominate, one finds the designation "household worker or employee." Whatever the title, the situations and working conditions of maids have changed little since the beginning of the century. The hours are excessive and there is little outside regulation or control. The only visible change is in nationality. French maids today are predominantly Spanish or Portuguese. In spite of often unfavorable treatment both literature and memoirs reveal that female domestics tend to assume the social and moral values of "their" homes.

FUGIER, ANNE-MARIE. La place des bonnes: la domesticité féminine à Paris en 1900 [The maids' place: female domestic service in Paris in 1900]. Paris: Grasset, 1979, 377 pp.

Anne-Marie Fugier reflects upon the ambiguity surrounding the feminine presence of the maid in the bourgeois family at the turn of the century and the maid's identity and rapport with family space within and without the household. There are tableaus of the times, the so-called belle époque, and vivid pictures of the mores of well-to-do French families. A sharp contrast existed between the living spaces of the maids and that of the comfortable family quarters. The maids were relegated to the attics. A room "au sixième," on the seventh floor, is as evocative a term as the student's garret. Yet the working spaces intersected. The troubling intimacy that ensued is analyzed.

Maids were thought to have unbridled sexual appetites. In reality, they were defenseless victims--often of both fathers and sons. Liaisons were tolerated, even expected. But the poor maid who became pregnant was quickly dismissed. Circumstances made it impossible for most to marry. If they somehow managed to marry, it was even more difficult to have children: ninety percent did not. The extensive documentation, including literature and historical materials, such as trial records and the press, combine to show that maids were women without lives or identities of their own.

GARNIER, CHRISTIANE. À chances égales . . . des femmes qui ont résolu d'étonner [With equal chances . . . women who resolved to amaze]. Paris: Hachette, 1971, 219 pp.

A book about some of France's outstanding women. Christiane Garnier endeavors to determine, in interviews, why and how they distinguished themselves. The Estates General of Women demanded that all notions of a "strong" or "weak" sex or notions of "superiority" cease. These women justify the claim that French women have excelled in professions along with men.

They include a woman deputy who devoted twenty-five years to political life. She insists that French women must become aware of their new responsibilities and that the struggle for equality and opportunity is far from being won. The surgeon is also a colonel, parachutist, and pilot of planes and helicopters with combat experience. The explorer recounts remarkable exploits and urges respect for all living things. The financial advisor who founded Femmes de Valeurs endeavors to introduce her countrywomen to the "mysteries" of the stock market. Here is a true shortcoming in women's education. She intends to "awaken" all the Mmes Bovaries in France. The journalist-mayor finds little difference between being mayor or mère, mother.

There are women in nontraditional fields. One has forsaken city life to take care of sheep. Another has pursued a life at sea and participated in oceanographic research. All reveal that, given equal opportunities, women can succeed.

GUIRAL, PIERRE, and GUY THUILLER. La vie quotidienne des domestiques en France au XIXe siècle [The daily life of domestics in nineteenth-century France]. Collection la vie quotidienne. Paris: Hachette, 1978, 288 pp.

This is one of a series of the author's studies of daily life in nineteenth-century France. Here, from the annals of anonymity, he presents a picture of an important though neglected group, the domestics. The majority of domestic servants are women. The book contains many details about how they lived, including clothes, housing, and hygiene, and how they worked: organization, salaries, and the invisible hierarchy of this demanding work. Most servants were of rural origin and remained quite pious. Employers sought passive qualities including sexual complacency. Only with their masters' growing concern with tuberculosis and venereal disease did their situation improve somewhat. By the eve of the First World War there was a shortage of servants. Many found better work elsewhere.

The 1870 article on "domestic" in the standard Larousse dictionary graphically describes their lot, an "impure and brutal servitude, vile and brutal slavery, of one who in fear answers to the wishes of the master by tears, to his kisses, by shudders of disgust and fear. And then, for the woman servant, what consequences: almost always degradation, poverty, prostitution, rape, sometimes infanticide."

The plight of the woman servant provided material for many writers of the time. There are many sensational details in Eugene Sue's Les mystères de Paris (1842-43); Eugène Labiche's play, Edgard et sa bonne, appeared in 1852; Guy de Maupassant describes the lonely life of servants in Une vie (1883); and Octave Mirabeau depicts the psychological effects of this life in Le journal d'une femme de chambre (1900). Proust's monumental À la recherche de temps perdu (1913-27) contains descriptions of life at the lower as well as upper levels of society. His famed Célestine has written an account of her life in the service of Monsieur Proust.

LABOURIE-RACAPÉ, MARIE-THÉRÈSE LETABLIER, and ANNE-MARIE VASSEUR. L'activité féminine: enquête sur la discontinuité de la vie professionnelle [Feminine activity: inquiry into the interruptions in professional life]. Paris: P.U.F., 1977, 204 pp.

This study endeavors to better understand the different components, the contributing factors, and the consequences of interruptions or continuity in the professional careers of working women. It had been found that women in the twenty-five to thirty-five year age group (those born in the years 1940 to 1949) were entering the work force at a higher rate. Yet this was precisely the age group in which career interruption usually occurred. To analyze this seemingly contradictory situation, 2,000 women from the towns of Lyons and Caën were interviewed in early 1975. All were married and had at least two children.

The findings disprove the longheld notions about the profiles of women's careers. Most interruptions take place before the age of twenty-five. Further, women who interrupt their work usually do so only once and for a relatively short period. The social, economic, occupational, and family circumstances that affect women's careers are analyzed. Not surprisingly, the likelihood of a career increases with the level of schooling, training, and qualifications. The two professions where women's activity is the most continuous are teaching and clerical work, particularly in government service. This is due in part to shorter, regular hours and job security provided by the public sector (French public school teachers are state employees).

LE GARREC, ÉVELYNE. <u>Les messagères</u> [The women heralds/forerunners]. Collection pour chacune. Paris: Éditions des femmes, 1976, 184 pp.

Évelyne Le Garrec holds that only through leaving home and going out to work can women become fully aware of the extent of their oppression. As messengers, they will meet each other and be able to participate in the fight against this oppression, an oppression that includes "alienating" work. This book, then, is not a plea for the right to salaried work, which has never "freed" anyone.

The author contends that the identity of women and their specific language must, of necessity, be the subject of research in which women intellectuals will play an important role. However, she feels it is essential that this research go beyond the theoretical level, a persistent problem in France. The activity of women intellectuals must not be separated from that of the majority of women who struggle daily both in their work and their lives. She notes that the promotion of women and feminism do not always go together. She feels that women who have made it, like Françoise Giroud and Simone Veil, do not like to be reminded that, in spite of all they have attained, they are still women.

Le Garrec deplores efforts to "neutralize" housewives. Consistent with her aim to consider all women, excerpts from various interviews are included. The opinions of factory workers, modest employees, peasants, and the female proletariat are heard. The women at the Lip factory resent that, after all the camaraderie with the men during the strike, things have now returned to their former situation. There were few positive gains. Nevertheless these interviews would seem to show that already a new feminine identity is asserting itself and that women's struggles are assuming forms adapted to their specific needs.

Women and Work

LESTERLIN, MARIE ADINE. Les femmes et la formation continue en 100 questions [Women and professional development in 100 questions]. Paris: Chotard & Associés, 1979, 154 pp.

The opportunities available to women who wish to undertake training or schooling in order to enter or reenter the work force, change fields, or upgrade skills are outlined. These possibilities and provisions are the outcome of a law pertaining to continuing training and education passed on July 17, 1978. While the law applies to men as well, it is French women who are expected to be the chief beneficiaries. Historically, women have been the least informed about such legislation. This book endeavors to correct that problem.

In question-and-answer form the main points of the law and its methods of application are covered. A second section provides information on how to undertake such training. It concludes with possible scenarios and a list of the national information centers for women, the CIFs.

Lip au féminin [Lip in the feminine]. Paris: Syros, 1977, 161 pp.

The strike at the Lip watch factory in Besançon, from April 1973 to March 1975, had a profound impact upon the women employed there. Most were at the lowest levels and at the lowest salaries. The takeover and prolonged occupation of the factory was for many the first chance to participate in a collective movement and exercise and extend their solidarity.

Exhausting but exhilarating, this experience in retrospect proved to have been a decisive moment in their lives. These factory women saw the extent--and the limits--of their male colleagues' concern for them. The women involved present their concerns, principally work and family. The language is simple and direct; cartoons dealing with the strike are included. The women of LIP hope to serve as an example to other women. They also want to educate men.

MARUANI, MARGARET. Les syndicats à l'épreuve du féminisme [Unions put to the test by feminism]. Paris: Syros, 1979, 271 pp., 80 pp. (Published with the assistance of the CNRS.)

In the past, there was little understanding between the worlds of trade unionism and feminism. The Couriau affair (1913-14) gives some idea of the ramifications of the problem. When Emma Couriau, who had been a typographer for seventeen years, applied for membership (theoretically possible) in the local union at Lyon, not only was she turned down, but her husband was expelled. Although he had been a militant union member for over twenty years, he was guilty of having permitted his wife to exercise the same profession. The issue was not just women's participation in the unions, but that of married women's right to work. Union strictures forced married women to find other, often more difficult and demanding, work. Feminists joined to support the couple but the advent of the war pushed the problem aside.

Has the situation changed noticeably with the new French feminist movement? Maruani studies recent publications and interviews feminists, women militants, and union members to examine this question. She finds that trade unions, like other groups, have been forced to pay attention to "their" women. Male members are "resigned" to seeing women workers among their ranks. Women's participation in strikes demonstrates that they can be comrades, not competitors. The chapter on the LIP strike shows that women fought for concerns that went well beyond conditions in the factory itself. The women held that militancy is also "their affair." Thus, in a major evolution feminist views, demands, and analyses have been introduced into union affairs. The ramifications of this conjecture are explored. The positions of the two principal unions, the CGT and the CFDT, are compared and their policy papers examined.

Maruani's analysis reveals that in some quarters there is still hostility to women's right to work. Antagonism results from two contradictory struggles among the women in these working-class organizations. One group is working for women's equality and a share of power; the other is antipower and antistructure, seeing any form of organization as necessarily masculine, hence oppressive. Another difficulty is that there is widespread hostility to the term feminist. Few women union members admit to being feminists. The term has had a bad press in these circles. However, the different meanings the term evokes illustrate that there are different feminist struggles taking place, both within and outside the unions.

MICHEL, ANDRÉE, ed. Les femmes dans la société marchande [Women in the market society]. Paris: P.U.F., 1978, 256 pp.

A Franco-American colloquium on the theme "The Economy and Sociology of the Family: Domestic Production" was held at Royaumont in January 1977. A number of the American papers have since been published in professional journals. This volume offers some of the French contributions.

Christine Delphy suggests that the concept of "domestic" work rather than "housework" be utilized when the subject under discussion is the unpaid work performed in the domus, in the sociological sense. The problem of the epistemology of economics is encountered in assessing the domestic production of women: Who produces and who holds the monopoly on economic discourse? Now more than ever, because of the rapid growth in the world's population, the unpaid labor of women must be recognized and accommodated. Outside the home, the work week must gradually be reduced. This will bring about moral and social autonomy that should result in a more equal distribution of domestic chores, including child care, among couples.

Women and Work

MICHEL, ANDRÉE, with CLAUDINE COLLET, and AGNÈS VIEILLE. Travail féminin: un point de vue [Feminine work: a point of view]. Travaux et recherches de prospective: schéma général d'aménagement de la France. Paris: Documentation Française, 1975, 158 pp.

This concise, well-documented study resulted from the conjunction of ten years of study by the delegation for the disposition of the territory and regional action and the occasion of the 1975 International Year of Woman. The history of women's work and its potential for the future is reviewed.

A brief survey on the introduction of industrial mechanization in the early nineteenth century precedes an analysis of the relationship between new techniques, such as computers and electronics, and female employment. The author argues that the slow but growing use of computers has been detrimental to women. Since current laws still "protect" women from night work (although not from jobs which start long before dawn), they are not trained as programmers. This problem is currently being addressed.

MONESTIER, MARIANNE. Femmes d'hier et de demain, d'ici et d'ailleurs [Women of yesterday and tomorrow, of here and there]. Paris: Plon, 1967, 384 pp.

This is a presentation and analysis of the advantages and difficulties involved when a husband and wife collaborate in their work. The most famous example studied is that of Pierre and Marie Curie.

*MONTESINOS, ANDRÉE. L'infirmière et l'organisation du travail hospitalier [The nurse and the organization of hospital work]. Paris: Centurion, 1973, 200 pp.

One of the main problems with nurses has been the high rate of turnover. Efforts have been undertaken to improve working conditions and hours. One successful innovation has been that of providing day-care facilities in the hospitals themselves.

PARENT-LARDEUR, FRANÇOISE. Les demoiselles de magasin [Lady clerks in the department store]. Paris: Éditions Ouvrières, 1970, 159 pp.

This brief study begins with the 1840s, when France was trying to adapt to rapid economic transformation. Society was not sufficiently prepared for this "progress." The fashion industry became mechanized and modernized. In the following decades the large Parisian department stores such as Le Bon Marché (1852), Le Louvre (1855), Au Printemps (1865), and La Samaritaine (1872), were founded. Their apogee was during the Second Empire.

Many of the young girls working in Paris in the last century were involved in one aspect or other of the garment industry. There was a hierarchy from demoiselles to grisettes for store girls. This classification is described by the 1842 Physiologie des demoiselles de magasin. Duties are detailed, as is the general appearance of the young women. Working conditions were deplorable. Some stood outside all day. Long hours were expected, particularly during busy seasons, but girls were fired or put on leave without pay during slow seasons.

There were contradictions in their situation. Subject to strict shop discipline, they were expected to show initiative, wit, and charm in order to sell. Leroy-Beaulieu's figures (1882) are used to show--and deplore, as he did--the disparity between the lives of the working women who lived in misery to provide the luxuries of other women who lived in affluence. Shop girls' salaries were about those of girls working in the mills. Only their social status was slightly more favorable.

Émile Zola describes the rise of the large department store in his novel Au bonheur des dames (1883). To document his work, the novelist took meticulous notes on many details pertaining to the lives of the young women in the department stores, particularly the Bon Marché and the Louvre. His notes have been preserved at the Bibliothèque Nationale, and Françoise Parent-Lardeur utilized them for her study.

See also Michael B. Miller's The Bon Marché: Bourgeois Culture and the Department Store 1869-1920 (1980).

PERROT, MICHELLE, ed. Travaux des femmes dans la France du XIXe siècle [Women's work in nineteenth-century France]. Paris: Éditions Ouvrières, 1978, 206 pp. (Special issue of Le Mouvement Social, no. 105 [October-December 1978].)

This collection of well-documented articles provides a graphic view of the long hours and difficult working conditions endured by the supposed "weaker sex." There is a brief outline of significant events from 1791 to 1913 and a bibliography that includes a number of unpublished doctoral dissertations as well as recent studies, along with several reviews of important books.

Michelle Perrot's opening article examines the changes in women's occupations in the course of the nineteenth century, from wet-nurse to employee. The wetnursing "industry" and its final demise is chronicled by Anne-Marie Fugier. Louise Tilly analyzes the structure of women's employment in the industrial cities of Anzin and Roubaix from 1872 to 1906. The situation of the silk-workers of Lyon (1835-1848) is Laura Strumhinger's subject. Marie-Hélène Zylberberg-Hocquard writes on the state employees of the tobacco and match factories, and Claudie Lesselier provides an overview of women employees in the large Parisian department stores before the First World War.

de PESLOUAN, GENEVIEVE. Qui sont les femmes ingénieurs en France? [Who are the women engineers in France?]. Paris: P.U.F., 1974, 179 pp.

To become an engineer in France requires from five to six years of study and competitive exams after having obtained the demanding baccalauréat. This means that women are at a disadvantage unless they defer having children. When one examines the fields where French women engineers are employed, yet another type of discrimination appears. They work principally in the chemical industry and, more recently, with electronic firms. Half are employed in the public sector although only a third of their male colleagues can be found there. Women engineers tend to be concentrated in research, teaching, documentation, and laboratory work.

Among other factors hindering women professionally are lack of contacts--the "old boy" networks that place most engineers--lack of mobility and, as in so many professions, family responsibilities. Yet in a world becoming increasingly more technical society needs women engineers. They can play an important role: women are sensitive to human problems and needs. Feminine sensibility can contribute to the amelioration of the conditions of workers. Too often their needs are forgotten. The data for Geneviève de Peslouan's study was obtained from questionnaires received from over 700 women holding engineering degrees. This was the first effort to obtain such data. The respondents were estimated to be about a third of the total number of female graduates.

PITON, MONIQUE. C'est possible [It's possible]. Paris: Éditions des femmes, 1975, 625 pp.

This is an account and reflection on the strike at the Lip factory. Piton, the oldest of six in a modest, small-town family, went to work early, first as maid, then as factory worker. Married before twenty, she divorced in her early thirties. Divorce meant assuming responsibilities for herself and her daughter. A series of jobs followed. She had been working at LIP for four years when the strike and occupation took place.

The women involved found that their obstacles were many and subtle. They had to struggle all the more tenaciously. For these women it meant a struggle together and a year of freedom discovering the world (the women strikers spoke at rallies throughout France to gain support). Above all, this experience proved that it was indeed possible for women to overcome great obstacles.

de SAIRIGNÉ, GUILLEMETTE. Les Françaises face au chômage [French women face to face with unemployment]. Paris: Denoël/Gonthier, 1978, 203 pp.

In part personal accounts, in part data, this volume documents the problem of female unemployment in France in the decade prior to its publication. In France as in other Western industrial societies, women are the first victims of unemployment. There are, however, significant regional differences. Unemployment among women is most prevalent in the industrial north, south, and southwest. The socioprofessional category most affected by unemployment is that of women who work in factories and service industries. Those under twenty-five have the greatest difficulty entering the work force. And, the last hired are inevitably the first fired. The author points to the major potential problem, the approximately two to four million women who, for a variety of reasons, are not working at the moment. They may enter the work market from one day to the next.

The preamble of the French Constitution of 1958 guaranteed women equal right to work. Since 1965 they have had an equal right to unemployment benefits. Even so, young men are automatically eligible to receive these benefits when they return from compulsory military service whether or not they have ever worked, while women of the same age who have not found a first position are not.

The law of 1975 guarantees equality of access to employment regardless of sex or family situation, including pregnancy. This law is not always obeyed. Further, figures indicate that women still receive lower salaries because they occupy lower level positions. Accordingly, their compensations are also lower. Feminists would abolish the practice of hiring women on short-term contracts, a practice that circumvents legal restrictions.

SULLEROT, ÉVELYNE. Les Françaises au travail [French women at work]. Paris: Hachette, 1973, 276 pp. (Inquiry undertaken by the IFOP with the aid of the journal Femmes d'aujourd'hui and with the support of the General Commissariat of the Plan.)

Running commentary accompanies this 126-question survey of 1,300 French women. They represent different ages, many milieus, and different occupations. Évelyne Sullerot decided to use this broad sample of French women to examine questions that previously had not been pursued in depth. Data was obtained on how French women cope with child care, to what extent the feminine work force was mobile, and what the pattern and impact of career interruption was during a woman's lifetime.

Approximately half the group changed jobs in order to advance professionally. The other half did so for family reasons that took precedence over professional concerns. A surprising discovery was that a quarter of those who left work returned in five years or less, and for three-quarters, it was in less than ten years. The implications of these findings led Sullerot to found the Retravailler Centers that help women of all ages and backgrounds enter or reenter the work force.

One of the pioneers in recent French feminist studies, Évelyne Sullerot (herself a reentry woman), is now a sociologist known throughout the world. She was a co-founder of the French Family Planning Movement. Many of her works have appeared in English. Earlier titles include:

Demain les femmes [Tomorrow women]. Paris: Robert Laffont, 1965, 271 pp. (Eleven translations thus far, but none in English.)

Women and Work

La vie des femmes [The life of women]. Paris: Denoël/Gonthier, 1965, 271 pp.

Histoire et sociologie du travail féminin [History and sociology of women's work]. Paris: Denoël/Gonthier, 1965, 296 pp. (Ten translations, but none in English.)

Les crèches et les équipments d'accueil pour la petite enfance [Day-care centers and equipment to accommodate young children]. Paris: Hachette, 1973, 250 pp. (Written in collaboration with Michèle Saltiel.)

Le travail des femmes en France [Women's work in France]. Paris: Documentation Française Illustrée, no. 278, 1973, 95 pp. (Prepared in collaboration with the Comité du Travail Féminin.)
  A short schema of the major aspects of women's work in France is presented. Among the topics covered are: choice of a position, professional training, the particular problems relating to women and work, French legislation, and the position of the major unions. A global view of the problem is also included.

TABARD, NICOLE. Enquête sur les besoins et aspirations des familles et des jeunes [Inquiry into the needs and aspirations of families and youth]. Paris: Centre de Recherche et de Documentation sur la Consommation/Caisse Nationale d'Allocations Familiales: CRDEOC/CNAF, 1974, 512 pp. (Preface by Pierre Boisard, with the participation of Ludovic Lebart, Danielle Prangère, and Benoît Riandey.)
  Results of a second national inquiry in 1971 among 2,000 families covered by family benefits from the national social security system. (The first was held in 1961.) The majority of these families were from towns of over ten thousand inhabitants. Among the many findings relating to women were attitudes toward and details of their participation in the work force. The problems of fertility, motherhood and employment, and family allowances are examined.
  Half the volume consists of statistics. Several chapters profile the socioeconomic characteristics of those interviewed. Tabard and her colleagues continue the study of families published in 1967 in Les conditions de vie des familles (Centre de Documentation sur la Consommation, Union Nationale des Caisses d'Allocation), an extensive work she undertook with Yvette van Effenterre, Michel Guillot, Agnès Pitrou, and others.

ZYLBERBERG-HOCQUARD, MARIE-HÉLÈNE. Féminisme et syndicalisme en France [Feminism and trade unions in France]. Paris: Anthropos, 1978, 326 pp.
  At the end of the nineteenth century syndicalism and feminism were two movements of growing importance in France. There were

parallel--and at times divergent--reactions as both movements became aware of what they thought was a new figure, the salaried woman. Discussion of the problem of women's growing opportunities to undertake salaried work had further ramifications. With the economic evolution of the country, women's place in French society was being redefined in new ways.

The author enumerates the myths and realities relating to women's salaried work: types of positions, working conditions, prevailing attitudes, etc. There are useful outlines of feminist associations, feminist journals, and the acts of feminist congresses. The most frequently asked question in the second half of that century centered upon the utility and value of women's work.

Women were reluctant to join the unions. This reluctance is attributed to the widely held view that women's work was supplemental. Further, women were rarely qualified and were seldom concentrated in large numbers. Most women were employed in small workshops or worked in isolation at home. French syndicalism was also more radical than that of England, another factor in discouraging feminine participation. Only belatedly did the unions come to recognize the role of women as fellow workers and their female comrades' potential to help in their struggles.

Relations between feminists and women workers were hindered by the fact that most feminists were from the middle class. Some had a condescending and paternalistic approach that women workers resented.

Bibliography of Earlier Works, 1830-1969

This bibliography provides titles of but some of the many works published in France on the topic of French women. Additional listings will be found in the bibliographies included in the Introduction under "Resources," as well as in some of the annotated entries and the recent studies in English that have been cited.

A useful early bibliographical source is the forty-five-volume Bibliographie universelle ancienne et moderne edited by Louis-Gabriel Michaud and published from 1854 to 1865. Another earlier work, Aglauro Ungherini's Manuel de bibliographie, de biographie et d'iconographie des femmes célèbres (1892-1905) was republished in 1968 in three volumes.

More recent reference works are the Bibliography in the History of European Women (1976) compiled by Joan Kelly with Barbara Alpern Engel and Women in Western European History: A Select Chronological, Geographical, and Topical Bibliography, from Antiquity to the French Revolution (1982) compiled and edited by Linda Frey, Marsha Frey, and Joanne Schneider.

These listings vary considerably. There are works destined for the general public as well as serious scholarly studies. As social historians have shown in recent years, to fully understand a society of any period, popular journals and untutored memoirs can be as useful and insightful as the most erudite dissertations.

ABENSOUR, LÉON. Le féminisme sous le règne de Louis-Philippe et en 1848. Paris: Plon & Nourrit, 1913, 337 pp.

———. La femme et le féminisme avant la Révolution. Paris: E. Leroux, 1923, 477 pp. (Twelve-page bibliography.)

———. L'histoire générale du féminisme des origines à nos jours. Paris: Delagrave, 1921, 326 pp.

Bibliography of Earlier Works

_____. Le problème féministe: un cas d'aspiration collective vers l'égalité. Paris: Radot, 1927, 185 pp.

_____. Les vaillantes: Héroïnes, martyres, et remplaçantes. Paris: P. Chapelot, 1917, 312 pp.

ACKER, PAUL. Oeuvres sociales des femmes. Paris: Plon, 1908, 287 pp.

D'ADHÉMAR, MARIE. La femme catholique et la démocratie française. 2d ed. Paris: Perrin, 1900, 316 pp.

D'AGOULT, MARIE [Daniel Stern]. Histoire de la Révolution de 1848. 3 vols. Paris: G. Sandré, 1850-53.

AIMERY de PIERREBOURG, MARGUERITE [Claude Ferval]. J.-J. Rousseau et les femmes. Paris: A. Fayard, 1934, 412 pp.

ALLART de MÉRITENS, HORTENSE [Mme P. de Saman]. Les enchantements de Prudence de l'Esbaix. Paris: Michel Lévy Frères, 1873, 366 pp. (Preface by George Sand.)

_____. La femme et la démocratie de nos temps. Paris: Delaunay, 1836, 124 pp.

d'ALLEMAGNE, HENRI-RENÉ. Les Saint-Simoniens, 1827-1837. Paris: Gründ, 1930, 453 pp.

d'ALMÉRAS, HENRI. Une amoureuse: Pauline Bonaparte. Paris: A. Michel, 1906, 365 pp.

_____. L'amour sous les verrous: les prisons révolutionnaires. Paris: A. Michel, 1936, 380 pp.

_____. Charlotte Corday d'après les documents contemporains. Paris: Annales Politiques et Littéraires, 1910, 276 pp.

_____. La femme amoureuse dans la vie et dans la littérature: étude psycho-physiologique. Paris: A. Michel, 1920.

_____. Le mariage chez tous les peuples. Paris: Schleicher Frères, 1903, 200 pp.

_____. Marie-Antoinette et les pamphlets royalistes et révolutionnaires. Paris: Librairie Mondiale, 1907, 424 pp.

ANCELLE, LISE. L'heure de la femme. Paris: Sansot, 1909, 229 pp.

ARIÈS, PHILLIPE. Histoire des populations françaises et de leurs attitudes devant la vie depuis le XVIIIe siècle. Paris: Self, 1948, 569 pp.

Bibliography of Earlier Works

ARMAND, ÉMILE. Libertinage et prostitution (grandes prostituées et fameux libertins): l'influence du fait sexuel sur la vie politique et sociale de l'homme. Paris: Éditions Prima, 1931, 436 pp.

_____. La révolution sexuelle et la camaraderie amoureuse. Paris: Critique et Raison, 1933, 342 pp.

ARMENGAUD, ANDRÉ. Démographie et société. Paris: Stock, 1966, 212 pp.

_____. La population française au XXe siècle. Paris: P.U.F., 1965, 126 pp.

ARON, MARGUERITE. Le journal d'une Sévrienne. Paris: F. Alcan, 1912, 241 pp.

ASSOLLANT, ALFRED. Le droit des femmes. Paris: Anger, 1868, 308 pp.

AUBERT, JEAN-MARC, et al. L'Église et la promotion de la femme. Paris: Éditions Fleurus, 1969, 143 pp.

AUBRY, O. Brelan de femmes; ou, le coup d'état de Brumaire. Paris: A. Fayard, 1927, 254 pp.

_____. L'impératrice Eugénie. Paris: A. Fayard, 1931, 446 pp.

AUCLAIR, MARCELLE, and MENIE GRÉGOIRE, eds. Femmes. 2 vols. Paris: Plon, 1967.

AUCLERT, HUBERTINE. L'argent de la femme. Paris: Pédone, 1904.

_____. Le droit politique des femmes, question qui n'est pas traitée au congrès international des femmes. Paris: Hugonis, 1878.

_____. L'égalité sociale et politique de l'homme et de la femme. Marseille: A. Thomas, 1879, 16 pp.

_____. Les femmes arabes en Algérie. Paris: Société d'Éditions Littéraires, 1900, 250 pp.

_____. Les femmes au gouvernail. Paris: Marcel Giard, 1923, 407 pp.

_____. Le vote des femmes. Paris: V. Giard & E. Brière, 1908, 220 pp.

AUDOUARD, OLYMPE. À travers l' Amérique, le Far-West. Paris: E. Dentu, 1869, 370 pp.

Bibliography of Earlier Works

_____. À travers l'Amérique, North America. États-Unis. Constitution, moeurs, usages, lois, institutions, sectes religieuses. Paris: E. Dentu, 1871.

_____. Guerre aux hommes. Paris: E. Dentu, 1866, 256 pp.

_____. Gynécologie: la femme depuis 6000 ans. Paris: E. Dentu, 1873, 332 pp.

_____. Voyage à travers mes souvenirs, ceux que j'ai connus, ce que j'ai vu. Paris: E. Dentu, 1884, 348 pp.

AUMONT, MICHÈLE. La chance d'être femme. Paris: Hachette, 1958, 205 pp.

_____. Femmes en usine: les ouvrières de la métallurgie parisienne. Paris: Éditions Spes, 1953, 158 pp.

AVRIL de SAINTE-CROIX, GHÉNIA. L'éducation sexuelle. Paris: F. Alcan, 1918, 40 pp.

_____. Le féminisme. Paris: V. Giard & E. Brière, 1907, 219 pp. (Preface by Victor Margueritte.)

BACQUES, HENRI. L'empire de la femme. Paris: E. Dentu, 1859, 108 pp.

BADER, CLARISSE. La femme française dans les temps modernes. Paris: E. Perrin, 1883, 574 pp.

BAISSAC, JULES. Les femmes dans les temps anciens. Paris: M. Lévy, 1857, 212 pp.

BARBEY D'AUREVILLY, JULES. Les bas bleus. Paris: V. Palme, 1873, 343 pp. Geneva: Slatkine, 1968.

_____. Femmes et moralistes. Paris: A. Lemerre, 1906, 340 pp.

BARRÈS, MAURICE. Le coeur des femmes en France: extraits de la chronique de la grande guerre (1914-1919). Paris: Plon, 1928, 239 pp.

BASCOU-BANCE, PAULETTE. La condition de la femme en France: son évolution. Paris: Institut Pédagogique National, 1964.

BAUMAL, FRANCIS. Le féminisme au temps de Molière. Paris: Renaissance du Livre, 1926, 162 pp.

BELILON, CAMILLE, and HYACINTHE BELILON. Ève dans l'humanité: sur le livre de Maria Deraismes. N.p., 1900, 132 pp. (Preface by G. Montorgueil.)

Bibliography of Earlier Works

BELSO, GUILLAUME [Fernand Goland]. Les féministes françaises. Paris: Francia, 1925, 344 pp.

BELTRAMI, GEORGES. La provocation à l'avortement et la propagande anti-conceptionnelle: la loi du 31 juillet 1920. Aix-Marseille: Université d'Aix-Marseille, 1921.

BENOIST, CHARLES. Les ouvrières de l'aiguille à Paris: notes pour l'étude de la question sociale. Paris: Chailley, 1895, 296 pp.

BERGER, IDA. Lettres d'institutrices rurales d'autrefois, rédigées à la suite de l'enquête de Francisque Sarcey en 1897. Paris: Association des Amis du Musée Pédagogique, 1961.

_____. Les maternelles. Paris: C.N.R.S., 1959, 195 pp.

BERGUES, HÉLÈNE, P. ARIÈS, E. HELIN, L. HENRY, R.P. RIQUET, A. SEVY, and J. SUTTER. La prévention des naissances dans la famille: ses origines dans les temps modernes. Paris: P.U.F., 1960, 400 pp.

BERTAUT, JULES. Amoureuses et femmes galantes. Lyon: Éditions de Lyon, 1955, 247 pp.

_____. Les belles émigrées: la Comtesse de Polastron, Madame de Flahaut, la Comtesse de Balbi, la Marquise de la Tour du Pin, la Princesse Louise de Bourbon-Condé. Paris: Flammarion, 1948, 281 pp.

_____. Égéries du XVIIIe siècle: Madame Suard, Madame Delille, Madame Helvétius, Madame Diderot, Mademoiselle Quinault. Paris: Plon & Nourrit, 1928, 257 pp.

_____. La Duchesse d'Abratès. Paris: Flammarion, 1949, 318 pp.

_____. L'Impératrice Eugénie et son temps. Paris: Amiot-Dumont, 1955, 309 pp.

BERTIN, CÉLIA. Le temps des femmes. Paris: Hachette, 1958, 202 pp.

BESSAND-MASSENET, PIERRE. Femmes sous la Révolution: la fin d'une société. Paris: Plon, 1953, 259 pp.

BILCESCO, SARMISA. De la condition légale de la mère en droit romain et en droit français. Paris: A. Rousseau, 1890.

BILLARD, MAX. Les femmes enceintes devant le tribunal révolutionnaire. Paris: Perrin, 1911, 225 pp.

BILLY, ANDRÉ. Hortense [Allart de Méritens] et ses amants. Paris: Flammarion, 1961, 234 pp.

Bibliography of Earlier Works

_____. La présidente [Aglaé Sabatier, 1821-1890] et ses amis. Paris: Flammarion, 1945, 260 pp.

BLANC, MARIE-THÉRÈSE [T. Bentzon]. Les Américaines chez elles. Paris: Calmann-Lévy, 18 , 411 pp.

_____. Choses et gens d'Amérique. Paris: Calmann-Lévy, 1898, 334 pp.

_____. Femmes d'Amérique. Paris: A. Colin, 1900, 331 pp.

BLANCHARD, MARIE [Berthe Dangennes]. Mariée ou non, la femme doit être indépendante. Paris: Nilsson, 1923, 128 pp.

BLUM, LÉON. Du mariage. Paris: Ollendorff, 1907, 342 pp.

BODIN, MARGUERITE. L'institutrice. Paris: Bibliothèque Sociale des Métiers; G. Doin, 1922, 347 pp.

BOEUF, MARIE [Camille Bos]. Pessimisme, féminisme, moralisme. Paris: F. Alcan, 1907, 173 pp.

BOGELOT, ISABELLE. Trente ans de solidarité 1877-1906. Paris: Maulde, Doumenc, 1908, 431 pp.

de BOIGNE, CHARLOTTE LOUISE. Mémoires de la Comtesse de Boigne, née d'Osmond. 4 vols. Paris: Plon & Nourrit, 431 pp.

BOIRON, J.F. La condition des femmes. Macon: Bellenand, 1882, 279 pp.

BOIS, JULES. Couple futur. Paris: Librairie des Annales, 1912, 450 pp.

_____. Ève nouvelle. Paris: Chailley, 1896, 381 pp.

_____. Le mystère et la volupté. Paris: Éditions Littéraires et Artistiques, 1901, 324 pp.

BOISGONTIER, HENRI. Les syndicats professionnels féminins de l'Abbaye de l'Union centrale des syndicats professionnels féminins. Paris: Jouve, 1927, 196 pp.

BONNEBAULT, ARMAND. Les groupements professionnels féminins: leur passé, leur présent, leur avenir. Paris: Rousseau, 1910, 200 pp.

BONNEFF, LÉON, and MAURICE BONNEFF. La classe ouvrière. Paris: Éditions de la Guerre Sociale, 1911, 400 pp.

BONNEFOY, ANTOINE. Place aux femmes: les carrières féminines administratives et libérales. Paris: Fayard, 1914, 382 pp.

BONNIER, CHARLES. La question de la femme. Paris: V. Giard & E. Brière, 1897, 59 pp.

BORDEAUX, HENRY. Louise de Savoie, régente et "roi" de France. Paris: Plon, 1954, 432 pp.

BOREL, Mme ÉMILE. La mobilisation féminine en France (1914-1919): documents rassemblés par la société "l'Effort féminin français." Paris: Imprimerie Union, 1919, 88 pp.

BORÉLY, MARTHE. L'appel au Françaises: le féminisme politique. Paris: Nouvelle Librairie Nationale, 1919, 125 pp.

_____. L'émouvante destinée d'Anna de Noailles. Paris: Albert, 1939, 220 pp.

_____. La femme et l'amour dans l'oeuvre d'Anatole France. Paris: Crès, 1917, 51 pp.

_____. Le génie féminin français. Paris: Éditions de Boccard, 1917, 296 pp.

BOSSU, JEAN. La femme et la libre pensée sous la IIIe République. Paris: Institut Français d'Histoire Sociale, 1957.

BOUGLÉ, CÉLESTIN. Chez les prophètes socialistes, saint-simoniens, et ouvriers: le féminisme saint-simonien. Paris: F. Alcan, 1918, 246 pp.

BOURDIN, ISABELLE. Les sociétés populaires à Paris pendant la Révolution française jusqu'à la chute de la royauté. Paris: Librairie du Recueil Sirey, 1937, 454 pp.

BOUVIER, JEANNE. Les femmes pendant la Révolution. Paris: Éditions Eugène Figuière, 1931, 346 pp.

_____. Histoire des dames employées dans les postes, télégraphes, et téléphones de 1714 à 1929. Paris: P.U.F., 1930, 359 pp.

_____. La lingerie et les lingères. Paris: G. Doin, 1928, 392 pp.

_____. Mes mémoires; ou, 59 années d'activité industrielle, sociale, et intellectuelle d'une ouvrière. Paris: Action Intellectuelle, 1936, 185 pp.

BOVERAT, FERNAND. Patriotisme et paternité. Paris: Grasset, 1913, 370 pp.

_____. La résurrection de la natalité. Paris: Hachette, 1941, 497 pp.

BRIDEL, LOUIS. La femme et le droit. Paris: Pichon, 1884, 148 pp.

BRIMO, ALBERT. La femme dans le droit publique français. Toulouse: Annales de la Faculté de Droit de Toulouse, 1968. Reprint. Paris: Montchrestien, 1975, 131 pp.

BUISSON, FERDINAND. Le vote des femmes. Paris: H. Dunod & E. Pinat, 1911.

CABET, ÉTIENNE. La femme: son malheureux sort dans la société actuelle, son bonheur dans la communauté. Paris: Bureau du Populaire, 1848, 32 pp. (There are at least twelve editions.)

CAPY, MARCELLE. Une voix de femme dans la mêlée. Paris: Ollendorff, 1916, 155 pp. (Preface by Romain Rolland.)

de CASTELLANE, MARIA. Souvenirs de la duchesse de Dino, publiés par sa petite-fille. Paris: C. Lévy, 1908, 363 pp.

CASTELNAU, JACQUES. Madame Tallien [Princesse de Chimay 1773-1835]: révolutionnaire, favorite, princesse. Paris: Hachette, 1938, 253 pp.

_____. Marguerite de Navarre, la reine Margot. Paris: Hachette, 1945, 255 pp.

CASTELOT, ANDRÉ. Josephine. Paris: Perrin, 1964, 629 pp.

_____. Marie-Antoinette d'après des documents inédits. Paris: Amiot-Dumont, 1953, 372 pp.

_____. Le secret de Madame Royale d'après des documents inédits. Paris: Sfelt, 1949, 351 pp.

de CASTRIES, RENÉ. Madame du Barry. Paris: Hachette, 1967, 288 pp.

CAUSSY, FERNAND. Laclos 1741-1803: d'après des documents originaux, suivi d'un mémoire inédit de Laclos. Paris: Mercure de France, 1905, 365 pp.

La cause de la femme. Paris: Alcan, 1900, 288 pp.

CAZIN, MADELEINE. Le travail féminin. Rennes: Imprimeries Réunies, 1943, 144 pp.

Bibliography of Earlier Works

CÉRATI, MARIE. Le Club des citoyennes républicaines révolutionnaires. Paris: Éditions Sociales, 1966, 190 pp.

CERMAKIAN, MARIANNE. La princesse des Ursins: sa vie et ses lettres. Paris: Didier, 1969, 716 pp.

CHABAUD, LOUIS. Les précurseurs du féminisme, Mesdames de Maintenon, de Genlis, et Campan: leur rôle dans l'éducation chrétienne de la femme. Paris: Plon, 1901, 330 pp.

CHAMPCEIX, LÉODILE [Andrée Léo]. La femme et les moeurs: liberté ou monarchie? Paris: Journal de Droit des Femmes, 1869, 174 pp.

CHANSON, PAUL. L'accord charnel. Paris: Éditions du Levain, 1950, 171 pp.

―――――. L'art d'aimer. Paris: Éditions Familiales de France, 1949, 159 pp.

―――――. La Fayette et sa femme. Paris: Éditions Familiales de France, 1947, 233 pp.

CHARLETY, SEBASTIEN. Histoire du saint-simonisme: 1825-1864. Paris: Hachette, 1896, 498 pp.

de CHARNAGE, GUY. Les femmes d'aujourd'hui; esquisses. Paris: Michel Lévy, 1867, 215 pp.

CHARRIER, EDMÉE. L'évolution intellectuelle féminine: la femme dans les professions intellectuelles, la femme étudiante. Paris: A. Mechelinck, 1931, 572 pp.

de CHASTENAY, VICTORINE LANTY. Mémoires de 1771 à 1815. 2 vols. Paris: Plon, 1896.

CHAUCHARD, Dr. PAUL. Amour et contraception. Paris: Mame, 1965, 293 pp.

―――――. Apprendre à aimer. Paris: Fayard, 1963, 206 pp.

―――――. La dignité sexuelle et la folie contraceptive. Paris: Éditions du Levain, 1965, 79 pp.

CHAUVIN, JEANNE. Étude historique sur les professions accessibles aux femmes: influence du sémitisme sur l'évolution de la position économique de la femme dans la société. Paris: V. Giard & E. Brière, 1892, 296 pp.

CHOMBART de LAÜWE, MARIE JOSÉ, et al. La femme dans la société: son image dans différents milieux sociaux. Paris: C.N.R.S., 1963, 439 pp.

———. La femme: nature et vocation. Recherches et débats du Centre Catholique des intellectuels Français. Paris: Fayard, 1963, 221 pp.

CHOMBART de LAÜWE, PAUL HENRY, ed. Images de la femme dans la société: recherche internationale. Paris: Éditions Ouvrières, 1964, 280 pp.

CLAMORGAN, PIERRE. Le travail de la femme et la bienfaisance privée à Paris. Paris: Bouvalot-Jouves, 1908, 233 pp.

CLARETIE, JULES. L'école des dames. Paris: Sansot, 1907, 292 pp.

———. La femme dans la nature, dans les moeurs, dans la légende, dans la société: tableau de son évolution physique et psychique. Paris: Bong, 1908-1910.

CLAVEL, SOLANGE. Professions féminines sociales: assistantes sociales, conseillères d'orientation, psychotechniciennes. Paris: P.U.F., 1963, 162 pp.

CLÉMENT, MARCEL. La femme et sa vocation. Paris: Éditions Latines, 1959, 231 pp.

COIRAULT, GASTON. Les 50 premières années de l'enseignement secondaire féminin 1880-1920. Tours: Université de Poitiers, 1940.

COMBARIEU, JULES. Les jeunes filles françaises et la guerre. Paris: A. Colin, 1916, 235 pp.

COMPAIN, LOUISE-MARIE. La femme dans les organisations ouvrières. Paris: V. Giard & E. Brière, 1910, 148 pp.

COMPAYRÉ, GABRIEL. Histoire critique des doctrines de l'éducation en France depuis le seizième siècle. 2 vols. Paris: Hachette, 1879.

CONFÉDÉRATION FRANÇAISE ET DÉMOCRATIQUE DU TRAVAIL [C.F.D.T.]. Femmes au travail: solutions pour aujourd'hui et demain. Paris: Formation, 1967, 47 pp.

COQUET, J. Les femmes ont la parole? Paris: Gallimard, 1955, 207 pp.

CORCOS, FERNAND. Les femmes en guerre. Paris: Montaigne, 1927, 191 pp.

CORDELIER, JEAN. Mme de Maintenon. Paris: Seuil, 1955, 555 pp.

CORDELIER, SUZANNE. Femmes au travail: étude pratique sur dix-sept carrières féminines. Paris: Plon, 1935, 232 pp.

CORMIER, MANON. Madame Juliette Adam; ou, l'Aurore de la IIIe République. Bordeaux: Delmas, 1934, 302 pp.

COTTI, COLETTE. La femme au seuil de l'an 2000. Paris and Tournai: Casterman, 1968, 200 pp.

COTTIN, PAUL, ed. Journal intime de Mme Moitte (1747-1807): un ménage d'artistes sous le Premier Empire. Paris: Plon, 1932.

COUSIN, VICTOR. Études sur les femmes illustres et la société du XVIIIe siècle. Paris: N.p., 1858.

_____. Jacqueline Pascal. Paris: Didier, 1845, 443 pp.

_____. La jeunesse de Mme de Longueville. Paris: Didier, 1864, 588 pp.

_____. Madame de Chevreuse et Madame de Hauteforte. 2 vols. Paris: Didier, 1856.

_____. Madame de Longueville. 2 vols. Paris: Didier, 1855-59.

_____. Madame de Longueville pendant la Fronde. Paris: Didier, 1867, 491 pp.

_____. Madame de Sablé. Paris: Didier, 1854, 464 pp.

CRETTÉ-BRETON, YVONNE. Mémoires d'une bonne, souvenirs 1908-1919. Paris: Éditions du Scorpion, 1966, 256 pp.

CUSENIER, MARCEL. Les domestiques en France. Paris: A. Rousseau, 1912, 376 pp. (Preface by Louis Puech.)

DAILLIER-CRETON. La paix du monde ou le droit commun rétabli pour tous par la baptême de la femme et son prochain avènement. Paris: E. Dentu, 1865, 375 pp.

DANIELOU, MADELEINE. Livre de sagesse pour les filles de France. Paris: Bloud & Gay, 1942, 247 pp.

DAPEFIGUE, Mme. La Comtesse du Cayla, Louis XVIII, et les salons du Faubourg Saint-Germain sous la Restauration. Paris: Amyot, 1886, 247 pp.

DARIO, JEAN. L'activité professionnelle des femmes en France: étude statistique, évolution, comparaisons internationales. Paris: P.U.F., 1947, 100 pp.

DAUBIÉ, JULIE-VICTOIRE. L'émancipation de la femme en dix livraisons. Paris: E. Thorin, 1871, 159 pp.

Bibliography of Earlier Works

_____. La femme pauvre au XIXe siècle. Paris: Guillaumin, 1866, 450 pp.

_____. Du progrès dans l'instruction primaire: justice et liberté. Paris: Imprimerie de Mme Claye, 1862, 157 pp.

DAYOT, ARMAND. L'image de la femme. Paris: Hachette, 1889, 397 pp.

DECAUX, ALAIN, ed. Grandes favorites de toutes les époques et dans tous les pays. Paris: Grasset, 1960, 493 pp.

DEFLOU, JEANNE (Mme ODDO). Le sexualisme: critique de la prépondérance et de la mentalité du sexe fort. Paris: J. Tallandier, 1906, 355 pp.

DEJEAN, ÉTIENNE. La Duchesse de Barry et les monarchies européennes (août 1830-déc. 1833). Paris: Librairie Plon, 1913, 393 pp.

DELATOUR, YVONNE. Les effets de la guerre sur la situation de la Française d'après la presse féminine 1914-1918. Paris: Université de Paris, 1965.

DELPECH, JEANINE. L'âme de la Fronde: Mme de Longueville (1619-1679). Paris: Fayard, 1957, 217 pp.

DERAISMES, MARIA. Ève contre M. Dumas, fils. Paris: E. Dentu, 1872, 71 pp.

_____. Ève dans l'humanité. Paris: L. Sauvaitre, 1891, 225 pp.

_____. France et progrès. Paris: Librairie de la Société des Gens de Lettres, 1873, 463 pp.

_____. Nos principes et nos moeurs. Paris: Michel Lévy, 1868, 328 pp.

DERBLAY, CLAUDE. Henriette d'Angleterre et sa légende. Paris: SFELT, 1950, 262 pp.

_____. Une héroïne de Brantôme: Renée de Bussy d'Amboise, Maréchale de Balagny, Princesse de Cambrai. Paris: Plon, 1935, 253 pp.

DEROGY, JACQUES. Des enfants malgré nous? Paris: Éditions de Minuit, 1956, 252 pp.

DEROIN, JEANNE. Almanach des femmes: Women's Almanac. London: J. Watson; Paris: St. Honoré, 1852-55.

DESCARMES, ALAIN. Histoire satirique de la femme à travers les âges. Paris: Éditions de Neuilly, 1947, 216 pp.

Bibliography of Earlier Works

DESMOTTES, G. Manuel pratique du service social. Les assistantes sociales: leur formation. Paris: Éditions Juridiques et Techniques, 1964, 167 pp.

DESSENS, ALFRED. Les revendications des droits de la femme au point de vue politique, civil, économique pendant la Révolution. Toulouse: C. Marquès, 1915, 208 pp.

DESSIGNOLLE, ÉMILE. Le féminisme d'après la doctrine socialiste de Charles Fourier. Lyon: A. Storck, 1903, 148 pp.

DEVALDÈS, MANUEL. La maternité consciente: le rôle des femmes dans l'amélioration de la race. Paris: Radot, 1927, 221 pp.

De DINO, (Duchesse) DOROTHÉE TALLEYRAND-PÉRIGORD. Chronique de 1831 à 1862. 4 vols. Paris: Plon & Nourrit, 1909-10.

DOGAN, MATTEI, and JACQUES NARBONNE. Les femmes françaises face à la politique: comportement politique et condition sociale. Paris: A. Colin, 1955, 192 pp.

DOLÉRIS, Dr. JACQUES. Hygiène et morale sociales: néo-malthusianisme, maternité et féminisme, éducation sexuelle. Paris: Masson, 1918, 270 pp.

DOLLÉANS, ÉDOUARD. George Sand: féminisme et mouvement ouvrier. Paris: Éditions Ouvrières, 1951, 177 pp.

DONNAY, MAURICE. La femme et sa mission. Paris: Plon, 1941, 274 pp.

_____. La Parisienne et la guerre. Paris: Crès, 1916, 163 pp.

DOURLEN-ROLLIER, ANNE-MARIE. La vérité sur l'avortement: deux enquêtes inédites. Paris: P. Maloines, 1963, 246 pp.

DROZ, GUSTAVE. Monsieur, Madame, et bébé. Paris: J. Hetzel, 1867, 392 pp. (There are many editions of this popular work cited by French Academy.)

DUCHÂTEL, SUZANNE BIDAULT. Le féminisme intellectuel. Mayenne: Floch, 1930, 390 pp.

DUCOT, LOUISE [Jacques Trève]. Du rôle de la femme dans la vie des héros. Paris: Figuière, 1913, 259 pp.

DUFRÉNOY, ADÉLAÏDE, and AMABLE TASTU. Le livre des femmes: choix de morceaux extraits des meilleurs écrivains français sur le caractère, les moeurs, et l'esprit des femmes. 2 vols. Paris: Persan, 1823.

Bibliography of Earlier Works

DULONG, CLAUDE. L'amour au XVIIIe siècle. Paris: Hachette, 1969, 322 pp.

DUMAS, ALEXANDRE, fils. Les femmes qui tuent et les femmes qui votent. Paris: Calmann-Lévy, 1880, 216 pp.

_____. La question du divorce. Paris: Calmann-Lévy, 1880, 417 pp.

_____. La question de la femme. Paris: Association pour l'Émancipation de la Femme, 1872, 64 pp.

_____. La recherche de la paternité. Lettre à M. Rivet, député. Paris: Calmann-Lévy, 1883, 138 pp.

DUMAS, ANDRÉ. Le contrôle des naissances, opinions protestantes. Paris: Bergers et Mages, 1965, 163 pp.

DUPANLOUP, FÉLIX ANTOINE PHILIBERT [Bishop of Orléans]. Aux femmes du monde. Paris: C. Douniol, 1868, 160 pp.

_____. Dernière réponse à M. Dury et à ses défenseurs. Paris: C. Douniol, 1868, 160 pp.

_____. La femme chrétienne et française. Paris: C. Douniol, 1870.

_____. Femmes savantes et femmes studieuses. Paris: C. Douniol, 1867, 80 pp.

_____. Lettres sur l'éducation des filles et sur les études qui conviennent dans le monde. 7th ed. Paris: P. Téquin, 1879, 467 pp.

_____. Opuscule sur l'éducation des femmes. 2 vols. Paris: C. Douniol, 1867-68.

de DURAS, Duchesse LOUISE [née Noailles]. Journal des prisons de mon père, de ma mère, et des miennes. Paris: Plon, 1888, 322 pp.

DUREIL, NICOLE. Femme et associée. Paris: Baudinière, 1934, 284 pp.

DUVERGER, MAURICE. La participation des femmes à la vie politique. Paris: UNESCO, 1955, 240 pp.

DYLE, JULIETTE. Au fil de Mars: journal d'une infirmière. Paris: Imprimerie Busson, 1926, 254 pp.

Bibliography of Earlier Works

d'EAUBONNE, FRANÇOISE. Le complexe de Diane: érotisme ou féminisme. Paris: R. Julliard, 1951, 301 pp.

_____. Une femme témoin de son siècle: Germaine de Staël. Paris: Flammarion, 1966, 285 pp.

L'emploi des femmes: séminaire syndical régional. Paris: OCDE, 1968, 423 pp.

ESQUIROS, ADÈLE. Les amours étranges. Paris: A. Courcier, 1853, 348 pp.

ESQUIROS, ALPHONSE. Les vierges folles. Paris: Le Gallois, 1841, 215 pp.

_____. Les vierges martyres. Paris: Delavigne, 1842, 156 pp.

Essai sur la condition des femmes en Europe et en Amérique. Paris: Ghio, 1882, 442 pp.

d'ESTERNO, HENRI. La femme envisagée au point de vue naturaliste, spiritualiste, philosophique, providentiel. Paris: Calmann-Lévy, 1882, 196 pp.

Examen de conscience des femmes honnêtes en France. Paris: E. Dentu, 1872, 59 pp.

EYQUEM, ALBERT. Le régime dotal. Son histoire, son évolution et ses transformations au XIXe siècle sous l'influence de la jurisprudence et du notariat. Paris: 1903, 586 pp.

FAGNIEZ, GUSTAVE. La femme et la société française pendant la première moitié du XVIIe siècle. Paris: J. Gamber, 1929, 397 pp.

FAGUET, ÉMILE. Le féminisme. Paris: Boivin, 1890, 380 pp.

FAHMY-BEY, JEANNE [Jehan d'Ivray]. L'aventure saint-simonienne et les femmes. Paris: Alcan, 1928, 232 pp.

FALLOT, TOMMY. La femme esclave. Paris: Fischbacher, 184, 78 pp.

FAVRE, JULES. Quatre conférences: "De la condition des femmes dans les sociétés démocratiques." Paris: Plon, 1874, 244 pp.

La femme émancipée. Edited by Cécile Brunschvig et al. Paris: Éditions Montaigne, 1927, 217 pp.

Les femmes dans la société actuelle. Paris: Spes, 1928, 290 pp.

Bibliography of Earlier Works

Femmes du XXe siècle: semaine de la pensée marxiste de janvier 1965. Paris: P.U.F., 1965, 234 pp.

FERRÉ, LOUISE MARIE. Féminisme et positivisme. Paris: the author, 1938, 129 pp.

FINOT, JEAN. Préjugé et problème des sexes. Paris: F. Alcan, 1912, 524 pp.

FLEISCHMANN, HECTOR. Dessous des princesses et maréchales d'Empire d'après des lettres inédites, des documents nouveaux, les journaux des modes et les témoignanges des contemporains. Paris: Librairie des Annales, 1905, 283 pp.

_____. Le dix-huitième siècle galant et libertin: recueil de documents curieux et très rares sur l'amour et les femmes galantes au XVIIIe siècle. Paris: A. Michel, 1913, 330 pp.

_____. Les femmes et la Terreur, d'après les documents des Archives Nationales. Paris: Charpentier & Fasquelle, 1910, 364 pp.

_____. Les filles publiques sous la Terreur. Paris: A. Méricant, 1908, 324 pp.

FRANK, LOUIS. Essai sur la condition politique de la femme: étude de sociologie et de législation. Paris: A. Rousseau, 1892, 596 pp.

_____. La femme avocat: exposé historique et critique de la question. Paris: V. Giard & E. Brière, 1898, 313 pp.

_____. Le grand catéchisme de la femme. Paris: Gilon, 1894, 124 pp.

FRÉVILLE, JEAN, ed. La femme et le communisme: anthologie des grands textes du marxisme. Paris: Éditions Sociales, 1950, 224 pp.

FROGER-DOUDEMONT, RAOUL. Que veulent donc ces féministes? Paris: V. Giard & E. Brière, 1926, 460 pp.

GABORTY, ÉMILE. Les femmes dans la tempête: les Vendéennes. Paris: Perrin, 1934, 262 pp.

GALICHON, CLAIRE. Ève réhabilitée: plaidoyer "pro fémina." Paris: Librairie Générale des Sciences Occultes, 1904, 460 pp.

GALOPIN, ARNOULD. Ninon de Lenclos d'après sa correspondance amoureuse, les témoignages et les récits de ses contemporains. Paris: A. Michel, 1910, 310 pp.

Bibliography of Earlier Works

GARÇON, MAURICE, ed. <u>Voyage d'une Hollondaise en France en 1819</u>. Paris: J.J. Pauvert, 1966, 187 pp.

GAUTHEROT, GUSTAVE. <u>Les supliciées de la Terreur</u>. Paris: Perrin, 1926, 328 pp.

GAY, JULES. <u>Bibliographie des ouvrages relatifs à l'amour, aux femmes, au mariage, et des livres facétieux, pantagruéliques, scatologiques, satiriques, . . .</u> 4 vols. Paris: Lemonnyer, 1894-1900.

GAZIER, CÉCILE. <u>Les belles amies de Port-Royal</u>. Paris: Perrin, 1930, 253 pp.

GEMÄHLING, PAUL. <u>Travailleurs au rabais: la lutte syndicale contre les sous-concurrences ouvrières</u>. Paris: Bloud, 432 pp.

GENNARI, GÉNEVIÈVE. <u>Le dossier de la femme</u>. Paris: Perrin, 1965, 361 pp.

GEX-LEVERREUR, M. <u>Une Française dans la tourmente</u>. Paris: E. Paul, 1945, 207 pp.

GIDE, PAUL, and ADHEMAR ESMEIN. <u>Étude sur la condition privée de la femme dans le droit ancien et moderne</u>. Paris: Durand & Pédone-Lauriel, 1867, 563 pp.

de GIRARDIN, ÉMILE. <u>L'égale de l'homme. Lettre à M. Alexandre Dumas fils</u>. Paris: Calmann Lévy, 1881, 140 pp.

_____. <u>L'homme et la femme: l'homme suzerain, la femme vassale. Lettre à M. A. Dumas fils</u>. Paris: M. Lévy, 1872.

GIRAUD, LÉON [Draigu]. <u>Des promesses du mariage: étude historique et juridique</u>. Paris: F. Pichon, 1888.

_____. <u>Le roman de la femme chrétienne: étude historique avec une lettre-préface par Mlle. Hubertine Auclert</u>. Paris: Ghio, 1880, 332 pp.

_____. <u>Essai sur la condition des femmes en Europe et en Amérique</u>. Paris: A. Ghio, 1882.

_____. <u>La femme et la nouvelle loi sur le divorce</u>. Paris: Pédone-Lauriel, 1885.

GIRAUDOUX, JEAN. <u>La Française et la France</u>. Paris: Gallimard, 1951, 247 pp. (Written in 1934.)

Bibliography of Earlier Works

GIROUD, GABRIEL. Cempius: éducation intégrale, co-éducation des sexes, d'après les documents officiels et les publications de l'établissement. Paris: Schleicher Frères, 1900, 394 pp.

_____. Moyens d'éviter la grossesse. N.p.: the author, 1908, 96 pp.

_____. Paul Robin. Paris: Éditions Mignolet & Storz, 1937, 317 pp.

de GONCOURT, EDMOND, and JULES de GONCOURT. La femme au XVIIIe siècle: la société, l'amour, et le mariage. Paris: Firmin Didot, 1862, 459 pp.

GONNARD, RENÉ. La femme dans l'industrie. Paris: A. Colin, 1906, 283 pp. (Contains an important bibliography.)

GOYAU, LUCIE FÉLIX FAURE. La femme au foyer et dans la cité. Paris: E. Perrin, 1917, 367 pp.

GRAVE, JEAN. La société future. Paris: Stock, 1895, 414 pp.

GRÉARD, OCTAVE. L'éducation des femmes par les femmes: études et portraits. Paris: Hachette, 1886, 360 pp.

_____. Mémoire sur l'enseignement secondaire des filles. Paris: Delalain Frères, 1882, 208 pp.

GRÉPON, MARGUERITE. Pour une introduction à une histoire de l'amour. Paris: J. Vigneua, 1946, 259 pp.

GRIMANELLI, PÉRICLÈS. La femme et le positivisme. Paris: Pelletan, 1905, 128 pp.

GRINBERG, SUZANNE. Historique du mouvement suffragiste depuis 1848. Paris: Goulet, 1926, 216 pp.

GRINDON, A. Étude sur l'amélioration progressive de la condition des femmes en droit romain et en droit français. Lyon: Girard & Josserand, 1860, 180 pp.

GUELAUD-LÉRIDON, FRANÇOISE. Recherche sur la condition féminine dans la société d'aujourd'hui. Paris: P.U.F., 1967, 128 pp.

GUÉROULT, GEORGES. Du rôle de la femme dans notre rénovation sociale. Caen: A. Domin, 1891.

GUESDE, JULES. La femme et la société bourgeoise. Paris: Librairie de l'Humanité, 1923, 44 pp.

GUILBERT, MADELEINE. La femme et l'organisation syndicale jusqu'en 1914. Paris: CNRS, 1966, 408 pp.

Bibliography of Earlier Works

_____. Les fonctions des femmes dans l'industrie. Paris and The Hague: Mouton, 1966, 408 pp.

GUILBERT, MADELEINE, and V. ISAMBERT-JAMATI, et al. Travail féminin et travail à domicile. Paris: CNRS, 1956, 222 pp.

GUILOU, ROBERT. La Française dans ses quatre âges: essai sur le XXe siècle. Paris: Levé, 1919, 254 pp.

GUITTON, THÉRÈSE. Professions féminines paramédicales. Paris: P.U.F., 1962, 117 pp.

GUYOT, YVES. Société pour l'amélioration du sort de la femme et la revendication de ses droits. Paris: Mayer, 1888, 79 pp.

D'HAUSSONVILLE, GABRIEL PAUL. Salaire et misère des femmes. Paris: Calmann-Lévy, 1900, 314 pp.

_____. Le Salon de Mme Necker. 2 vols. Paris: N.p., 1882.

_____. Le travail de la femme à domicile. Paris: Blond, 1909.

HAVEL, J.E. La condition de la femme. Paris: A. Colin, 1961, 224 pp.

HEIM, MAURICE. François I et les femmes. Paris: Gallimard, 1956, 301 pp.

d'HÉRICOURT, JENNY. La femme affranchie: réponse à MM. Michelet, Proudhon, E. de Girardin, A. Comte et aux autres novateurs modernes. 2 vols. Paris: Bohne, 1860.

HUISMAN, GEORGES. La vie privée de Mme Roland: Marie Jeanne Philipon (1754-1793). Paris: Hachette, 1955, 254 pp.

HUMBERT, JEANNE. Eugène Humbert, la vie et l'oeuvre d'un néo-malthusien. Paris: Grande Réforme, 1947, 333 pp.

HUZARD, ANTOINETTE de BOURGEVIN [Colette Yver]. Dans le jardin de féminisme. Paris: Clamann-Lévy, 1929, 209 pp.

IBERT, JEAN-CLAUDE. Les femmes à travers le monde. Paris: Hachette, 1960, 342 pp.

Bibliography of Earlier Works

JACQUES, ANNE. Journal d'une Française. Paris: P.U.F., 1946, 328 pp.

JEANSON, FRANCIS. Simone de Beauvoir, ou l'entreprise de vivre, suivi d'entretiens avec Simone de Beauvoir. Paris: Seuil, 1966, 302 pp.

JOBEZ, ALPHONSE. La femme et l'enfant; ou, misère entraîne oppression. Paris: Lévy, 1852, 384 pp.

JORAN, THÉODORE. Au coeur du féminisme. Paris: A. Savaète, 1908.

―――. Autour du féminisme. Paris: C. Poussielgue, 1906, 219 pp.

―――. Les féministes avant le féminisme. Paris: A. Savaète, 1910, 243 pp.

―――. Le mensonge du féminisme. Paris: H. Jouve, 1905.

―――. Le suffrage des femmes. Paris: A. Savaète, 1914, 384 pp.

―――. La trouée féministe. Paris: A. Savaète, 1909.

JOURDAIN, CHARLES-MARIE. L'éducation des femmes au moyen âge. Paris: Didot Frères, 1871, 32 pp.

JOURDAN, LOUIS. Les femmes devant l'échafaud. Paris: Ballay, 1862, 317 pp.

―――. Les mauvais ménages. Paris: Librairie Nouvelle, 1859, 344 pp.

KAHN, GUSTAVE. La femme dans la caricature française. Paris: Méricant, 1907, 470 pp. (Orné de 448 illustrations dans le texte et 72 gravures hors teste en noir et en couleurs, d'après les plus rares et les plus amusantes caricatures de toutes le époques.)

KATSCHER, LÉOPOLD. A sa majesté la femme. Paris: P.U.F., 1926, 123 pp.

de LABOULAYE, ÉDOUARD. Recherches sur la condition civile et politique des femmes, depuis les Romains jusqu'à nos jours. Paris: A. Durand, 1843, 528 pp. (Commended by the Académie des Sciences Morales et Politiques.)

LACORE, SUZANNE. L'émancipation de la femme. Paris: Éditions de la Perfrac, 1945, 69 pp.

―――. Femmes socialistes. Paris: Librairie Populaire du Parti Socialiste, 1932, 52 pp.

Bibliography of Earlier Works

LACOUR, LÉOPOLD. Humanisme intégral. Le duel des sexes: la cité future. Paris: Stock, 1897, 360 pp.

_____. Les origines du féminisme contemporain. Trois femmes de la Révolution: Olympe de Gouges, Théroigne de Méricourt, Rose Lacombe. Paris: Plon & Nourrit, 1900, 432 pp.

LAFARGUE, PAUL. La question de la femme. Paris: Éditions Oeuvres Nouvelles, 1904, 24 pp.

de LA GUETTE, CATHERINE. Mémoires de Madame de la Guette [c. 1613-80] écrites par elle-même. Paris: P. Jannet, 1856, 223 pp. (New edition edited and with a preface by M. Moreau.)

LAGROUA WEILL-HALLÉ, Dr. ANDRÉE MARIE. La grand'peur d'aimer: journal d'une femme médicin. Paris: Gonthier: Julliard, 1960, 196 pp. (Preface by Simone de Beauvoir.)

_____. La libre conception à l'étranger. Paris: Maloine, 1958, 192 pp.

_____. Le "planning familial." Paris: Maloine, 1959, 87 pp. (Preface by Simone de Beauvoir.)

_____. Pour la pilule et le planning familial. Nancy: Berger-Lévrault, 1967, 79 pp. (Printed with Paul Chauchand's Contre la pilule, 80 pp.)

de LA HIRE, MARIE. Le féminisme en France et les sociétés féministes. Paris: N.p., 1907.

_____. La femme française: son activité pendant la guerre. Paris: Taillandier, 1917.

LAIGLE, MATHILDE. "Le Livre de Trois Vertus" de Christine de Pisan et son milieu historique et littéraire. Paris: H. Champion, 1912, 375 pp.

LAINÉ, ANDRÉ. La situation des femmes employées dans les magasins de vente à Paris. Paris: A. Rousseau, 1911, 270 pp.

LAMBER[T], JULIETTE (Mme ADAM). Idées anti-proudhonniennes sur l'amour, la femme, et le mariage. Paris: Taride, 1858, 196 pp. (There are many subsequent printings of this work by an author who lived to be a hundred.)

_____. Mes sentiments et nos idées avant 1870. 6th ed. Paris: Alphonse Lemerre, 1895, 480 pp.

LAMBERT, PIERRE, and MARGUERITE LAMBERT. 3,000 foyers parlent: une enquête de "Clair Foyer" sur la régulation des naissances. Paris: Éditions Ouvrières, 1966, 296 pp.

de LA MAGDELEINE, P. L'Agnès d'aujourd'hui, ou la femme moderne. Paris: Éditions de la Jeune Académie, 1934, 361 pp.

de LAMOTTE, ARMAND. Étude sociale: la femme en ville et à la campagne, salaires et conditions diverses. Paris: M. Rivière, 1910, 102 pp.

LAMPÉRIÈRE, ANNA. La femme et son pouvoir. Paris: V. Giard & E. Brière, 1909, 308 pp.

──────. Le rôle social de la femme: devoirs, droits, éducation. Paris: F. Alcan, 1898, 174 pp.

LAMY, ÉTIENNE. La femme de demain. Paris: Perrin, 1901, 291 pp.

LARCHER, LOUIS JULIEN. Ce qu'on dit du mariage et du célibat. Paris: Magnin & Blanchard, 1858, 292 pp.

──────. Les femmes jugées par les bonnes langues dans tous les temps et dans tous les pays. Paris: Magnin, 1859, 245 pp.

──────. La femme jugée par les grands écrivains des deux sexes. Paris: Simon, 1846, 586 pp.

──────. Les femmes peintes par elles-mêmes. Paris: Magnin & Blanchard, 1858, 269 pp.

──────. Opinions des anciens et des modernes sur l'éducation des filles, ou, le livre des institutrices et des mères de famille. Paris: Larousse & Boyer, 1859, 384 pp.

──────. Satires et diatribes sur les femmes, l'amour, et le mariage, avec une réfutation. Paris: Delahaye, 1860, 282 pp.

LASSERRE, ADRIEN. La participation collective des femmes à la Révolution française: les antécédents du féminisme. Paris: Félix Alcan, 1906, 349 pp.

de LAURIBAR, PAUL. Le Code de l'éternelle mineure: philosophie du droit féminin, précédé d'une étude sur la situation juridique et sociale de la femme à travers les âges. Paris: Plon, 1922, 419 pp.

de LA VARENDE, JEAN. Les belles esclaves. Paris: Flammarion, 1949 334 pp.

LEBRUN, Mme ÉMILE [Vérine]. L'art d'aimer ses enfants. Paris: Spes, 1943, 284 pp.

Bibliography of Earlier Works

_____. La famille nouvelle. Paris: Spes, 1944, 95 pp.

_____. La femme et l'amour dans la société de demain. Paris: Spes, 1930, 215 pp.

LE BRUN, PIERRE. Questions actuelles du syndicalisme. Paris: Seuil, 1965, 171 pp.

LECLERC, ANDRÉ. Le vote des femmes en France. Paris: Marcel Rivière, 1929, 236 pp.

LECLERC, JACQUES. La femme: aujourd'hui et demain. Paris and Tournai: Casterman, 1968, 134 pp.

_____. Vers une famille nouvelle. Paris: Éditions Universitaires, 1962, 188 pp.

LEDUC, LUCIEN. La femme et les projets de lois relatifs à l'extension de sa capacité. Paris: V. Giard & E. Brière, 1898.

LEFEBVRE, CHARLES. La famille en France dans le droit et dans les moeurs. Paris: M. Giard, 1920, 222 pp.

LEFEVRE, MAURICE. La femme à travers l'histoire. Paris: A. Fontemoing, 1902, 328 pp.

LÉGIER-DESGRANGES, HENRY. Madame de Moysan et l'extravagante affaire de l'Hôpital général, 1749-1758: du Jansénisme à la Révolution. Paris: Hachette, 1954, 478 pp.

LEGOUVÉ, ERNEST. La femme en France au XIXe siècle. Paris: Didier, 1864.

_____. Histoire morale des femmes. Paris: Sandré, 1848, 450 pp. (Many subsequent editions.)

_____. La question des femmes. Paris: Hetzel, 1881, 47 pp.

LEGOUVÉ, GABRIEL. Le mérite des femmes. Paris: Didot l'aîné, 1801, 92 pp. (Numerous editions of this didactic poem were printed until 1850.)

LEHMANN, ANDRÉE. De la réglementation légale du travail féminin. Étude de législation comparée. Paris: H. Arthez, 1924, 216 pp.

_____. Le rôle de la femme dans l'histoire de France au moyen âge. Paris: Berger-Levrault, 1952, 526 pp.

_____. Le rôle de la femme dans l'histoire de la Gaule. Paris: P.U.F., 1944, 150 pp.

Bibliography of Earlier Works

---. Le rôle de la femme française au milieu du XXe siècle. Paris: Éditions de la Ligue Française pour le Droit des Femmes, 1950, 35 pp.

LE ROUX, HUGUES. Nos filles, qu'en ferons nous? Paris: Calmann-Lévy, 1898, 267 pp.

LEROUX, PIERRE. De l'égalité, suivi d'aphorismes sur la doctrine de l'humanité. Boussac: P. Leroux, 1848, 272 pp.

LEROY-BEAULIEU, PAUL. La question ouvrière au XIXe siècle. Paris: Charpentier, 1872, 340 pp.

---. Rapport sur le concours relatif à l'instruction et au salaire des femmes dans les travaux d'industrie. Paris: Firmin-Didot, 1871, 341 pp.

---. Le travail des femmes au XIXe siècle. Paris: Charpentier, 1873, 468 pp.

de LESCURE, MATHURIN FRANÇOIS ADOLPHE. Les grandes épouses: études morales et portraits d'histoire intime. Paris: Firmin-Didot, 1884, 528 pp.

---. Les maîtresses du Régent: études d'histoire et de moeurs sur le commencement du XVIIIe siècle. Paris: E. Dentu, 1860, 483 pp.

---. Marie-Antoinette et sa famille, d'après les nouveaux documents. Paris: E. Ducrocq, 1854, 668 pp.

---. Les mères illustres: études morales et portraits d'histoire intime. Paris: Firmin-Didot, 1882, 436 pp.

LETOURNEAU, CHARLES. La condition de la femme dans les diverses races et civilisations. Paris: V. Giard & E. Brière, 1903, 508 pp.

---. L'évolution du mariage et de la famille. Paris: Delahaye & Lecrosnier, 467 pp.

LEVINCK, ANNE. Les femmes qui ne tuent ni ne votent. 3d ed. Paris: C. Marpon & E. Flammarion, 1882, 155 pp.

LÉVY-LEBOYER, C. Les infirmières. Paris: École Pratique des Hautes Études, 1967, 158 pp.

LI, DZEH DJEN. La presse féministe en France de 1869 à 1914. Paris: L. Rodstein, 1934, 236 pp.

Bibliography of Earlier Works

Ligue française pour le droit des femmes (also entitled Cinqante ans de féminisme, 1870-1920). Paris, 1921, 148 pp.

LILAR, SUZANNE. Le couple. Paris: Grasset, 1963, 305 pp.

LIPINSKA, MÉLINA. Les femmes et le progrès des sciences médicales. Paris: Masson, 1930, 235 pp.

_____. Histoire des femmes médecines. Paris: Jacque, 1900, 586 pp.

LOLIÉE, FRÉDÉRIC. La femme dans la nature, dans les moeurs, dans la légende, dans la société: tableau de son évolution physique et psychique . . . . Paris: Bong, 1908-10.

_____. Les femmes du second empire. 3 vols. Paris: Félix Juven, 1906.

LOMBROSO, GINA. La femme dans la société actuelle. Paris: Payot, 1959, 398 pp.

LOURBET, JACQUES. La femme devant la science contemporaine. Dernier mot: liberté entière pour la femme!! Paris: Félix Alcan, 1896, 178 pp.

_____. Le problème des sexes. Paris: V. Giard & E. Brière, 1900, 298 pp.

de LUPPÉ, ALBERT. Les jeunes filles dans l'aristocracie et la bourgeoisie à la fin du XVIIIe siècle. Paris: Champion, 1924, 256 pp. (This work was reissued as Les jeunes filles à la fin du XVIIIe siècle by the same publisher in 1925; it contains previously unpublished letters of the period and a fifteen-page bibliography.)

_____. Les jeunes Françaises au XVIIIe siècle. Paris: Alex Redier, 1932, 217 pp.

MACHARD, RAYMONDE. Les Françaises: ce qu'elles valent . . . ce qu'elles veulent. . . . Paris: Flammarion, 1945, 219 pp.

MADAY, ANDOR. Le droit de la femme au travail: étude sociologique. Paris: V. Giard & E. Brière, 1905, 260 pp.

_____. Les femmes et les tribunaux de prud'hommes. Neuchâtel: Attinger Frères, 1917, 22 pp.

MAGNE, ÉMILE. Le coeur et l'esprit de Madame de La Fayette: portraits et documents inédits. Paris: Émile-Paule Frères, 1927, 402 pp.

MALLET, FRANCINE. La victoire de la femme: histoire universelle de la condition féminine. Paris: Pont Royal, 1964, 202 pp.

MALLET-JORIS, FRANÇOISE. Marie Mancini, le premier amour de Louis XIV. Paris: Hachette, 1964, 311 pp.

MARTIAL, LYDIE. La femme intégrale. Paris: the author, 1901, 40 pp. Reprinted in L'éducation humaine: la femme et la liberté, le féminisme, la grandeur de son but; la femme intégrale (Paris: Union de la Pensée Féminine, 1902).

———. Misère sociale de la femme du XVIIe et XIXe siècles. Paris: G. Weil, 1911.

MARTIN, LOUIS-AUGUSTE. Histoire de la condition des femmes chez les peuples de l'antiquité. Paris: Chez Ebrard, 1839, 246 pp.

———. Histoire de la femme: sa condition politique, civile, morale, et religieuse. Vol. 1, Paris: Didier, 1862, 391 pp. Vol. 2, 1863, 300 pp.

MARTIN, MARGUERITE. Les droits de la femme. Paris: Marcel Rivière, 1912, 129 pp.

MARTIN, MARIE-ADÈLE. La jeune fille française dans la littérature et dans la société 1850-1914. Rennes: Maurice Simon, 1938, 213 pp.

MARTIN, MARIE-MADELEINE. Le "génie" des femmes. Paris: Éditions du Conquistador, 1950, 220 pp.

de MAULDE LA CLAVIÈRE, MARIE A. Les femmes de la Renaissance. Paris: Perrin, 1898, 717 pp.

MAURETTE, MARCELLE. La vie privée de Mme de Pompadour. Paris: Hachette, 1951, 302 pp.

———. La vraie dame aux camélias, ou l'amoureuse sans amour. Paris: . Michel, 1939, 219 pp.

MAURRAS, CHARLES. Le romantisme féminin. Paris: Cité des Livres, 1926, 214 pp.

MAY, GITA. De Jean-Jacques Rousseau à Madame Roland: essai sur la sensibilité préromantique et révolutionnaire. Geneva: Librairie Droz, 1964, 271 pp.

de MENERVILLE, Mme [née Fougeret]. Souvenirs d'émigration. Paris: P. Roger, 1934, 299 pp.

MENY, GEORGES. Lutte contre le sweating-system. Paris: Rivière, 1910, 447 pp.

Bibliography of Earlier Works

MEYER, Dr. ALEXANDRE. Des rapports conjugaux considérés sous le triple point de vue de la population, de la santé, et de la morale publique. Paris: Baillière, 1857, 384 pp.

MICHEL, ANDRÉE, and GÉNEVIÈVE TEXIER. La condition de la Française d'aujourd'hui. Vol. 1, Mythes et réalités. Vol. 2, Les groupes de pression: perspectives nouvelles. Paris: Denoël/Gonthier, 1964-65.

MICHEL, LOUISE. La Commune. Paris: Stock, 1898, 423 pp.

_____. Mémoires. Paris: E. Roy, 1886, 490 pp.

MICHELET, JULES. L'amour. Paris: Hachette, 1858, 414 pp.

_____. La femme. Paris: Hachette, 1860, 396 pp. (Many reprints, including Calmann-Lévy, 1879, 468 pp.)

_____. Les femmes de la Révolution. Paris: A. Delahayes, 1854, 327 pp.

_____. Le prêtre, la femme, et la famille. Paris: Chamerot, 1845, 356 pp.

_____. La sorcière. Paris: E. Dentu, 1862, 456 pp.

MILHAUD, CAROLINE. L'ouvrière en France: sa condition présente, les réformes nécessaires. Paris: F. Alcan, 1907, 202 pp.

MILHAUD-SANUA, LOULI. Figures féminines, 1909-1939. Paris: Librairie Beaufils, 1946, 106 pp.

MOKÉ, HENRI. Du sort de la femme dans les temps anciens et modernes. Ghent: A. Carel, 1860.

MONESTIER, MARIANNE. Les sociétés secrètes féminines. Paris: Production de Paris, 1963, 265 pp.

MONGRÉDIEN, GEORGES. Madame de Montespan et l'affaire des poisons. Paris: Hachette, 1953, 222 pp.

_____. Madeleine de Scudéry et son salon d'après des documents inédits. Paris: Tallandier, 1946, 235 pp.

_____. Marion de Lorme et ses amours. Paris: Hachette, 1940, 254 pp.

_____. Les précieux et les précieuses. Paris: Mercure de France, 1939, 350 pp.

Bibliography of Earlier Works

MONOD, ADOLPHE. La femme, deux discours: I. La mission de la femme; II. La vie de la femme. Paris: Ducloux, 1848, 111 pp.

MONOD, MARIE-OCTAVE. Daniel Stern Comtesse d'Agoult, de la Restauration à la IIIe République. Paris: Plon, 1937, 313 pp.

de MONTJOIE, CAMILLE. L'égale. Paris: Sansot, 1911, 207 pp.

MORET, E. Les femmes sous la Terreur. Paris: Lasseray, 1872, 420 pp.

MORIN, PIERRE. Les droits de la femme mariée sur les produits de son travail. Paris: Rousseau, 1908, 367 pp.

MORNET, JACQUES. La protection de la maternité en France: étude d'hygiène sociale. Paris: M. Rivière, 1910, 315 pp.

MORTIER, AURÉLIE [Aurel]. L'art d'aimer. Paris: A. Fayard, 1927, 363 pp.

———. Le miracle de la chair. Paris: A. Fayard, 1928, 354 pp.

———. Le couple: essai d'entente. Paris: E. Figuière, 1935, 350 pp.

———. Les Françaises devant l'opinion masculine. Paris: Sansot & Chiberre, 1922, 30 pp.

———. Nouvel art d'aimer. Paris: P.U.F., 1941, 171 pp.

———. Une politique de la maternité. Paris: Éditions Médicales, 1923, 61 pp.

———. Rodin devant la femme. Paris: Maison du Livre, 1919, 231 pp.

———. Simplicité féminine au secours! La physique de l'influence. Paris: R. Chiberre, 1921, 64 pp.

———. Voiçi la femme. Paris: Sansot, 1909, 343 pp.

MULDORF, BERNARD. Sexualité et féminité. Paris: Centre d'Études et de Recherches Marxistes, 1965, 48 pp.

NAUDET, PAUL ANTOINE. Pour la femme: études féministes. Paris: Fontemoing, 1904, 330 pp.

NETTER, YVONNE. La femme face à ses problèmes: défense quotidienne de ses intérêts. Paris: Pichon & Durand-Auzias, 1962, 94 pp. (Preface by Marie Bonaparte.)

Bibliography of Earlier Works

_____. Le travail de la femme mariée, son activité professionnelle. Paris: P.U.F., 1923.

NEUWIRTH, LUCIEN. Le dossier de la pilule. Paris: Éditions de la Pensée Moderne, 1967, 350 pp.

NIBOYET, EUGENIE. Le vrai livre des femmes. Paris: E. Dentu, 1863, 245 pp.

NICOLITCH, SUZANNE. Le socialisme et les femmes. Paris: Librairie Populaire, 1946, 38 pp.

NIEL, MATHILDE. Le drame de la libération de la femme. Paris: Le Courrier du Livre, 1968, 127 pp.

NOVICOW, JACQUES. L'affranchissement de la femme. Paris: F. Alcan, 1903, 296 pp.

OBERKIRCH, HENRIETTE-LOUISE. Mémoires de la Baronne d'Oberkirch sur la cour de Louis XIV et la société française avant 1789. Edited by Suzanne Burkard. Paris: Mercure de France, 1970, 556 pp.

OULMONT, CHARLES. Les femmes peintres du XVIIIe siècle. Paris: Riever, 1928, 64 pp. and 60 plates.

OSTROGORSKI, MOÏSE. La femme au point du vue du droit public: étude d'histoire et de législation comparée. Paris: A. Rousseau, 198 pp.

PAILLERON, MARIE-LOUISE. George Sand, historie de sa vie. 3 vols. Paris: Grasset, 1938-53.

PAIN, JEAN. Le duel des sexes: causes et origines. Paris: Radot, 1927, 223 pp.

de PANGE, JEAN (Comtesse). Comment j'ai vu 1900. Paris: Grasset, 1962, no pagination.

PARENT-DUCHÂTELET, Dr. ALEXANDRE JEAN-BAPTISTE. De la prostitution dans la ville de Paris, considérée sous le rapport de l'hygiène publique, de la morale, et de l'administration; ouvrage appuyé de documents statistiques puisés dans les archives de la Préfecture de la police. 2 vols. Paris: J.-B. Baillière, 1836.

PARIAS, LOUIS-HENRI, ed. Histoire générale du travail. 4 vols. Paris: Nouvelle Librairie de France, 1959-61.

PARIS, FERNANDE. Le travail des femmes et le retour de la mère au foyer. Paris: Sirey, 1943, 445 pp.

PASTEUR, CLAUDE. Pionnières de l'histoire. Paris: Éditions du Sud, 1963, 302 pp.

de PAYER, ALICE. Le féminisme du temps de la Fronde. Paris: Fast, 1922, 207 pp.

PELLETAN, EUGÈNE. La femme au XIXe siècle. Paris: Pagnerre, 1869, 35 pp.

PELLÉ-DOUEL, YVONNE. Être femme. Paris: Stock, 1967, 271 pp.

PELLETIER, Dr. MADELEINE. L'éducation féministe des filles. Paris: V. Giard & E. Brière, 1915, 76 pp.

_____. La femme en lutte pour ses droits. Paris: V. Giard & E. Brière, 1908, 79 pp.

PELLOUTIER, FERNAND, and MAURICE PELLOUTIER. La vie ouvrière en France. Paris: Schleicher, 1900, 344 pp. (Reedited by Maspero in 1975.)

PICARD, ROGER. Les salons littéraires et la société française 1660-1789. New York: Brentanos, 1943, 353 pp.

PIERRARD, PIERRE. La vie ouvrière à Lille sous le Second Empire. Paris: Bloud & Gay, 1965, 532 pp.

PINET, MARIE-JOSEPH. Christine de Pisan (1365-1430): étude biographique et littéraire. Paris: Champion, 1927, 463 pp.

PINSET, JACQUES, and YVONNE DESLANDRES. Histoire des soins de beauté. Paris: P.U.F., 1960, 124 pp.

PIRET, R. Psychologie différentielle des sexes. Paris: P.U.F., 1965, 154 pp.

POIRIER, M. L'infériorité sociale de la femme et le féminisme. Paris: Marchal & Bellard, 1900, 186 pp.

de POMPERY, ÉDOUARD. La femme dans l'humanité, sa nature, son rôle, et sa valeur sociale. Paris: Hachette, 1864, 392 pp.

_____. Quintessences féminines. Paris: Reinwald, 1893, 340 pp.

POTHIER, ROBERT JOSEPH. Traité de la puissance du mari sur la personne et les biens de la femme. Vol. 1, Oeuvres. Paris: Coss & Marchal, 1861.

PROUDHON, PIERRE-JOSEPH. De la justice dans la Révolution et dans l'Église. 3 vols. Paris: Garnier Frères, 1858.

Bibliography of Earlier Works

———. La pornocratie, ou les femmes dans les temps modernes. Paris: A. Lacroix, 1875, 269 pp.

PUECH, JULES. Femmes, 1932: vaines redites. Paris: Imprimerie du Palais, 1932, 201 pp.

———. La vie et l'oeuvre de Flora Tristan, 1803-1844. Paris: Union Ouvrière; Marcel Rivière, 1925, 514 pp.

QUERRÉ-JAULMES, FRANCE. La femme; grands textes des Pères de l'Église. Paris: Grasset, 1968.

RAT, MAURICE. Aventurières et intrigantes du grand siècle. Paris: Plon, 1957, 585 pp.

———. Dames et bourgeoises, amoureuses, et galantes du XVIe siècle. Paris: Plon, 1955, 230 pp.

———. Femmes de la Régence. Paris: Berger Levrault, 1961, 268 pp.

RAUZE, MARIANNE. L'anti guerre: féminisme économique. Paris: Éditions de l'Équité, 1915, 31 pp.

RÉDIER, ANTOINE. La guerre des femmes: histoire de Louise de Bettignies et ses compagnes. Paris: Éditions de la Vraie France, 1935, 333 pp.

de RÉMUSAT, CLAIRE (Comtesse). Mémoires de Madame de Rémusat, 1802-08. 3 vols. Paris: Calmann-Lévy, 1880.

REMY, JACQUES, and ROBERT WOOG. La Française et l'amour. Paris: R. Laffont, 1960, 337 pp. (Survey by Institut Français d'Opinion Publique.)

RENARD, MARIE-THÉRÈSE. La participation des femmes à la vie civique. Paris: Éditions Ouvrières, 1965, 175 pp.

RENAUDOT, MAURICE. Le féminisme et les droits publics de la femme. Niort: Clouzot, 1902, 158 pp.

RÉVAL, GABRIELLE [pseud.]. L'avenir de nos filles. Paris: Hatier, 1904, 303 pp. (Édition illustrée des portraits des principales personalités féminines.)

———. Madame Campan, assistante de Napoléon. Paris: A. Michel, 1931, 318 pp.

Bibliography of Earlier Works

_____. Les Sèvriennes. Paris: Société d'Éditions Littéraires et Artistiques, 1900, 368 pp.

REYNIER, GUSTAVE. La femme au XVIIe siècle, ses ennemis et ses défenseurs. Paris: J. Tallandier, 1929, 276 pp.

RICHER, LÉON. Le code des femmes. Paris: E. Dentu, 1883, 402 pp.

_____. Le divorce: projet de loi proposé à la nouvelle Assemblée. Paris: A. Sagnier, 1873, 268 pp.

_____. La femme libre. Paris: E. Dentu, 1877, 340 pp.

_____. Le livre des femmes. Paris: Librairie de la Bibliothèque Démocratique, 1873, 191 pp.

RIGAUD, ROSE. Les idées féministes de Christine de Pisan. Neuchâtel: University of Neuchâtel, 1911, 151 pp. Reprint. Geneva: Slatkine, 1973.

ROCHE, LINE. Ce que vaut une femme: traité d'éducation morale et pratique des jeunes filles. Reims: Dubois-Poplinot, 1888, 113 pp.

ROCHEBLAVE-SPENLÉ, ANNE-MARIE. Les rôles masculins et féminins: les stéréotypes, la femelle, les états intersexuels. Paris: P.U.F., 1964, 347 pp.

ROLAND, PAULINE. Lettres. Edited by C. Perroud. 2 vols. Paris: Imprimeries Nationales, 1900.

ROLAND de LA PLATIÈRE, MARIE-JEANNE PHILIPON. Mémoires de Madame Roland. 2 vols. Paris: Baudouin Frères, 1820.

ROLIN, CÉLINE. La femme devant le divorce. Paris and Tournai: Casterman, 1968, 264 pp.

ROMIER, LUCIEN. Promotion de la femme. Paris: Hachette, 1930, 253 pp.

ROMIEU, MARIE. La femme au XIXe siècle. Paris: Amyot, 1859, 364 pp.

ROUSSEL, NELLY. Paroles de combat et d'espoir. Épone: L'Avenir Social, 1919, 64 pp.

_____. Quelques lances rompues pour nos libertés. Paris: V. Giard & E. Brière, 1910, 231 pp.

_____. Trois conférences. Paris: Giard, 1930, 123 pp.

Bibliography of Earlier Works

ROUSSELOT, PAUL. Histoire de l'éducation des femmes en France. 2 vols. Paris: Didier, 1883.

_____. La pédagogie féminine: extraits des principaux écrivains qui ont traité de l'éducation des femmes depuis le XVIe siècle. Paris: C. Delagrave, 1881.

ROUSSY, BAPTISTE. Éducation domestique de la femme et rénovation sociale. Paris: Delagrave, 1916, 254 pp.

SAINT-ANDRÉ, CLAUDE. Madame du Barry, d'après des documents authentiques. Paris: E. Paul, 1908, 303 pp.

SAND, GEORGE [Amandine Aurore Lucille Dupin (baronne DUDEVANT)]. Le journal d'un voyageur pendant la guerre. Paris: Michel Lévy, 1871, 310 pp.

_____. Souvenirs de 1848. Paris: Calmann-Lévy, 1880, 434 pp.

SARTIN, PIERRETTE. La promotion de la femme. Paris: Hachette, 1964, 304 pp.

_____. Une femme à part entière. Paris: Casterman, 1966, 265 pp.

SAUMONEAU, LOUISE. Le mouvement féministe socialiste. Paris: Femme Socialiste, 1903.

SAUREL, LOUIS. Les femmes héroïques de la Résistance: Bertie Albrecht, Danielle Casanova. Paris: F. Nathan, 1945, 32 pp.

SAUVY, ALFRED. La prévention des naissances. Paris: P.U.F., 1962, 128 pp.

SCHIFF, MARIO. La fille d'alliance de Montaigne, Marie de Gournay. Paris: P. Champion, 1910, 147 pp.

SCHOELL, FRANCK. La femme française: petite introduction à l'examen de la société française contemporaine. New York and London: G. Putnam, 1924, 384 pp.

SCHUYTEN, M. C. L'éducation de la femme. Paris: O. Doin, 1908.

SÉCHÉ, LÉON. Muses romantiques: Hortense Allart de Méritens dans ses rapports avec Chateaubriand, Béranger, Lamartine, Saint-Beuve, George Sand, Mme d'Agoult. Paris: Mercure de France, 1908, 338 pp.

SECRETAN, CHARLES. Le droit de la femme, suivi des études sociales. 5th ed. Paris: Fischbacher, 1908, 323 pp.

Bibliography of Earlier Works

SEE, CAMILLE. L'université et Madame de Maintenon. Paris: Cerf, 1894, 185 pp.

_____. Lycées et collèges de jeunes filles. Paris: Cerf, 1884, 580 pp.

SERTILLANGES, Reverend Père ANTONIN GILBERT. Féminisme et Christianisme. Paris: Lecoffre, 1920, 343 pp.

_____. Prière de la femme française pendant la guerre. Paris: Art Catholique, 1916, 35 pp.

SÉVERINE [pseud. of CAROLINE RÉMY (GUEBHARD)]. En marche . . . . Paris: Simonis-Empis, 1896, 320 pp.

_____. Notes d'une frondeuse. Paris: Simonis-Empis, 1894, 320 pp.

_____. Pages mystiques. Paris: Simonis-Empis, 1895, 322 pp.

_____. Pages rouges. Paris: Simonis-Empis, 1893.

_____. Vers la lumière . . . Affaire Dreyfus . . . impressions vécues. Paris: Stock, 1900, 464 pp.

SIMENON, GEORGES. La femme en France. Paris: Presse de Cité, 1959, no pagination. (Many photographs by Daniel Frasnay.)

SIMON, JULES. L'ouvrière. Paris: Hachette, 1861, 388 pp.

SIMON, JULES, and GUSTAVE SIMON. La femme du vingtième siècle. Paris: Calmann-Lévy, 1892, 410 pp.

SOLENTE, SUZANNE. Christine de Pisan. Paris: Klincksieck, Imprimerie Nationale, 1969.

SOULIÉ, FRÉDÉRIC. Physiologie du bas-bleu. Paris: Aubert, 1840, 124 pp.

STEENBERGHE, F., et al. La femme catholique dans le monde contemporain. Paris: Plon, 1939, 239 pp.

STENGER, GILBERT. Grandes dames du XIXe siècle: chronique du temps de la Restauration. Paris: Perrin, 1911, 462 pp.

SULLEROT, EVELYNE. Histoire et sociologie du travail féminin. Paris: Denoël/Gonthier, 1968, 397 pp.

_____. La vie des femmes. Paris: Denoël/Gonthier, 1965, 158 pp.

Bibliography of Earlier Works

TABOUIS, GENEVIÈVE. <u>Vingt ans de suspense diplomatique</u>. Paris: A. Michel, 1958, 411 pp.

TALMY, ROBERT. <u>Histoire du movement familial en France (1896-1939)</u>. 2 vols. Paris: Union Nationale des Caisses d'Allocations Familiales, 1962.

TEINTURIER, F. <u>Les femmes</u>. Paris: Sartorius, 1860, 312 pp.

TERRISSE, MARIE. <u>Notes et impressions à travers le "féminisme."</u> Paris: Fischbacher, 1896, 224 pp.

TEUTSCH, ROBERT. <u>Le féminisme</u>. Paris: Malfère, 1934, 297 pp.

THIBERT, MARGUERITE. <u>Le féminisme dans le socialisme français de 1830-à 1850</u>. Paris: Giard, 1926, 377 pp.

THIÉBAUX, CHARLES. <u>Le féminisme et les socialistes, depuis Saint-Simon jusqu'à nos jours</u>. Paris: Rousseau, 1906, 178 pp.

THOMAS, EDITH. <u>Les femmes de 1848</u>. Collection du centenaire de la révolution de 1848. Paris: P.U.F., 1948, 80 pp.

_____. <u>George Sand</u>. Paris: Éditions Universitaires, 1959, 139 pp.

_____. <u>Pauline Roland: socialisme et féminisme au XIXe siècle</u>. Paris: Marcel Rivière, 1956, 222 pp.

_____. <u>Les Pétroleuses</u>. Paris: Gallimard, 1963, 288 pp.

THOUZERY, PAUL. <u>La femme au XIXe siècle. Ce qu'elle est; ce qu'elle n'est pas</u>. Paris: Achille Faure, 1866, 224 pp.

THULIÉ, HENRI. <u>La femme: essai de sociologie psychologique</u>. Paris: Delahaye & Lecrosnier, 1885, 517 pp.

TIXERANT, JULES. <u>Le féminisme à l'époque de 1848 dans l'ordre politique et dans l'ordre économique</u>. Paris: V. Giard & E. Brière, 1908, 209 pp.

de TOURZEL, LOUISE ÉLISABETH. <u>Mémoires de Mme la duchesse de Tourzel, gouvernante des enfants de France pendant les années 1789 à 1795</u>. 2 vols. Pt. 1, Paris: Plon, 1883-93. Pt. 2, Paris: Mercure de France, 1969, 479 pp.

de TRAILLES, PAUL, and HENRY de TRAILLES. <u>Les femmes de France pendant la guerre et les deux sièges de Paris</u>. Paris: Polo, 1872, 234 pp.

Bibliography of Earlier Works

TOLÉDANO, ANDRÉ-MICHEL. <u>La vie de famille en France sous la Restauration et la Monarchie de Juillet</u>. Paris: A. Michel, 1943, 254 pp.

TROUARD-RIOLLÉ, YVONNE. <u>Les activités féminines en agriculture</u>. Paris: Spes, 1935, 267 pp.

TRUC, GONZAGUE. <u>Histoire illustrée de la femme</u>. 2 vols. Paris: Plon, 1940-41.

_____. <u>Madame de Montespan</u>. Paris: A. Colin, 1936, 214 pp.

TURGEON, CHARLES. <u>Le féminisme français</u>. Vol. 1, <u>L'émancipation individuelle de la femme</u>, 458 pp.; vol. 2, <u>L'émancipation politique et familiale de la femme</u>, 500 pp. Paris: Larose & Forcel, 1902.

TURMANN, MAX. <u>Initiatives féminines</u>. Paris: Lecoffre, 1905, 430 pp.

TURQUAN, JOSEPH. <u>Les femmes de l'émigration (1789-1815)</u>. Paris: E. Paul, 1911, 371 pp.

UZANNE, LOUIS OCTAVE. <u>Le célibat et l'amour: traité de vie passionnelle et de dilection féminine</u>. Paris: Mercure de France, 1912, 350 pp. (Preface by Rémy Gourmont.)

_____. <u>Études de sociologie féminine: Parisiennes de ce temps en leurs divers milieux, états, et conditions; études pour servir à l'histoire des femmes, de la société, de la galanterie française, des moeurs contemporaines, et de l'égoïsme masculin. Ménagères, ouvrières et courtisanes, bourgeoises et mondaines, artistes et comédiennes</u>. Paris: Mercure de France, 1910, 483 pp.

_____. <u>La femme à Paris: nos contemporaines. Notes successives sur les Parisiennes</u>. Paris: Imprimeries Réunies, 1894, 329 pp.

_____. <u>Les femmes de France pendant l'invasion</u>. Paris and Nancy: Berger-Levrault, 1893, 445 pp.

_____. <u>La Française du siècle: la femme et la mode. Métamorphoses de la Parisienne de 1792-1892: tableau de moeurs et usages aux principales époques</u> . . . . Paris: Librairies-Imprimeries Réunies, 1892, 246 pp.

_____. <u>Madame de Montesson, douanière d'Orléans (1738-1806)</u>. Paris: Émile-Paul, 1904, 332 pp.

_____. <u>Madame Récamier</u>. Paris: Tallandier, 1902, 432 pp.

Bibliography of Earlier Works

VACHET, PIERRE. La femme: cette énigme. Paris: Grasset, 1966, 268 pp.

VAILLAND, ROGER. Laclos par lui-même. Paris: Seuil, 1953, 190 pp.

VAÏSSE, JEAN-LOUIS. Les droits de la femme. Paris: Cherbuliez, 1871, 392 pp.

VALABRÈGUE, CATHÉRINE. La condition masculine. Paris: Payot, 1968, 185 pp.

VALIN, A. La femme salariée et la maternité. Paris, 1911.

VALMOR, JOSEPH. Ce que nous devons à la femme. Paris: M. Rivière, 1913, 272 pp.

VANIER, HENRIETTE. La mode et ses métiers: frivolités et luttes des classes (1830-1870). Paris: A. Colin, 1960, 287 pp.

de VARIGNY, C. La femme aux États-Unis. Paris: A. Colin, 1893, 322 pp.

VATEL, CHARLES. Bibliographie dramatique de Charlotte de Corday. 2 vols. Paris: Plon, 1872.

_____. Charlotte Corday et les Girondins. 3 vols. Paris: Plon, 1864.

_____. Dossiers du procès criminal de Charlotte de Corday devant le tribunal révolutionnaire. Paris: Poulet-Malassis, 1861, 108 pp.

_____. Histoire de Madame Du Barry. 3 vols. Versailles: L. Bernard, 1883.

VÉRECQUE, CHARLES. Histoire de la famille des temps sauvages à nos jours. Paris: V. Giard & E. Brière, 1914, 282 pp.

VÉRONE, MARIA. La femme et la loi. Paris: Larousse, 1920, 48 pp.

VÈZE, RAOUL. Les femmes et la galanterie au XVIIe siècle. . . . Paris: P.H. Daragon, 1907, 280 pp.

_____. La galanterie parisienne sous Louis XV et Louis XVI. Paris: Bibliothèque des Curieux, 1910, 304 pp.

VIER, JACQUES. La Comtesse d'Agoult et son temps. 6 vols. Paris: A. Colin, 1955-56.

de VILLERMONT, MARIE (Comtesse). Histoire de la coiffure féminine. Brussels: A. Mertens, 1891, 822 pp.

Bibliography of Earlier Works

———. Le mouvement féministe: ses causes, son avenir, solution chrétienne. 2 vols. N.p., 1900-14.

de VILLIER du TERRAGE, MARC. Histoire des clubs de femmes et des légions d'Amazones, 1793-1848-1871. Paris: Plon & Nourrit, 1910, 422 pp.

VINCENT, JACQUES. Parisiennes de guerre, 1914-1918. Paris: Édition de France, 1918, 301 pp.

VINDRY, FLEURY. Les demoiselles de St. Cyr (1686-1793). Paris: H. Champion, 1900, 459 pp.

VIRET, FRÉDÉRIC. Des femmes, ou quelques mots sur leur position morale et matérielle, et plus particulièrement sur celle de la fille du peuple, dans l'organisation sociale actuelle. Paris: Martinon & Durupt, 1850, 108 pp.

WEISS, LOUISE. Ce que femme veut: souvenirs de la IIIe République. Paris: Gallimard, 1946, 332 pp.

———. Mémoires d'une Européenne. 3 vols. Paris: Payot, 1968-70.

de WITT-SCHLUMBERGER, Mme PAUL. Une femme aux femmes: pourquoi les femmes doivent étuder la question des moeurs. Paris: Fischbacher, 1909, 63 pp.

ZANTA, LÉONTINE. Psychologie du féminisme. Paris: Plon & Nourrit, 1922, 214 pp. (Preface by Paul Bourget.)

Subject Index

abortion, xii, xvi, 23-24, 70, 111 112-13, 114, 119-25, 129, 141, 148, 155
Albistur, Maïté, 14, 31, 34, 63
Albrecht, Bertie, 23-24, 112
Alquier, Henriette, 23, 112
American women, xii-xiii, xvi, 67-69, 78-79, 80, 107, 111, 134, 163
ancien régime, xiv, 5, 18, 131, 145, 152
Ariès, Phillipe, 144-45, 151
Aristotle, 101, 161
Armogathe, Daniel, 14, 31, 34, 63
Auclair, Marcelle, 45
Auclert, Hubertine, 8, 9, 32, 49
Autriche, Anne d', 1

Balzac, Honoré de, 84, 95, 149
Barthes, Roland, 75, 106
Bazard, Claire, 7
Beauvoir, Simone de, xii, 16, 25, 27, 34, 43-44, 50, 52-53, 67, 69, 76, 80-81, 83-84, 90, 95, 98-99, 103, 108, 112, 116, 120
Belladonna, Judith, 113, 118, 126
Bergman, Ingmar, 92
Bonald, Louise de, 13
Bouchardeau, Huguette, 31, 35
Boucher, Victorine, 36
Brel, Jacques, 149
Bres, Madeleine, 21
Brunschvicg, Cécile, 35, 64

Cabet, Étienne, 7
Cahiers de doléances, 3, 12, 17

Catherine de Medicis, 1, 15, 48, 71
Catholic church, 3, 12-14, 17-20, 22, 25, 40, 45, 64, 70, 77, 82, 121, 126-27, 144, 147-48, 153, 155-58, 159, 165
Chabrol, Claude, 106
Charles V, 14
Charles IX, 48
Châtelet, Mme de, 62-63
Chirac, Jacques, 149
Civil Code. See Napoleanic Code
Cixous, Hélène, 84
Colette, 45, 86
Condorcet, Antoine-Nicolas de, 4, 16, 37, 82
Contemporary French Civilization, xxiii
contraception, xvi, 22-24, 52, 70, 111-13, 119, 122-25, 131-34, 136, 141, 144-46
Couriau affair, 185
Couriau, Emma, 185
Cousin, Victor, 7, 18
Curie, Marie, 21, 187

Dalsace, Jean, 112
Daubié, Julie, 20
daycare, 91-93, 142-43, 148, 166, 187, 191
de Gaulle, Charles, 11, 38, 67
Delphy, Christine, 186
Démar, Claire, 18, 32, 48-49
Deraismes, Maria, 9, 49-50
Deroin, Jeanne, 6, 8, 72
Descartes, René, 101
Devaldés, Jeanne, 23

Subject Index

Devaldés, Manuel, 23
Diderot, Denis, 3, 16, 86, 149
divorce, 3, 8, 11-13, 24, 93, 139-40, 141
Dreyfus Affair, the, 8
Duhet, Paule-Marie, 37
Dumas, Alexandre, 92
Dupanloup, Monseigneur, 19
Durand, Marguerite, xviii, 8, 59, 97, 155
Duras, Marguerite, 97, 102, 103
Duruy, Victor, 19

education, 4, 13-22, 32, 134-36, 140, 142-43, 149-55, 166
Effenterre, Yvette van, 191
Elle, xiii, 75, 78, 102, 106, 162, 167
Emile, (Rousseau), 17, 32
Enfantin, Prosper, 6, 82
enfranchisement, 4-11, 26-27, 34-35, 48-49
Engels, Friedrich, 61, 78, 113
Ernst, Max, 80
Excoffans, Béatrix, 37

family, the, 82-84, 131-34, 139-48
family planning, 22-25, 112-13, 131-34
Faure, Edgar, 177
Feminine Mystique, The, (Friedan), 26, 80, 168
Fénelon, 15
Ferry, Jules, 19, 153
Festival of Women's Films, 98-99
Forrester, Vivianne, 118
Foucault, Michel, 165
Fourier, Charles, 6, 61, 82, 84
French International Congress on the Rights of Women, 9, 49
French Revolution, 3-4, 8, 37, 111
Freud, Sigmund, 52, 70, 77, 82, 85, 88, 93, 102
Friedan, Betty, xii, 26, 80, 99, 107, 163, 168
Fronde, La, 8, 72, 109
Fugier, Anne-Marie, 188

Gauthier, Xavière, 84, 99, 111, 117-18
Gennari, Geneviève, 51
Gérard, Claude, 36

Giroud, Françoise, xv, 27, 114, 159, 166, 184
Giscard d'Estaing, Valéry, 25, 107, 162, 166
Goldman, Emma, 58
Goncourt brothers, the, 17
Gouges, Olympe de, 4, 37
Gournay, Marie de, 2, 34
Grégoire, Marie, 52
Groult, Benoîte, 51-52, 84, 111, 112
Guillot, Michel, 191
Guizot, François, 18
Guyon, Jeanne, 56-57

Halimi, Gisèle, 25, 70, 120, 123, 129
Henri II, 48
homosexuality, 111-12, 116, 170
Hugo, Victor, 36, 47, 54
Humbert, Eugene, 23
Huot, Marie, 23

International Year of Woman, xviii, 93, 128, 187
Irigaray, Luce, 84, 102, 118, 168

Jeanne d'Arc, 46, 71
John XXIII, 157
Jolas, Betsy, 102
Jung, Carl, 77

Krasucki, Henri, 179

Labé, Louise, 34
Labiche, Eugène, 183
Lacan, Jacques, 85, 88, 102
Laclos, Choderlos de, 171
Lacombe, Claire, 4, 37
La Fayette, Mme de, 2
Laguiller, Arlette, 53
Lakanal, 17, 37
Lamber, Juliette, 31
Laot, Jeanette, 53-54
Laurencin, Marie, 45
LeClerc, Annie, 84
Legouvé, Gabriel, 7
Lemmonier, Elisa, 134
Lenin, Nikolai, 164, 167
Léon, Pauline, 4
Lesselier, Claudie, 188
Lévi-Strauss, Claude, 32, 85, 134

Subject Index

Lougee, Caroline, 2
Louis XIV, 3, 41-42, 57
Louis XV, 16
Louis Philippe, 7

Maintenon, Mme de, 41-42
Malraux, Andre, 57
Malraux, Clara, 57, 80
Marie-Claire, 45, 57, 73, 162
Marx, Karl, 77, 78, 113, 166-68
Maupassant, Guy de, 183
May, Picqueray, 58
Mead, Margaret, 52
Médicis, Catherine de, 1, 15, 48
Méricourt, Thérgoine, 4, 37
Michel, Louise, 8, 32, 37, 54-56
Michelet, Jules, 4, 32, 39-40, 46-47, 88, 96, 171
Mill, Stuart, 82
Millet, Kate, xii, 163
Ministry of the Rights of Women, 26, 111, 159
Mink, Paule, 23
Mirabeau, Octave, 183
Misme, Jane, 9
Mitterand, François, 26, 168
Molière, 2, 13, 16
Moll-Weiss, August, 181
Monnier, Suzanne, 63
Momod, Jacques, 25, 120
Montaigne, xv, 2, 15, 86
Montesquieu, 12, 100
Morin, Edgar, 75
motherhood, 82-84, 85-86, 88-89, 91, 93, 96, 107, 131-34, 140, 142-43, 146-47, 151
Mouvement de Libération des Femmes (MLF), xii, 44, 93, 118-19, 165
Musidora, 71, 98

Napoleon, 5, 15, 17-18, 131
Napoleonic Code, 5-6, 12, 64, 70, 93, 131, 159, 181
Naquet, Alfred, 13
Navarre, Marguerite de, 1
Navarre, Phillip de, 14
neo-Malthusians, 23, 75
Noailles, Duchesse de, 41
Notebooks of grievances. See Cahiers de doléances

Owens, Robert, 7

Packard, Vance, 107
Parker, Dorothy, 51
Payen, Alix, 36
Philip V, 41
Philip of Burgundy, 14
Philosophes, the, 3, 12
Piton, Monique, 172
Pitrou, Agnès, 191
Lizan, Christine de, 14, 34, 71
Poullain de la Barre, François, 2, 16, 34, 82
pornography, xiii, 118
pronatalist policy, xvi, 23, 76, 113, 120-23, 125
Proudhon, Pierre-Joseph, 7, 31
prostitution, 4-6, 59, 73, 77, 89, 99, 111-13, 118, 126-128
Proust, 183
Psych et Po, 26, 119

Rabaut, Jean, 31, 69
Rabelais, 15
rape, xiii, xvi, 111, 114-15, 129-30
Réage, Pauline, 118
religion, 12-14, 18-20, 40, 45, 64, 70, 76-77, 82, 121, 127, 136-37, 144, 148, 152, 153, 155-58, 165
Rémy, Caroline, 8
Resistance, the, 11, 36-38, 46, 48, 56-57, 177
Revolution of 1848, 8
Richard, Marthe, 58-59
Richelieu, Cardinal, 141
Richer, Leon, 9
Rilke, Rainer M., 88, 104
Rimbaud, Arthur, xii
Robespierre, Maximilien de, 5
Robin, Paul, 23
Rochefort, Christine, 59
Roland, Pauline, 6, 37
Rostand, Jean, 25, 120
Roudy, Yvette, 26-27, 159-60, 168
Rousseau, Jean-Jacques, 17, 55, 132, 144
Roussel, Nelly, 23, 35, 59-60, 132

Saint-Simon, Duc de, 6, 7, 40-41, 165
Saint-Simoniens, 6-7, 8, 40-42,

Subject Index

48-49, 63, 72, 75
Sand, George, 39, 62, 86
Sarrazin, Albertine, 170
Sartre, Jean-Paul, 76, 84, 99
Saunier-Seïté, Alice, 47-48
Second Sex, The (de Beauvoir), xii, 16, 34, 52-53, 80, 83, 103
Sée, Camille, 19
Séverine, 72
Sévigné, Mme de, 2
sexual politics, 111-30
Shulman, Alix, 68
Staël, Mme de, 17, 37, 44, 45-46
Stalin, Joseph, 167
Starobinski, Jean, 104
Stendhal, 61, 95
Stone, Lucy, 68
Strumhinger, Laura, 188
Sue, Eugene, 183
Sullerot, Évelyne, xv

Tallyrand, 37
Teilhard de Chardin, Pierre, 77
Theresa, Saint, 45, 77
Tocqueville, de, 67
Tristan, Flora, 6, 32, 36, 39, 50, 60-62
Trotsky, Leon, 58

unemployment, 180, 189-90
Union des Femmes Francaises, 37-38, 81, 93
unions, 9, 35-38, 50, 53, 75, 81, 93, 114, 142, 162, 172, 178-80, 184-85, 191, 192; Confederation Française, 53; Confédération Générale du Travail, 53, 162, 178-80; Couriau affair, 185; Démocratique du Travail, 53
Ursins, Princesse des, 41

Valabrègue, Catherine, 71
Vallès, Jules, 72
Vaugelas, 2
Veil, Simone, 25, 184
Vernet, Madeleine, 59
Vérone, Maria, 10
Voilquin, Suzanne, 7, 32, 36, 49, 63-64, 72
Voltaire, François, 41, 56, 62

Weiss, Louise, 10, 64, 65
Wilde, Oscar, 104
witchcraft, 37, 39-40, 44-45
Woolf, Virginia, 80, 118
World War I, 10, 20, 22-23, 132, 154, 183, 188
World War II, 10-11, 36-38, 46, 48, 56-59, 113, 177

Zetkin, Clara, 164
Zola, Émile, 22, 53, 124, 188
Zwang, Dr., 117-18
Zylberberg-Hocquard, Marie-Hélène, 172, 188

Author Index

Adler, Laure, 105
Agulhon, Maurice, 94
Aimé, Martin, 134
Albistur, Maïté, 29, 34, 59, 63
Allauzen, Marie, 175
Armogathe, Daniel, 29, 34, 59, 63
Arondo, Marie, 175
Association Choisir, 119, 129, 162
Aubert, Jean-Marie, 155
Auclair, Marcelle, 45

Badinter, Elisabeth, 138
Baelen, Jean, 62
Baker, Catherine, 156
Balayé, Simone, 45
Ballorain, Rolande, 67
Barbara, 127
Bardèche, Maurice, xix
Barthes, Roland, 47
Basile, Colette, 176
Bastide, Huguette, 149
Beauvoir, Simone de, 43, 81, 108, 120, 139
Bécane, Geneviève, 176
Bédarida, François, 61
Bédrine, Nicole, 149
Bell, Susan Groag, xxi, 29, 30, 174
Belladonna, Judith, 126
Bellan, Claude, 150
Bénabou, Maxime, 116
Benoît, Nicole, 75
Berger, Henry, 120
Bertrand, Micheline, xix
Bidault, Suzanne, 46, 177

Bidelman, Patrick Kay, xxi, 29, 137
Blanquart, Louisette, 162
Bolster, Richard, 95
Boncoeur, Jean-Louis, 44
Borgal, Clément, xix
Bosmans, Fernand, 125
Bouchardeau, Huguette, 35
Boulineau, Annie, 36
Bourg, Claude, 177
Bouyer, Louis, 156
Briac, Aurélia, 76
Brion, Hélène, 35
Brimo, Albert, 162
Brisset, Claire, 125
Bruhat, J., 179

Cabanis, José, 46
Callet, Christine, 177
Calo, Jeanne, 96
Cardinal, Marie, 96
Carisse, Colette, 76
Carlander, Ingrid, 67
Carlier-Mackiewicz, Nicole, 139
Castelot, André, xx
Cayron, Claire, 139
Cauvin, Claire, 163
Cérati, M., 179
CGT (Confédération Générale du Travail), 178
Chabaud, Jacqueline, 155
Chabauty, Marie-Luce, 140
Chabrol, Claude, 105
Chalon, Marie-Thérèse, 47
Champion, Jean, 169
Charles-Roux, E., 179
Charzat, Gisèle, 163, 164

Author Index

Chatel, Nicole, 36
Cheverny, Julien, 76
Chiappe, Jean-Françoise, xx
Choffel, Jean, 47
Choisy, Maryse, 77
Chombart de Laüwe, Marie-José, 150
Cixous, Hélène, 96
Clark, Frances I., 29
Clément, Catherine, 77, 96
Cloulas, Yvan, 48
CNRS (Centre National de la Recherche Scientifique), 181
Cohen, Suzy, 148
Colin, Madeleine, 174, 179
Collange, Christiane, 77, 78, 150
Collet, Claudine, 187
Collins, Marie, 28
Colloques du Centre Catholique, 121
Comité pour la liberté de l'avortement et de la contraception, 121
Coninck, Christine, 127
Constant, Louis, 36
Corbin, Alain, 127
Courtivron, Isabelle de, xxi
Cressanges, Jeanne, 116
Crozet, René, 37

Daco, Pierre, 94
Dallayrac, Dominique, 117
Dana, Jacqueline, 140
Dardigna, Anne-Marie, 106
Darmon, Pierre, 165
Decaux, Alain, xx
Decroux-Masson, Annie, 150
Delais, Jeanne, 169
Démar, Claire, 48
Deraismes, Maria, 49
Desanti, Dominique, 50, 61
Dhavernas, Odile, 165
Donzelot, Jacques, 137
Dourlen-Rollier, Anne-Marie, 125
Duby, Georges, 138
Duché, Jean, 78
Dufour, Antoine, xx
Dufrancatel, Christine, 38
Duhet, Paule-Marie, 37
Dumazedier, Joffre, 76
Dumont, Yvonne, 164

Duras, Marguerite, 97
Durca-Journet, Isabelle, 169
Dzeh Djen, Li, 109

d'Eaubonne, Françoise, 79
Elhadad, Lydia, 63
Ely, Marie, 180
Erhel, Catherine, 170

Fairchild, Cissie, 131, 137
Falconnet, Georges, 151
Fargier, Marie-Odile, 130
Fauchery, Pierre, 98
Faure, Christine, 38
Femmes de Musidora, des, 98
Femmes de Nice, les, 80
Flamant-Paparatti, Danielle and Emmanuelle, 151
Flandrin, Jean-Louis, 125, 141
Fouquet, Catherine, 139
Fraisse, Geneviève, 38, 181
Francis, Claude, 50, 98
Francos, Ania, 38
Friang, Brigitte, 65
Fritz, Paul S., 27
Fruchet, Hélène, 157
Fugier, Anne Martin, 137, 182

Garnier, Christiane, 182
Gascard, Françoise, 50
Gaudilla, Naty Garcia, 73
Gauthier, Xavière, 99, 100, 117
Gelis, Jacques, 138
Gennari, Genevieve, 51
Geraud, Roger, 125
Gilles, C., 179
Giroud, Françoise, 166, 169
Gontier, Fernande, 51, 98
Granrut, Claude de Renty, 177
Grégoire, Menie, 52
Grimal, Pierre, xx, 29
Gros, Brigitte, 142
Groult, Benoîte, 81, 82, 89, 112, 124
Guelaud-Leridon, Françoise, 82
Guérrand, Roger-Henri, 122
Guidici, Maurice, 169
Guilbert, Madeleine, xviii, 179
Guiral, Pierre, 183
Guitton, Jean, 148
Gutman, Colette, 107

Author Index

Guy, Alice, 100
Guy, François, 126
Guy, Michèle, 126

Halimi, Gisèle, 119, 123, 129
Hans, Marie-Françoise, 118
Hareven, Tamara K., 138
Hassoun, Jacques, 148
Hermann, Claudine, 101
Hoffmann, Paul, 101
Houray, Pierre, 118
Horer, Suzanne, 102
Houle, Ghislaine, xix

Irigaray, Luce, 102
Istin-Aulite, Paulette, 169

Jacob, Madeleine, 65
Jaget, Claude, 128
Jourcin, Albert, xx

Knibiehler, Yvonne, 138
Krakovitch, Odile, 49

Labourie-Racapé, Marie-Thérèse Letablier, 183
Lagroua Weill-Hallé, Marie A., 123
Laguiller, Arlette, 53
Laïk, Madeleine, 152
Lainé, Pascal, 83
Laot, Jeanette, 53
Lapouge, Gilles, 118
Larrive, Hélène, 142
Lascault, Gilbert, 103
La Tour du Pin, Marquise de, 65
Laurent, Alain, 83
Laurent, Charles, 137
Laurent, Michelle, 103
Lauwick, Françoise, 83, 143
Lavoisier, Bénédicte, 107
LeBrun, Annie, 84, 103
Lebrun, François, 143
Leclerc, Annie, 104
Leclerq, Jacques, 157
Lefaucheur, Nadine, 151
Le Garrec, Evelyne, 84, 184
Leger, Danièle, xxi, 73
Léguay, Catherine, 170
Lejeune, Jérôme, 126
Lejeune, Paule, 54

Lemoine-Luccioni, Eugenie, 85
Leprohon, Pierre, 62
Leroy, Roland, 121
Leroy, Suzanne, 85
Lesperance, Emmanuel, 85
Lesterlin, Marie-Adine, 185
Le Triudic, Dominique-Martin, 56
Leulliette, Pierre, 112
Leutrat, Paul, 45
Lilenstein, Régine, 149
Lottin, Alain, 138
Lougee, Caroline C., 27, 29
Lowit, Nicole, xviii

Macciocchi, Maria A., 166
Maillard, Claude, 85, 124, 129
Mallet-Joris, Françoise, 56
Malraux, Clara, 57
Mandrou, Robert, 39
Markale, Jean, 40
Marks, Elaine, xxi
Maruani, Margaret, 172, 185
Masnata, Claire Rubattel, 68
Massip, Renée, 86
Mauduit, Jean, 167
Maure, Huguette, 119
Mayeur, Françoise, xiv, 152, 153
McMillan, James, xxi, 28
Menasseyre, Christiane, 87
Métral, Marie-Odile, 144
Michel, Andrée, 27, 87, 138, 145, 186, 187
Michel, Claude, 88
Molette, Charles, 157
Moll-Weiss, Augusta, 181
Monestier, Marianne, 57, 65, 187
Montesinos, Andrée, 187
Montrelay, Michèle, 88
Morière, Huguette, 124
Morin, Edgar, 75
Muhlstein, Anka, 40

Niepce, Janine, 50
Noël, Michele, 88
Nokovitch, Milena, 89

Offen, Karen, xxi, 28, 29, 30, 137, 174
Oraison, Marc, 129

Paillard, Bernard, 75

Author Index

Parent-Duchâtelet, Alexandre, 128
Parent-Lardeur, Françoise, 187
Parturier, Françoise, 89, 90
Pellaumail, Marcelle Maugin, 90
Pelletier, Madeleine, 154
Pelosse, Valentine, 49
Perasso, Élaine, 91
Perrein, Michèle, 91
Perrot, Michelle, 38, 188
Peslouan, Genevieve de, 188
Peyret, Claude, 125
Picqueray, May, 58
Piettre, Monique, 28, 42
Pillorget, René, 145
Pisan, Annie de, 43
Piton, Monique, 172, 189
Pitrou, Agnès, 146
Poitiers, University of, 44
Poncet, Dominique, 163
Porte, Michelle, 97
Prévost, Françoise, 45
Prost, Antoine, 30, 134

Quéré, France, 92
Quiguer, Claude, 104

Rabaut, Jean, 29, 30, 41
Raimond, Anne-Marie, 167
Renard, Marie-Thérèse, 167
Renaudin, Edmée, 58
Rey, Pierre Louis, xx
Ribeaud, Marie-Cathérine, 146
Richard, Marthe, 58
Righini, Marielle, 92
Rocard, Geneviève, 107
Rocheblave-Spenlé, Anne-Marie, 155
Rochefort, Christiane, 59
Roudy, Yvette, 168
Roussel, Louis, 138
Roussel, Nelly, 59

Sacotte, Marcel, 129
Sairigné, Guillemette de, 189
Saltiel, Michèle, 148
Salvaresi, Elisabeth, 38
Samson, Marcelle Germain, xix
Samuel, Pierre, 43
Sarrazin, Albertine, 170
Sartin, Pierette, 92

Sayre, Sylvie Weil, 28
Sebbar, Leila, 147
Shorter, Edward, 138
Simon, Jules, 172
Socquet, Jeanne, 102
Sowerwine, Charles, xxi
Strumingher, Laura, 174
Sullerot, Évelyne, 108, 109, 138, 148, 190, 191

Tabard, Nicole, 191
Taüb, Edith, 29
Texier, Catherine, 129, 138
Thiam, Awa, 112
Thomas, Edith, 56
Thuiller, Guy, 183
Touati, Claude-Rose, 149
Toulat, Jean, 125
Traer, James E., 137
Tristan, Anne, 43
Tristan, Flora, 60, 61, 62

Vaillot, Rene, 62
Valabrègue, Catherine, 93
Valensin, Georges, 126
Van Tieghem, Philippe, xx
Vasseur, Anne-Marie, 183
Vellay, Pierre, 126
Vergez, Suzi, 119
Vézina, Marie-Odile, 129
Victor, Éliane, 109
Vieille, Agnès, 187
Villeneuve, Roland, 44
Villette, Pierre, 45
Vincent, Madeleine, 93
Voilquin, Suzanne, 63

Weiss, Louise, 64
Weitz, Margaret Collins, xi, 73

Yaguello, Marina, 104

Zegel, Anne, 180
Ziegler, G., 179
Zylberberg-Hocquard, Marie-Hélène, xviii, 172, 191

Title Index

(The titles listed here are those that have been annotated or referred to in the essays. Additional titles will be found in the bibliography which is arranged alphabetically by author.)

À chances égales . . . des femmes qui ont résolu d'étonner, 182
Activité féminine: enquête sur la discontinuité de la vie professionnelle, 183
Activité professionnelle de la femme et vie conjugale, 145
L'affranchissement des femmes, 48
Ainsi soit-elle, 51, 81, 112
L'alternative: libérer nos corps ou libérer l'avortement, 119
À l'aube du féminisme: les premières journalistes, 1830-1850, 105
Amazones, guerrières, et gaillardes, 43
Les Américaines, 67
L'amour au féminin, 119
"An Annotated Bibliography of Recent Studies on French Women," xi
Apprenons à faire l'amour, 116
Aujourd'hui la femme, 92
Autobiographie d'une pionnière du cinéma (1873-1968) [Alice Guy], 100

Autrement dit, 96
Les avantages que les femmes peuvent recevoir de la philosophie, 16
L'avenir des femmes, 92
L'avortement: crime ou libération?, 125
Avortement: histoire d'un débat, 120
Avortement: les pieces du dossier, 124
Avortement: pour une loi humaine, 125
Avortement: une loi en procès, l'affaire Bobigny, 119
L'avortement de Papa: essai critique pour une vraie réforme, 123
Avortement et libre choix de la maternité: textes et documents, 121
Avortement et respect de la vie humaine, 121

Les babarotes, 80
Benoîte Groult, 51

Cahiers de civilisation médiévale, Xe-XIIe siècles, 44
Cahiers de doléances des femmes en 1789 et autres textes, 28
Cahiers sur la femme et la criminalité, 169
Catherine de Médicis, 48
La cause des femmes, 123
Les causes de l'absentéisme féminin, 178

Title Index

Ce n'est pas d'aujourd'hui, 174, 179
Cent mesures pour les femmes, 166
130,000 familles prennent la parole, 147
Ce que femme veut, 89
Ce que les femmes reclament, 167
Ce que veulent les femmes: articles et discours de 1869 à 1894, 49
Ce sexe qui n'en est pas un, 102
C'est dur, la solitude, 85
C'est possible, 172, 189
"Cherchez la femme: recherches sur les femmes," xi
La cité des dames, 14
La Citoyenne, 8, 9, 29
Le Code des femmes, 9, 28
Le Code des femmes: . . . , 28
Combats pour les femmes, 64
Le commerce des dames, 88
Les communistes et la condition de la femme, 164
Comprendre les femmes et leur psychologie profonde, 94
La condition de la Française d'aujourd'hui, 138
La condition féminine, 78
La condition féminine à travers les âges, 42
Les contemplatives, des femmes entre elles, 156
Contemporary French Civilization, xi, xxiii, 30, 115
Contraception et avortement: dix ans de débat dans la presse (1965-1974), 122
Le "corps" feminin, 65
La création de la femme chez Michelet, 96
La création étouffée, 102
Les crèches, 148
Les crèches: des enfants à la consigne?, 142
Les cris de la vie, 52

Déclaration des droits de la femme et de la citoyenne, 4
Déclaration des droits de l'homme et du citoyen, 4, 37

De la drague, 76
De la justice dans la Révolution et dans l'Église, 7
De l'éducation des dames, 16
De l'éducation des deux sexes, 16
De l'éducation des femmes, 16, 37
De l'inégalité des sexes, 2
Les demoiselles de magasin, 187
Derniers combats, 60
Des Femmes dans la Résistance, 36
Des livres et des femmes, xix
La destinée féminine dans le roman européen du XVIIIe siècle, 98
Dictionnaire des femmes célèbres, xx
Dictionnaire érotique, 105
Dire nos sexualités, 117
Divorce en France, 139
18 millions de bonnes à tout faire, 180
Domestic Enemies: Servants and Their Masters in Old Regime France, 131, 137
Dossier de la femme, 51
Le Droit des femmes, 8, 9, 49
Droits des femmes, pouvoirs des hommes, 165

L'école des femmes, 113
Écologie, féminisme: révolution ou mutation?, 79
Écoute ma différence, 92
Les écrits de Simone de Beauvoir: la vie, l'écriture, 98
Edmée au bout de la table, 58
L'éducation des filles, 15
L'éducation des filles en France au XIXe siècle, 152
L'éducation féministe des filles, 154
Elles étaient cent et mille, 57
Émile, 17, 30, 132
Emmanuelle ou l'enfance au féminin, 151
En portées, 103
Encyclopedia, 16, 29
Les enfants de la maternelle, 14
Enfants de l'image, 150
Les enfants de exclus, 146
Enquête sur les besoins et

Title Index

aspirations des familles et de jeunes, 191
L'enseignement secondaire des jeunes filles sous la Troisième République, xiv, 153
Entre chienne et louve, 91
Entrer dans la vie: naissances et enfances dans la France traditionnelle, 138
L'ère de la femme moderne: essai sur le féminisme, 85
Et nous aurions beaucoup d'enfants, 140
Et pourtant j'étais libre, 57
L'éternelle sacrifiée, 59
Être femme après 40 ans, 116
Eux, les hommes, 93

La fabrication des mâles: du sexisme ordinaire aux pièges de la libération sexuelle, 151
La famille, 141
La famille dans la vie de tous les jours, 146
Familles: parenté, maison, sexualité dans l'ancienne société, 141
Fécondité, 22
Le féminisme, 27, 87
Le féminisme au masculin, 51, 82
Le féminisme en France, xxi, 73
Féminisme et syndicalisme en France, 172, 191
Le féminisme ou la mort: ou la subjectivité radicale, 79
Féminin-masculin: le nouvel équilibre, 83
La femme, 32, 46
La femme: anti-féminisme et christianisme, 155
La femme: aujourd'hui et demain, 157
La femme: de la belle Hélène au mouvement de libération des femmes, xx
La femme au XVIIIe siècle, 17
La femme avenir, 92
La femme celte: mythe et sociologie, 40

La femme dans la pensée des lumières, 101
La femme dans la vie et dans l'Église, 157
Une femme du réseau Shelburn: l'histoire de Marie-Thérèse Le Calvez de Phouha en Bretagne, 56
La femme en marge, 26, 168
Femme et chef d'entreprise, 177
La femme et l'amitié, 86
La femme et la formation continue en 100 questions, 185
La femme et la loi, 28
La femme et la société québécoise, xix
La femme et ses images, 83
La femme liberée?, 92
La femme majeure: nouvelle féminité, nouveau féminisme, 75
La femme pauvre au XIXe siècle, 20
Les femmes, xviii
Femmes: l'âge politique, 162
Femmes: quelle libération?, 93
Les femmes à la mairie: nous, conseillères municipales, 166
Les femmes aujourd'hui, 168
Les femmes dans la Résistance, 37
Les femmes dans la Révolution, 28, 46
Les femmes dans la société marchande, 186
Les femmes de Giscard, 163
Femmes d'hier et de demain, d'ici et d'ailleurs, 187
Les femmes en France dans une société d'inegalités, 73, 159
Femmes et immigrées: l'insertion des femmes immigrées en France, 181
Les femmes et la Révolution, 3
Les femmes et leurs maîtres, 166
Les femmes et le travail du Moyen Âge à nos jours, 179
Femmes et machines de 1900: lecture d'une obsession moderne style, 104

Title Index

Femmes-femmes sur papier glacé, 106
Les femmes françaises face au pouvoir politique, 162
Les femmes innovatrices, 76
Les femmes, la pornographie, l'érotisme, 118
Les femmes salariées, 178
Les femmes savantes, 16
Les femmes s'entêtent, 80
Femmes, sexisme, et société, 87
La femme soleil: les femmes et le pouvoir, une relecture de Saint-Simon, 40
Femmes toutes mains: essai sur le service domestique, 181
Femmes tragiques de l'histoire, xx
Femmes, violence, pouvoir, 163
Figurées, défigurées: petit vocabulaire de la feminité représentée, 103
Fille ou garçon, 152
Les filles de noces: misère sexuelle et prostitution (19e et 20e siècles), 127
Les fils de Freud sont fatigués, 77
Flora Tristan, 62
Flora Tristan: oeuvre et vie mêlées, évoquées, commentées, et choisies, 50
F Magazine, 30, 89, 112, 173
Folles femmes de leurs corps: les prostitutées, 126
Les Française aujourd'hui, 87
Les Françaises au travail, 190
Les Françaises face au chômage, 189
Les Françaises sont-elles des citoyennes?, 164
La Fronde, 8, 72, 109

La Gazette des femmes, 67
Génération consciente, 23
La grève des ventres: propogande néo-malthusienne et baisse de natalité française, XIXe-XXe siècles, 30
Le grief des femmes, 34
Le guerre des sexes, 77

Histoire de la presse féminine en France dès origines à 1848, 109
Histoire de l'enseignement en France, 1800-1967, 30, 134
Histoire des féminismes français, 29, 42, 69
Histoire des femmes, xix
Histoire des Françaises, xx
L'histoire des mères du moyen âge à nos jours, 138
Histoire du féminisme français, 34
Histoire du MLF, 43
Histoire et actualité du féminisme, 80
Histoire illustrée de la femme, xx
Histoire mondiale de la femme, xx
Histoire morale des femmes, 28
L'histoire sans qualités: essais, 38
Housewife or Harlot: The Place of Women in French Society, 1870-1940, xxi, 28

Idées reçues sur les femmes, 149
Il était des femmes dans la Résistance,
L'important, c'est la femme, 117
L'infirmière et l'organisation du travail hospitalier, 187
Les initiées: les femmes, l'esotérisme, et les sociétés secrètes, 65
Institutrice de village, 149

Jeanne Guyon: le siècle des femmes savantes, 56
Le jeune née, 96
Je veux rentrer à la maison, 77
Le Journal de la femme, 47
Le Journal des femmes, 72
Journal d'une bourgeoise, 51

Lâchez-tout, 84, 103
Lettre ouverte aux femmes, 89
Libération des femmes: le MLF, 73
Libérons l'avortement, 121

Title Index

La libre maternité, 122
Les lieux de Marguerite Duras, 97
Lip au féminin, 172, 185
Un lit a soi: itinéraires des femmes, 84
Le livre noir sur l'avortement, 45
Louise Michel: ou la Valléda de l'anarchie, 56
Louise Michel l'indomptable, 54

Madame du Châtelet, 62
Madame et le Management, 78
Madame de Staël: lumières et liberté, 45
Madame et le bonheur, 150
Madame le . . . , 50
Ma loi d'avenir, 49
Le mariage: les hésitations de l'Occident, 144
Le mariage dans la société française contemporaine, 138
Marianne au combat: l'imagerie et la symbolique républicaines de 1789 à 1880, 94
Le masochisme "dit" féminin, 90
La maternité en milieu sous-proletariat, 146
Les matriarches: essai sur la fin du pouvoir mâle, 76
Ma vie comme je peux, 176
Ma vie revue et corrigée par l'auteur, 59
May la réfractaire: pour mes 81 ans d'anarchie, 58
Mémoire de femmes: mémoire du peuple, 36
Mémoires d'une Européenne, 64
Mémoires d'une Européene, 64
Le mérite des femmes, 7
Le métier de femme, 52
Les messagères, 184
Michelet, 47
Michelet, le prêtre, et la femme, 46
Moi, Claire, 81
Moi, la bonne, 175
Moi, une militante, 53
Mon corps, ton corps, leur corps: le corps de la femme dans la publicité, 107
Le Monde, 30
Le monde au féminin: encyclopédie des femmes célèbres, xx
Mon destin de femme, 58
Montesquieu et la feminité, 100
Mother Love: Myth and Reality, 138
Les mots et les femmes, 104
Les mots pour le dire, 96
La Muse Historique, 8
Mystères et ministères de la femme, 156

Ne pleure pas, hurle, 91
New French Feminisms, xxi, 69
Le nouveau féminisme américain: étude historique du Women's Liberation Movement, 67
Nouvelle encyclopédie de la femme, xix
Les nouvelles femmes, 89

L'ombre et le nom: sur la féminité, 88
On tue les petites filles, 147

Papa lit, maman coud, 150
Le paradis des femmes: Women, Salons, and Social Stratification in Seventeenth Century France, 27, 29
Les Paradisiennes, 142
Pariahs Stand Up! The Founding of the Liberal Feminist Movement in France: 1858-1889, xxi, 29, 137
Les parleuses, 97
Parole au négresses, 112
Parole de femme, 104
Paroles . . . elles tournent, 98
Partage des femmes, 85
La partagée, 127
La participation des femmes à la vie civique, 167
Par une porte entrebaillée: ou comment les Françaises entrent dans la Carrière, 177
Pas d'histoire, les femmes: 50 ans d'histoire des femmes, 35

Title Index

La paysanne française d'aujourd'hui, 175
Le pédophile et la maman: l'amour des enfants, 147
Pénélope, 73, 138
La physiologie du mariage, 84
Pipi debout, quelle injustice, 119
Place aux femmes, 177
La place des bonnes: la domesticité féminine à Paris en 1900, 182
The Policing of Families, 137
La pornocratie, ou les femmes dans les temps modernes, 7
The Position of Women in Contemporary France, 29
Possession et sorcellerie au XVIIe siècle: textes inédits, 39
Pour la libération de la femme, 118
Le premier sexe, 78
Le présent des femmes, 85
La presse féminine, 108
La presse féminine: fonction idéologique, 106
La presse féministe en France de 1869 à 1914, 109
Prisonnières, 170
Procès de sorcellerie, 44
Le programme commun des femmes, 162
Promenades dans Londres: ou, l'aristocracie et les prolétaires anglais, 61

Quelle drole de veuve, 83, 143
La question sexuelle, 23
Questions féministes, 73
Quinze femmes célèbres, xix
Qui sont les femmes ingénieurs en France?, 188

Recherches sur la condition féminine dans la société d'aujourd'hui, 82
Le récit féminin, 105
Regarde-toi qui meurs, 65
Research Resources: France, xvii

La révolte des Américaines, 68
La révolte des femmes, 167
Revue du Nord, 33
La robe rouge, 51
Les rôles masculins et féminins, 155

San fleur au fusil, 58
The Second Sex, xii, 16, 34, 52, 53, 80, 83, 103
Seule une femme . . . , 47
Séverine: une rebelle, 72
Le sexisme ordinaire, 108
Simone de Beauvoir et le cours du monde, 50
Sisters or Citizens: Women and Socialism in France since 1876, xxi
Sois belle et achète: la publicité et les femmes, 107
La sorcellerie en Auvergne, 37
La sorcellerie et sa répression dans le nord de la France, 45
La sorcellerie lyonnaise, 45
La sorcière, 39
Sorcières, 100
Souvenirs de guerre et d'occupation, 46
"The Status of Women in France Today," xi
Le statut matrimonial: ses conséquences juridiques, fiscales et sociales, 138
Stendhal, Balzac, et le féminin romantique, 95
Stratégie pour les femmes, 53
Sur l'admission des femmes au droit de cité, 4
Surréalisme et sexualité, 99
Suzanne Voilquin: mémoires d'une Saint-Simonienne en Russie, 1839-1846, 63
Suzanne Voilquin ou la Saint-Simonienne en Egypte, 63
Les syndicats à l'épreuve du féminisme, 172, 185

Telle que je suis, 52
Third Republic: Troisième République, xxi, 28

Title Index

La tige et le rameau: familles anglaise et française, 16e-18e siècles, 145
Le Torchon Brûle, xiii, xxi, 118
Le Tour de France, 36, 62
Tous les métiers pour les femmes, 180
Toutes les mêmes?, 88
Travail à temps partiel dans la fonction publique, solution ou palliatif aux difficultés de la femme fonctionnaire, 176
Travail des femmes en France, 191
Travail et condition féminine: bibliographie commentée, xviii
Travail féminin: un point de vue, 187
Travaux des femmes dans la France du XIXe siècle, 188
Tribunal de l'impuissance: virilité et défaillances conjugales dans l'ancienne France, 165
La Tribune des femmes, 49, 72

Les veuves et leurs familles dans la société d'aujourd'hui, 139
Une vie comme un jour, 47
La vie conjugale sous l'ancien regime, 143
La vie de Flora Tristan, 62
Une vie de putain, 128
La vie et l'oeuvre de Flora Tristan, 1803-44, 62
La vie quotidienne des domestiques en France au XIXe siècle, 183
Les vies des femmes célèbres, xx
Le village au sortilège: chroniques singulières sur la magie rustique dans les pays du coeur de France, 44
Le viol, 130
Viol: le proces d'Aix, avec un texte inédit de Gisèle Halimi, 129
Le voil des viols, 112
Vivre avec la peur au ventre, 124
Vivre au féminin, 94
La voie féministe, 35
La Voix des femmes, 72
Les voleuses de langue, 101
Le vote des femmes, 29
Voyage en Icarie, 7
La vraie vie des femmes commence à 40 ans, 116

"The Woman Question as a Social Issue in Republican France before 1914," xxi, 28
Women in France, 28
"Women, Socialism and Feminism, 1872-1922," xxi
Women, the Family, and Freedom: The Debate in Documents (1750-1950), xxi, 29

Ref Z 7964 .F8 W44 1985
Weitz, Margaret Collins.
Femmes

APR 8 1986